OPEN LETTERS

Russian Popular Culture
and the Picture Postcard, 1880–1922

During the fin-de-siècle and early revolutionary eras, picture postcards
were an important medium of communication for Russians of all backgrounds. In *Open Letters,* the most comprehensive study of Russian
picture postcards to date, Alison Rowley uses this medium to explore
a variety of aspects of Russian popular culture. The book is lavishly
illustrated with more than 130 images, most of which have never been
published before.

Through her examinations of postcards, Rowley addresses a diverse
range of topics: how landscape postcards conveyed notions of imperialism; the role of postcards in the rise of celebrity culture; depictions of
the body on erotic and pornographic postcards; how postcards were employed to promote differing interpretations of the First World War; and
the use of postcards by revolutionary groups seeking to overthrow the
tsarist government. Rowley determines the extent to which Russia was
embedded in Europe-wide cultural trends by situating the Russian case
within a larger European context.

ALISON ROWLEY is an associate professor in the Department of History at
Concordia University.

Open Letters

*Russian Popular Culture
and the Picture Postcard, 1880–1922*

ALISON ROWLEY

UNIVERSITY OF TORONTO PRESS
Toronto Buffalo London

© University of Toronto Press 2013
Toronto Buffalo London
utorontopress.com

Reprinted in paperback 2021

ISBN 978-1-4426-4706-0 (cloth)
ISBN 978-1-4875-4528-4 (paper)

Cataloguing in Publication information available from Library and Archives Canada.

This book has been published with the help of a grant from the Canadian Federation for the Humanities and Social Sciences, through the Awards to Scholarly Publications Program, using funds provided by the Social Sciences and Humanities Research Council of Canada.

University of Toronto Press acknowledges the financial assistance to its publishing program of the Canada Council for the Arts and the Ontario Arts Council, an agency of the Government of Ontario.

**Canada Council
for the Arts**

**Conseil des Arts
du Canada**

**ONTARIO ARTS COUNCIL
CONSEIL DES ARTS DE L'ONTARIO**

an Ontario government agency
un organisme du gouvernement de l'Ontario

Funded by the
Government
of Canada

Financé par le
gouvernement
du Canada

Canada

Contents

Illustrations

Acknowledgments

My father's intellectual footprints are all over this book. As a professor whose interests led him to publish on a wide array of subjects, he has always encouraged me to read widely and to never fear leaping into unknown topics. My mother's contribution has been just as valuable. An unending source of support, she believed deeply in this book project and was not averse to giving me postcards as birthday and Christmas presents, no matter how strange the individual requests may have seemed.

Other scholars have shaped the contours and contents of my book. Lars Lih offered valuable suggestions that expanded my thinking in the final stages of writing. Carter Elwood backed the project from the very beginning and made sure that I got into contact with Richard Ratzlaff at the University of Toronto Press. Richard has been a delight to work with, and I could not have asked for a better editor. In addition, I benefited greatly from those who commented on my research at conferences, in particular, Ron Bobroff, Sally Boniece, Kris Groberg, Sue McCaffray, Megan Swift, Connie Wawruck-Hemmett, and Mary Vipond. Thank you also to Erik Zitser who insisted that the book would not be complete without the chapter on erotic postcards, and to Sergey Lobachev who has been patient while I periodically shelved a project we are working together on in order to focus on the final revisions to this book.

At Concordia University, I am grateful for the support of my fellow Europeanists as well as my friend Donna Whittaker. Bob Tittler was particularly instrumental in the earliest stage of my research; he was the one who made sure I knew about Semmerling's *Israeli and Palestinian Postcards*. My sabbatical in 2010–2011 enabled me to finish the first draft of the entire manuscript.

Friends around the world have bolstered my spirits at key moments. I wish to thank Michael Bowling, Denise Comeau, Erika Golart, Pam Jackman, Carrie Levesque, Ilya Popov, and Manon Roy. I have also bounced ideas off a number of students as the book took shape. Olivier Button, Jess Gold, James Leduc, Richard Pilkington, Thomas Szwedska, and Nick Tošaj should be singled out for having listened patiently to my many ramblings about postcards.

Finally, I dedicate this book to my husband David. He is the other anchor of ABCD, and while he cannot always stop our sons Christopher and Benjamin from disturbing me as I try to work, he has *never ever* asked how much I have spent on postcards over the years.

Open Letters

More than "Wish You Were Here"

The mutilated postcard offers a stark commentary on Russian Emperor Nicholas II's prowess as a military commander. Having replaced his cousin, the popular Grand Duke Nikolai Nikolaevich, as commander-in-chief, in August 1915, Nicholas oversaw a seemingly endless series of defeats and the eventual disintegration of the Russian Army. His failures contributed greatly to the revolution that, in February 1917, swept him from his throne.

Disappointment with Nicholas as a military leader is palpable when you hold in your hands the postcard shown here as Figure I.1. It was published in Riga by the firm of V.A. Zol'man, and the original image was passed by the Russian censor on 30 March 1915. At first glance, the postcard seems no different from others made in the first month or so of the Great War. They, too, featured portraits of military leaders whose chests were adorned with a reassuring array of decorations (see Figures I.2 and I.3). But, those very decorations have been very carefully and deliberately effaced from our image.

Perhaps its owner was a frustrated foot soldier unable to comprehend the war aims of his government and simply wanting to go home. Or, more likely, the postcard was in the possession of a disgruntled officer, who would have understood the visual language of military decorations. Someone like that would have seen his world collapse with the advent of the Russian Revolution and, while he might not have completely broken with the idea of the monarchy as an institution (after all, Nicholas's face escaped the blade obliterating his decorations), he could have rejected this particular monarch in one of his most important roles. Ultimately, we will never know for certain who bought this postcard, why it was defaced, and why it was kept. Like with so many of the illustrations that

ОТКРЫТОЕ ПИСЬМО.

Е. И. В. Государь Императоръ
НИКОЛАЙ АЛЕКСАНДРОВИЧЪ
Самодержецъ Всероссійскій.

Изд.: В. А. ЗОЛЬМАНЪ, г. Рига, Гертрудинская 25, почт. ящ. 844.

Разрѣшено придворной цензурой 30 марта 1915 г.

I.1 Postcard of His Imperial Highness Emperor Nicholas Alexandrovich, Auto-crat of All-Russia. Manufactured by V.A. Zol'man, Riga, 1915. Image passed by the censor on 30 March 1915.

grace the following pages, this postcard remains at least a partial mystery that refuses to yield all of its secrets to historians.

Picture postcards are tantalizing objects, central to understanding the social history and visual culture of fin-de-siècle Russia. Produced in numbers dwarfing the print runs of posters or popular prints and available in every corner of the empire, picture postcards had the power not only to reflect popular culture, but also to shape it. Through picture postcards, it is possible to discern the multiplicity of the often-contradictory attitudes, beliefs, and values swirling through popular culture at the time.

Still, picture postcards are far from perfect sources. Given the number of small firms involved in their manufacture – businesses that have disappeared from history without leaving archival traces – we have no way of knowing exactly how many picture postcards were made between 1880 and 1922. Nor is it possible to determine what percentage of them may have survived the three revolutions, two world

Военный министръ Сухомлиновъ.

Дозволено цензурою. Рига, 30 августа 1914 г.

I.2 Postcard of War Minister Sukhomlinov. A.K. Gul'be and A.I. Gol't, Riga. Image passed by the censor 30 August 1914.

I.3 Postcard of Grand Duke Nikolai Nikolaevich. Tip. G. Gempel' i Ko., Riga.
Image passed by the censor 29 August 1914.

wars, and one civil war that Russians endured in the century that separates the "golden age" of the picture postcard from our own time. Today, a large number of Russian postcards remain in private hands rather than in public collections maintained by libraries and archives. Once treasured parts of individual collections, the postcards are slowly being discarded or sold off as grandchildren and great-grandchildren fail to see the value of such "clutter" except perhaps in monetary terms.

That reality has shaped this book in a fundamental way – one that may disconcert readers used to more archivally based studies. I never set out to write a book about, or even using, postcards. Indeed, my research focus a decade ago was solidly situated on Soviet visual propaganda in the 1930s. Intrigued by the question of pervasiveness, I pursued it by incorporating more and more media into my work. That, of course, eventually led to postcards, particularly, the advertising-agitational postcards of the late 1920s and early 1930s made with print runs numbering into the millions of copies. Slowly, I began to move backwards in time, as I uncovered the rich potential of postcards as sources. I immersed myself in the world of online auctions. At the time, eBay was a new phenomenon, and certainly not one consulted by most historians. Day after day, I would look at hundreds of auctions and make purchases if the family budget, or later, my university professional development account, would allow them. The emerging collection remained unfocused, however. Then a colleague passed me a review of *Israeli and Palestinian Postcards: Presentations of National Self.*[1] I bought the book straight away and liken the experience of reading it to being hit by lightning. Suddenly, I knew why I had been acquiring so many pieces of old cardboard: I was, of course, creating my own archive.

As I embraced this rather unorthodox methodological approach, I became more systematic in my acquisitions, structuring them around the broad categories (such as postcards of landscapes or images of royalty) that I observed in the surviving postcards. It did not take long to see that these categories reflected the segments, or niches, of the original market for picture postcards, and that they would make sense as chapters in the book that I was now envisioning. I checked my observations against references made about picture postcards in Russian diaries and memoirs from the era. As readers will see, I quote liberally from these sources throughout *Open Letters* in the hopes of conveying an accurate sense of the postcard market and the social conventions that shaped their various usages.

The greatest challenge then became making sure the picture post-cards I wanted to use as illustrations were unique enough to interest readers and to underscore the conclusions I wanted to draw about Russian popular culture, while also being sufficiently similar to others that they could unquestionably serve as representative examples. As I quickly learned, the ideal postcard was often impossible to find, particularly in certain categories that may have been dangerous to own (as was the case with postcards created by revolutionary groups) or where the postcards could have led to social opprobrium (read pornographic post-cards here). The more rare the postcard, the more I had to contend with collectors. Their interest in certain niches meant the costs involved for some chapters escalated rapidly. For instance, while it is still possible to purchase landscape postcards for $10 each, images of the Russian royal family at the time of writing average $50 to $150 a piece. The most I have paid for a postcard was $350. It was for a pornographic alphabet postcard that appears as an illustration in chapter 4. Such postcards have their own unique difficulties. They have to be purchased privately from dealers since eBay frowns on pornography and places auctions for what it deems adult materials in a special restricted section of its website. Finding the proper lexicon to navigate the parameters of such things takes time, too. Postcard sellers, for example, prefer the terms "nude" and "risqué" to "naked" and "pornographic." I also remain fuzzy on some of the legal niceties involved in mailing hundred-year-old erotic postcards. Fortunately, none of the envelopes containing my purchases was ever opened by Canada Post so the question of whether I was involved in the trafficking of pornography across international borders – as opposed to doing academic research – never had to be resolved.

I did find that patience and persistence were ultimately rewarded. Over a decade, for instance, I might only have seen, and bought, one postcard of Vera Zasulich, but I did acquire half a dozen images of Ekaterina Breshko-Breshkovskaia and even more of Maria Spiridonova. This leads me to believe my analysis of how picture postcards depicted women in the revolutionary movement is an accurate one. Moreover, that one case was replicated time and again as I moved through the various subjects I treat in *Open Letters*. Ultimately, I am confident the images presented here are representative of the postcards of their era.

I make no such claims concerning reception, however. Acquiring post-cards that would have let me consistently gauge the intentions of senders or the reactions of recipients has proven to be impossible. The vast majority of surviving Russian postcards were never postally used. Affixed into albums or pinned to walls to serve as reminders or decorations, they have no writing on their reverse sides and, hence, leave no clues in that regard for the historian.

Just as I have built my source base in a rather unorthodox manner, I have relied on an array of non-Russian scholarship to interpret the materials. This decision may alienate or provoke some readers who will, perhaps, question the use of such analytical tools. Nevertheless, it was a deliberate, and in some places necessary, choice. Cultural trends do not respect international borders. They fly across continents and oceans via technologies like picture postcards. As I intend to demonstrate in *Open Letters*, the Russian Empire was deeply embedded in the attitudes and crazes of the fin-de-siècle era. The only way to highlight these synergies is to openly and unapologetically draw upon scholarship that discusses cultural developments in Europe and North America. In other places, notably, when addressing the rise of celebrity culture and pornography, I was forced to look further afield since these are subjects that have not garnered much attention from specialists in Russian history. In addition, I have deliberately incorporated European postcards into my analysis in a couple of places. Russians had access to these images. Foreign postcards were, after all, sometimes mailed to Russia, and Russians travelling on the continent were free to purchase as many foreign postcards as they wished. It makes sense to include these examples into the narrative since they reflect the pan-European cultural dialogue that is central to this book.

The first full draft of *Open Letters* was written while I was on sabbatical in 2010–11. As coincidence would have it, I also read Claudia Verhoeven's *The Odd Man Karakozov* at the onset of writing. Verhoeven's book intrigued me, not only for its contents, but also for the approach the author took to its construction. In a brief section entitled "Plan," Verhoeven outlines her vision of the book's structure and then goes on to imply that one should feel free to read the contents in a different order should one so desire. Such flexibility with the text is possible because, as Verhoeven writes, "Each chapter narrates the case from its own angle, was written in such a way as to be largely autonomous, and can be read quite independently of the others."[2] I am not following the intricacies of one law case; however, I decided to structure my book in a similar way. Given the rather disparate nature of the subjects covered, it made sense to me to treat them as independently as possible. There is, as I will describe below, a logic to the ordering of the chapters, but it is also possible to read each one in a stand-alone fashion.

The first chapter explains the importance of picture postcards in the fin-de-siècle period. Picture postcards are a relatively overlooked historical source, certainly in Russian history, but also in European history more generally. Only a handful of books explore the way they express cultural values.[3] Other works remain more descriptive in nature or consist simply of anthologies of reproductions.[4] But, this does not mean postcards should continue to be ignored and underappreciated. Picture postcards emerged at a key moment in the nineteenth century – when, for the first time, the discovery of photography could be combined with new industrial techniques to create a mass visual popular culture. Now, unlike in past centuries, when works of art were expensive to produce and beyond the means of all but society's elites, visual images could be consumed regularly by every group in society. This chapter shows how they did so by focusing on the history and usage of picture postcards. First, it explains how changes to, and the expansion of, the Russian postal system established the infrastructure needed for postcards to circulate on a vast scale. Attention then shifts to the creation of postcards and the exploding market for them in both Russia and the rest of Europe. More than a century separates us from the first postcards and we are now so accustomed to them, it is difficult to overcome our prejudices and recapture the sense of wonder with which they were initially greeted. The chapter seeks to do so by explaining how postcards came to be collectible items. It then goes on to describe the more practical uses for postcards such as those connected with commerce, charity, and tourism.

After this introduction to the postcard market, the second chapter, "The Landscapes of Russian Imperialism," changes the focus to the pictures on Russian postcards. I begin with landscapes for two reasons. First, a vast quantity of landscape postcards has survived to the present day. I do not think this is an historical accident. Rather, it speaks to how many such postcards were manufactured in the first place. Given the centrality of these items to the market, they offer a natural starting point for my analysis. Also, I wanted to begin with the familiar and then stretch beyond it. In this increasingly digital age, the modern reader may only have encountered postcards in conjunction with travel, where postcards offer convenient photographs of places visited. As we shall see, landscape postcards were much more than this, and there are whole categories of other postcards waiting to be discussed.

The scholarly literature on landscape and its connection to imperialism in Russia is relatively sparse, certainly, when compared with the vast number of works devoted to these subjects in other national traditions.

Picture postcards illuminate ideas in Russian popular culture concerning Russia's status as a European nation in the midst of rapid industrialization. Using an interpretive framework that draws upon scholarship on American and British colonial landscapes, as well as Benedict Anderson's notion of "official nationalism," this chapter reveals how four kinds of landscape postcards created visions of the Russian Empire. Postcards with maps, coats of arms, and statues legitimized the political status quo and connected the idea of the Russian nation to the existing political system. Other picture postcards of the formal gardens constructed across the empire imposed a standardized, Europeanized image of public spaces. By projecting only images of social harmony, they suggested that Russian imperialism fostered no local resistance. Economic nationalism, too, found its way onto picture postcards, particularly those celebrating new infrastructure in peripheral regions. These images showed the government actively engaged in economic development such as the construction of railways and bridges and, hence, in building a modern nation. Finally, economic nationalism was also at the forefront on postcards connected to tourism. Here, too, Europeanized features (hotels, spas, and resorts) dotted the landscapes, and postcards of them constituted another way of visualizing the Russian Empire.

Following this discussion of landscapes, I turn in the next three chapters to questions of celebrity culture and depictions of the body. Chapter 3, "Gender and Celebrity Culture via the Lens of the Picture Postcard: The Case of Vera Kholodnaia, the 'Queen of the Russian Screen,'" traces the creation of celebrity culture in late Imperial Russia. Little work has been done on the subject in those years, with the exception of Louise McReynolds' *Russia at Play*, so looking further afield, this chapter taps works on the development of a star system in the United States.[5] Similar methods were used by Russian film studios, and there was a strong connection between such images of celebrities and changing notions of fashion and femininity in Russia's urban centres. The end of the nineteenth century saw the blurring of social boundaries and changing definitions of what constituted acceptable behaviour for Russian women. New ideas about consumption were literally embodied by actresses and other performers, whose sense of aesthetic selfhood was expressed by their clothes and public personas. Celebrities came to be influential fashion makers at a time when the Russian market was increasingly embracing Western clothing as a sign of modernity.[6] The example of Vera Kholodnaia, one of Russia's first film celebrities, and someone whose image circulated widely in picture postcard form, serves as a nexus for the chapter, although postcards are perhaps less central here than in subsequent chapters.

A different interpretation of the bodies displayed on picture postcards is found in chapter 4, which looks at romantic and erotic postcards in Russia. In the preceding chapter, I assumed, by and large, that most people consuming celebrity images were female. In this chapter, on the other hand, I assumed a mostly male audience, certainly, as the discussion moves to the most explicit images. The binarism set up by this approach does not necessarily hold true in all cases. Instead, it is meant to reflect notions held by Russian subjects in the fin-de-siècle era. Just as they believed women could become crazed fans of film stars, they thought of men when confronted with the existence of pornography. As this chapter reveals, Russia was deeply embroiled in the European market for such materials. The kinds of images produced stretched from romantic or humorous postcards that could be read in a suggestive manner (and be used by both genders) to full-blown pornography. Among the subjects the chapter considers are the alternative readings possible for postcards reproducing works of art as well as those meant to publicize acts of artistic protest, such as nudism. Meant to enlighten or shock, these postcards could also arouse and commodify the body.

In chapter 5, "Monarchy and the Mundane: Picture Postcards and Images of the Romanovs," I return to the question of celebrity culture, but instead of actresses, I focus on the mass-produced images of royalty that circulated widely by the end of the nineteenth century. I examine a noticeable shift in the perception of the Russian throne from an object of awe to one of celebrity and, at times, even notoriety. The existing scholarship has looked at this change in terms of the impact of ceremonial occasions,[7] or of pornographic cartoons of the tsar, the tsarina, and Rasputin.[8] What have usually been overlooked are the ramifications of another dialogue, one that involved members of the royal family being shown simply as ordinary people. Of great significance was Queen Victoria's decision to allow portraits of the British royal family to appear in new media, and the literature concerning the manipulation of her image forms a point of departure for this chapter since members of her extended family all came to employ similar methods of publicity.[9] However, what in the British context created a sense of attachment to the monarchy, proved detrimental in Russia. Images of the tsar, including some of his private family life, did little to improve his standing with his subjects. Instead, members of the royal family came to be seen as "bourgeois," with all the negative connotations that word implies in Russian.

These postcards point to how the tsar, by tolerating the production of royal kitsch, was himself implicated in undermining his position as a divine right monarch. Here, questions of celebrity culture become politicized, so it is fitting that this chapter serves as a kind of bridge to the final two, which connect picture postcards to the First World War and the Russian Revolution, respectively.

Building on Janet Watson's idea of "fighting different wars," chapter 7 looks at how Russian postcards moved beyond patriotic discourse during the Great War.[10] Because earlier historians have, by and large, focused exclusively on the connections between visual materials, including picture postcards, and patriotism, other stories have been neglected. Notably, other attempts to construct universalizing narratives of the war and private initiatives that captured the war as lived experience for individual soldiers have not been discussed. The purpose of this chapter is twofold: to describe the picture postcards produced by the Russian government and charitable organizations that fixed identities on prisoners of war and refugees; and then to discuss how picture postcards were, in fact, used by soldiers and their families during the conflict. In the process, the chapter shows how picture postcards frequently contradicted the patriotic discourse so carefully crafted by the Russian government, thereby, in their own way, complicating the war effort.

More deliberate efforts to destroy the tsarist regime are the focus of chapter 7. By studying the picture postcards generated, usually illegally, by revolutionary groups, I demonstrate how popular culture became politicized after the 1905 Revolution, and how revolutionaries, in turn, also became articles of popular consumption. These postcards deepen our understanding of how hotly contested Russia's new political arena was in the few short years between the 1905 and the 1917 revolutions, as disparate groups had to learn how to debate one another and create a visual language that was supposed to win them followers. As a widely employed form of political mobilization, postcards introduced new heroes for the masses, while also chronicling events as the monarchy and later the provisional government collapsed.

Finally, *Open Letters* ends with an epilogue, "Picture Postcards across the Revolutionary Divide," which takes the broad categories of analysis offered in the preceding chapters firmly into the Soviet period. In terms of celebrity, picture postcards were an important component of the cult of Lenin, proving that methods of publicity first introduced in the late imperial era continued to be employed long after Russia's first generation of film stars had been supplanted and the Romanovs had been swept from power. As time passed, and the new regime's grasp on power solidified, a pantheon of other celebrities was regularly promoted to the Soviet public. Picture postcards, like all forms of media in the USSR, were mobilized to promote these icons of the new era, who included women settling the frontier, using the latest technologies, or breaking production norms at work. Postcards eventually even constructed picture personalities for Soviet film stars such as Liubov' Orlova, who came to dominate the screen starting in the 1930s. While celebrity culture persisted, one aspect of the picture postcard market seemingly disappeared from view: pornography. It is doubtful that new erotic postcards were made in the early Soviet period, given the level of state-imposed control over photography. But, as scholars such as Mikhail Zolotonosov have posited, it was possible for new kinds of images to fill the void.[11] Postcards of sportswomen provided eroticized images that now put Soviet bodies on display. Finally, as we will see, some Soviet landscape postcards used familiar elements, like maps and symbols of state, to define the boundaries of the country, while others offered images of economic nationalism – images that connected progress to the construction of modern infrastructure.

Chapter One

The Market for Picture Postcards in Russia

In his memoirs, Soviet writer and journalist Ilya Ehrenburg described how, as a teenager, he used to buy pictures postcards of chorus girls, in his words "preferably naked ones," at a stationer's in Moscow. He decorated his room with postcard reproductions of artistic works, and when, in 1907, the tsarist secret police searched the lodgings of this student convert to Bolshevism, they found he had more than just art postcards. The official report showed that some revolutionary postcards, as well as a musical score for the Russian "Marseillaise," were confiscated from Ehrenburg.[1] These three tidbits of information tucked within Ehrenburg's reminiscences are suggestive of the ways in which picture postcards formed part of the everyday experience of Russians at the end of the nineteenth and start of the twentieth centuries.

What was the attraction of postcards? Why and how did they become such a crucial part of popular visual culture at the end of the nineteenth century? This chapter explores the process by which a market for picture postcards developed in Russia. It begins with a brief overview of the changing postal system since a well-functioning postal network was a vital component in what came to be known as the "golden age" of the postcard. Given the vast majority of postcards were bought to be used, rather than kept in collections, the demand for them hinged on the knowledge that picture postcards could and would reach the desired recipients. A second focus of this chapter is on the creation and growth of the postcard market, first in general, and then more specifically in Russia. The invention of the postcard coincided with significant advances in paper-making, photography, and printing, all of which contributed to the eventual emergence of a truly mass market for postcards. Throughout this book, it is emphasized that Russian postcards were part of a Europe-wide, if not global, phenomenon. Hence, an examination of how postcards arrived in Russia, the important role played by foreign manufacturers at first, and the ties between Russian and European collectors is in order. Next the chapter describes how people obtained and used postcards. Particular attention is paid to the use of postcards by businessmen, tourists, and collectors, although other constituencies will be discussed in passing (with more attention given to them in later chapters). Finally, the chapter ends with a discussion of censorship and postcards. Not everyone greeted the invention of the picture postcard with enthusiasm. As we shall see, apart from private concerns about manners and morality, the Russian government consistently supervised the use of postcards by people it deemed suspicious and, in times of war, postal communications came under even greater scrutiny.

The Development of the Russian Postal System

The roots of the Russian postal system stretch back to the country's diplomatic correspondence, which continued to make up the vast majority of mail sent until the mid-nineteenth century.[2] In 1833, the first city post was established in the capital, St. Petersburg. However, its functioning was hampered by unnamed streets and by houses without numbers, so home delivery was not possible.[3] Instead, the system relied on drop points for both arriving and departing letters. At this point, specifically affixed postage stamps were not used; instead, ink stamps marked the place and date of the letter. The system expanded slowly. Moscow did not have city post until 1845, but in the 1850s, similar systems spread to regional centres such as Kazan', Warsaw, Saratov, Kiev, Riga, Khar'kov, and Odessa. At the same time, the use of special envelopes became common. Called "stamp covers" (*shtempel'nye kuverty*), the envelopes began the practice of using the imperial double-headed eagle on Russian mail. The official state coat of arms, the eagle, was stamped onto the upper left-hand corner of the envelope in inks in varying colours depending on the city of origin.[4]

It was not until the 1850s that the idea of creating postage stamps was raised and, even then, the idea originated unexpectedly. At the start of the 1850s, the government sent A.P. Charukovskii to Europe to investigate the use of railways to speed up the postal system.[5] Charukovskii saw the effective use of both railways and postage stamps. Upon his return, his report found favour, and in 1856, F.M. Kepler was instructed to design the first stamp. Stamps were then placed under the jurisdiction of the Ministry of Finance, and in early 1858, their domestic use was announced in the newspapers of European Russia. They were sold at the postal installations in major cities and in downtown St. Petersburg shops, provided the owners agreed to do so.[6] Stamps for international mail lagged behind those for domestic consumption. In 1852, the Prussian government approached its Russian counterpart about employing stamps for correspondence between the two countries, but it was not until more than a decade later that the first designs were made. Again, the coat of arms of the country was chosen for the image. By the end of the 1860s, postage stamps were on mail to all European countries.

At the same time as Russian postage stamps were being designed and coming into use, the postal infrastructure of the empire was undergoing some significant changes. When the nineteenth century began, the postal system relied on horses to relay mail between the 3,200 or so post offices then in existence.[7] While horse power continued to play an important role in mail delivery, especially to outlying areas, into the 1930s, other forms of transportation were introduced mid-century, and they gradually expanded the area that could be reached, while also cutting delivery times quite dramatically. For instance, when Russia's first railway link between St. Petersburg and Moscow opened in 1851, mail immediately began to be carried by train between these two most important cities in the empire. Delivery time was cut from three or four days to twenty-four hours.[8] A decade later, the first special mailcars were added so letters could be sorted while the train was en route, further reducing the time it took to process items. By the end of 1874, mail was being carried along thirty-five separate railway lines.[9] Despite these advances, Russia's rail network developed rather more slowly than those in other parts of Europe, at least until the final decade of the nineteenth century.[10] As a result, the postal system also increased its reliance on steamships. In the 1860s and 1870s, mail in Russia came to be transported along a number of important rivers and across the empire's major lakes.[11]

These developments at the centre were matched by an expansion of postal infrastructure at the local level. By 1874, forty-seven cities had some form of local post.[12] In rural areas, postal affairs fell into the hands of the zemstva, created by one of Alexander II's Great Reforms in 1864. Even though zemstva posts were treated by the government with some suspicion – the competition for postal revenue was fierce – their number continued to grow rapidly. At their peak, zemstva posts could be found in thirty-four provinces and 365 districts.[13] A decline set in towards the end of the century, but the 1896–97 Russian census still noted the existence of 190 districts with zemstva posts.[14]

The infrastructure improvements outlined above allowed the volume of mail sent to increase exponentially. From 1875 to 1900, the total number of items sent through the Russian mail service grew by more than 530 per cent.[15] Hundreds of millions of individual letters and postcards were behind this growth – which suggests that mail, by the end of the nineteenth century, had become an increasingly accepted part of everyday life for members of Russia's upper, and newly emerging middle, classes.

The postal system, however, had to be rebuilt in the wake of the chaos engendered by the First World War and the 1917 revolutions. Despite the creation of the People's Commissariat of Post and Telegraph (Narkompochtel'), it initially proved difficult for the Bolsheviks to establish regular routes and central control. Uncertain local conditions during the civil war meant that frequently newly designed Soviet stamps and other postal materials were simply not available across the country.[16] Moreover, even explicit decrees from Moscow went unheeded. For example, in the spring of 1919, the Council of People's Commissars (Sovnarkom) issued a decree authorizing the establishment of three thousand local village post and telegraph offices. However, only 607 were actually set up.[17] In an effort to encourage people to use the mail system again, Sovnarkom also issued a decree stating that personal letters and postcards could be sent free of charge from 1 January 1919 to 15 August 1921. The decree did help to revive the postal system, for in the first few months the number of private letters sent rose by 34 per cent.[18] Still, not until the mid-1920s did mail consistently penetrate the countryside again. In 1924, the so-called circular post, where horse-drawn carts were driven on regular routes delivering all types of mail, was organized. At each predetermined stopping point, the driver, sometimes using only his cart as a shop and at other times setting up in a public building, would distribute the mail and sell postal supplies. By the end of 1925, the network encompassed 275,000 kilometres with 4,279 routes and 43,103 stopping points.[19] In 1925, some larger stopping points were turned into permanent postal installations, and the position of village postman was created. A version of the "circular post" continued in the 1930s, as what were termed "agit carts" were used to deliver mail and periodical literature to Red Army soldiers, often while they were on manoeuvres. For civilians, postal service further improved when, in 1930, home delivery replaced delivery to only one spot in the village and by then, it can be said with some confidence that letters and postcards were delivered to any home in the USSR.

This postal system built, and then rebuilt in the wake of revolution and civil war, was crucial to the market for picture postcards. It allowed Russians to become dependent on letters and postcards for all kinds of communications. But, the improved postal system was not the only factor that accounted for the popularity of picture postcards. Technological advances in papermaking and printing – subjects addressed below – were instrumental as well.

The Postcard Explosion

The popularity of, and mass market for, picture postcards could never have emerged without dramatic changes in papermaking and printing technology in the nineteenth century. At the beginning of the century, paper was an expensive and precious commodity – so much so that letters were still often sent simply folded and sealed rather than put in envelopes.[20] Paper was made from cotton and linen fibres, and little of the process for making it was mechanized. As the demand for paper grew, despite the cost, the international trade in rags did, too. By mid-century, most countries either prohibited the export of rags or charged export duties in an effort to protect their domestic papermaking industries. The situation changed quite dramatically when a German invention of 1847 – the first successful process for grinding wood and turning it into pulp – began to spread. Wood pulp paper was significantly cheaper. Hence, the price of paper products fell dramatically in the second half of the nineteenth century, and the widespread adoption of wood pulp paper allowed for a mass market in paper items, such as picture postcards, to develop since the lower prices attracted middle- and lower-class buyers for the first time.[21]

More elaborate paper products had already been emerging before the nature of papermaking changed so dramatically. The first half of the nineteenth century saw the use of illustrated writing paper and, in the 1840s, pictorial envelopes as well.[22] But, these items remained beyond the means of most people and, while the writing paper was available in stores in Moscow and St. Petersburg in the 1830s, its use was anything but widespread. A far more immediate precursor to the postcard was the pictorial visiting card, commonly referred to by its French name, carte-de-visite.[23] Cartes-de-visite flourished in the 1860s and continued to appear as late as the 1920s. They marked a dramatic shift in the nature of photography since, for the first time, multiple prints of a negative were available on the open market rather than simply made for a specific customer. Suddenly, portraits of royalty, politicians, celebrities, and everyday people were widely available. The popularity of cartes received a tremendous boost when Queen Victoria allowed J.E. Mayall to reproduce photographs of the British royal family, and let it be known she was an avid collector of cartes-de-visite. A mania for cartes-de-visite soon followed. For most of the 1860s, three to four hundred million cartes were sold each year in Britain alone.[24] But, Britain was only the tip of the iceberg, so to speak; cartes-de-visite were produced in vast quantities across the globe. The key manufacturers in Russia were A. Denier (St. Petersburg), S.L. Levitsky (St. Petersburg), N. Lorenz (St. Petersburg), and M. Panov (Moscow).[25] (See Figure 1.1.)

Building on the demand established by cartes-de-visite, the reproduction of photographic images expanded in the 1870s when bromide paper was invented in England. It spurred the development of rapid printing machines. Such machines were first adopted for postcard production in 1884 by a German firm, Neue Photographische Gesellschaft, and then their use spread to such other major producers as Raphael Tuck Ltd. Both bromide view postcards and portraits of celebrities could now be produced in larger print runs,[26] and this was a result of advances in printing technology. Hand-powered flat-bed presses were replaced in Russia by steam-powered ones in the 1870s. By the 1880s, rotary presses were introduced into Russia's largest publishing houses, leading to a dramatic expansion in the number of items printed. The inclusion of pictures in printed items also became the norm.

The timing could not have been better, since the first postcard appeared in Austria in October 1869. The invention quickly caught on, with almost three million postcards sold in the Austro-Hungarian Empire within next three months.[27] By July 1870, the first illustrated postcards were introduced by a German bookseller, and similar items were for sale in Britain and Switzerland by the end of the year. From these early beginnings, the market simply exploded. Firms and retail outlets spread quickly across Europe and into North America.[28] The new industry soon required intervention on the part of postal authorities, who needed to determine what kinds of postcards were acceptable for mailing and what rates would apply to postcards that often differed quite dramatically in size. Standardization came at the first World Postal Congress, held in Berne in 1874. Russia was one of twenty-two countries agreeing to abide by its rules concerning postal rates and transit between countries. The Congress established a uniform size (9 × 14 cm) for postcards. Postcard use continued to skyrocket: in the year following the Congress, the

1.1 Carte-de-visite of unknown subject. Manufactured by Denier, n.d.

member nations of the International Postal Union handled 231.5 million postcards. By 1900, that figure had grown to 2.8 billion.[29]

Postcards caught the attention of the Russian government as soon as they appeared elsewhere in Europe. Their use was authorized right away, but the first unstamped, plain postcards were not mailed in Russia until 1 January 1872. Initially, the size of postcards was set at 1/16th of a blank piece of paper, and production was centralized in the hands of postal authorities. The government monopoly on postcards was transferred to the Ministry of the Interior, in December 1894. For four more years, the market continued to be restricted; until 1898, when the Society of St. Eugenia (Obshchina sv. Evgenii krasnogo kresta) was permitted to enter the postcard market, the only non-government–issued postcards were made by foreign firms who imported their wares into Russia. Firms such as Granberg (based in Stockholm), Lapin (based in Paris), and Diakov (based in Berlin) flooded the Russian market with designs largely indistinguishable from those circulating in the rest of Europe.

Among the most notable developments was the introduction of "Greetings from" (*Gruss aus*) postcards. Originally created in Germany, in 1890, but available across the globe within a decade, this type of postcard fit neatly into a niche created by Europe's expanding tourist industry. The typical "Greetings from" postcard incorporated a number of small city views into the overall design, cataloguing what the maker considered to be the most distinguishing features of a given location (see Figure 1.2). For tourists, these postcards not only neatly summarized the highlights of their trip, but also gave them a sense of what to see in the first place. Hence, these postcards informed their notions of seeing and shaped perceptions of what was important and picturesque about a given location. For postcard collectors, the desire for ever more exotic locations and ingenious designs spurred manufacturers to expand the number of images they produced and to market novelty cards such as those with foldout series of city views (see Figure 1.3).[30]

Foldout postcards were not the only kind of novelty picture postcards introduced into the Russian market by foreign producers. Indeed, at some point, Russian examples of most fads could be found.[31] Figure 1.4, for instance, shows a postcard where only a part of the image has been hand-tinted, hence highlighting certain aspects of the scene. Other postcards were relief printed so certain aspects of the design were raised to the touch; some sellers today refer to these postcards as "pressed."

Judging by how many examples have survived to the present day, the market was particularly strong for holiday greeting postcards. Issued for

1.2 "Greetings from Petrograd." Manufactured by Fotopech. A.I. Tsenter. Postally used in 1915.

each of the year's three major holidays – Christmas, New Year, and Easter – the postcards frequently relied on sentimental scenes featuring children. They also initially had a strong non-Russian flavour about them since manufacturers used the same designs for multiple markets, changing only the language of the caption. Holiday postcards proved popular with consumers and continued to circulate for years after the revolution did away with public celebrations of these holidays.[32] Efforts to introduce similar postcards celebrating the anniversary of the October Revolution apparently did not garner the same enthusiasm from Soviet citizens, and they were not widely used even if they were produced in large quantities.[33]

The first Russian-made picture postcards were produced by the St. Eugenia Society in 1898. The Society had been founded in the wake of the Russo-Turkish War (1877–78), and its most significant early patron was Princess Evgeniia Maksimilianovna Ol'denburgskaia, a granddaughter of Emperor Nicholas I. It sought to train future generations of nurses; some of its students were eventually dispatched to the far reaches of

1.3 "Greetings from Riga." The camera is a flap that when opened reveals a series of views of Riga. Manufactured by Ernst G. Svanström, n.d.

1.4 "Happy New Year." The bottles and a flower on the woman's chest are tinted bright green; the lilacs at the bottom of the picture have a slight purple tint. No manufacturer listed. No date listed but was used privately in 1951.

the empire, including the Far East and Sakhalin Island, in order to improve medical practices. In St. Petersburg, the Society's complex, which included a hospital, a surgery, and a pharmacy, provided care for many of the city's poorest residents. The Society also provided funds for various tearooms and cafeterias maintained by temperance groups.[34]

To raise funds, the Society's leadership decided to issue special envelopes for Easter 1896. Their success suggested to the organization that picture postcards, too, could be profitable, and the Society soon became one of the most dominant actors in the Russian postcard market. Over a twenty-year period, it published 6,406 different images and issued about thirty million postcards.[35] At first, the print runs for the Society's postcards were modest, numbering only a few hundred copies. By 1907, however, print runs grew to ten thousand copies for each postcard, and the most popular postcards sold out five or six editions. Some, featuring works by E.M. Bem, even went to twenty editions.[36] The Society further expanded its reach by issuing eleven postcard catalogues between 1901 and 1915, and by briefly publishing a journal, *Otkrytoe pis'mo*, from 1904 to 1906. The journal gave recommendations to collectors and included articles suggesting how postcards could be used in schools. In order to sell its wares, the Society opened two stores: at 4 Kuznechnyi Most in Moscow (in 1903) and at 38 Bolshoi Morskoi Street in St. Petersburg (in 1904). Its postcards were also available for purchase at Red Cross kiosks in railway stations across the empire.[37]

The St. Eugenia Society benefited from close ties to the artistic community. Alexander Benois sat on the board of its Commission for Artistic Publications. Reproductions of works by Ilia Repin and members of the World of Art (Mir Iskusstvo) movement, among others, featured prominently among the Society's postcards. Indeed, the Society came to be known for popularizing Russian art in general, for the reproduction of scenic landscapes, and for issuing special thematically arranged series of postcards. It also held a number of design competitions for special occasions like the hundredth anniversary of Pushkin's birth and the two-hundredth jubilee in honour of the founding of St. Petersburg.[38] The influence of the Society was recognized in its own time. In September 1912, *Utro Rossii*, a progressive Moscow newspaper, stated that the "Society of St. Eugenia produced a revolution in the history of Russian postcards. It enhanced claims of the refined values of art and made postcards a weapon in the popularization of artistic works."[39] Indeed, the St. Eugenia Society proved to have such a strong cultural role that it was not destroyed by the Bolsheviks after the October Revolution. Instead, it was renamed the Committee on Popularizing Artistic Editions (Komitet populiarizatsii khudozhestvennykh izdanii) and incorporated into the State Academy of Material Culture (Gosudarstvennaia akademiia material'noi kul'tury). In the late 1920s, the renamed organization was still issuing postcards for the now Soviet market.

The success of the St. Eugenia Society spawned a number of imitators, especially since the fin-de-siècle saw increasing middle-class involvement in voluntary and philanthropic organizations together with a corresponding rise in civic consciousness.[40] Charitable and social welfare organizations produced and sold postcards to raise funds and awareness. Richard Bartmann, author of *Picture Postcard Encyclopaedia of Russia*, had a vast collection that included postcards from the Committee for the Resurrection of Russian Art, the Lyubanski Committee for Relief of the Poor, and the Committee for the Construction of a House for Teachers.[41] These cards were identifiable by the unique crests imprinted on their reverse sides, near where a user would write a message (see Figure 1.5). Other organizations, such as the Aleksandr Nevskii Temperance Society, printed their name on the front of the postcard with the picture (see Figure 1.6).

The number of these fundraising committees mushroomed once the First World War broke out, and similar efforts continued into the mid-1920s under the Soviet government. New organizations sought to assist wounded soldiers, war widows, and orphans. Some, such as the Royal Philanthropic Association to Assist Wounded Soldiers of the Lower Ranks and Their Families or the Special Petrograd Committee under the Auspices of H.M. Princess Olga Nikolaevna, continued to rely on patronage at the highest levels. The need for relief was so great other groups, such as the Petrograd City Committee for Soldiers and Their Families, often with roots in civil society rather than in the government bureaucracy or among the nobility, also emerged during the war years.

Their mandate was continued in the early Soviet period by groups established by the government, at both the national and regional levels, to provide financial assistance to Red Army veterans as well as to homeless children and victims of famine. Selling postcards, where a portion of the price was diverted to these social welfare organizations, again, proved to be a popular method of fundraising (see Figure 1.7).[42]

Postcards were also used by the American Relief Administration as it battled famine in Russia in the early 1920s. The starving who had relatives abroad were given special postcards with which to contact them. The postcards explained how drafts could be purchased so people in

1.5 Back of a postcard showing a large field gun. The caption at the bottom says the postcard was produced under the auspices of the Skobolev Committee with the approval of the emperor. Manufactured by the Skobolev Committee, 1916.

Soviet Russia would receive food packages. By September 1922, a hundred thousand packages per month were arriving in the afflicted regions.[43]

Alongside groups with patronage and causes to promote were a number of private entrepreneurs. Among the best-known Russian firms in the picture postcard market were Edition "Richard," founded in St. Petersburg in 1899 by P. Neustroev; Izdanie D.P. Efimov, founded in Moscow in 1902; and Izdanie fotografa M. Dmitriev, in Nizhnii-Novgorod. The latter was particularly noted for the high quality of its photographs, with Dmitriev winning a Golden Prize at the 1892 Paris Exposition for his work. Examples from other smaller firms can still be found today, but the firms themselves have disappeared largely unnoticed by history. The geographical space covered by local postcard manufacturers is staggering. They were dispersed across the country, in such disparate locations as Astrakhan, Samara, Odessa, Kishinev, Riga, Vilnius, Tiflis, Smolensk, and

1.6 Postcard showing the dangers of drinking. Manufactured by the Aleksandr
Nevskii Temperance Society, n.d.

Chita. Local producers also looked to larger firms to print postcards for
them. For instance, Granberg printed postcards of Kislovodsk for a firm
named Raev and views of Tomsk for P.I. Makushin's bookstore there. The
connection between postcard manufacturers and booksellers was, indeed, a strong one. Postcards were normally sold in bookstores, and it
was not uncommon to find booksellers branching out into postcard production themselves.[44] Other postcards were sold alongside foodstuffs in
small supermarkets as these began to appear in urban areas at the end of
the century.[45] Postcards sometimes reached the countryside owing to the
efforts of foreigners residing in Russia. H.V. Keeling, a British worker
who spent five years living in Russia, recalled that he was popular with
villagers "because I had a camera and took their photographs, printing
them post cards at a nominal price."[46] Finally, the distribution of picture
postcards was further facilitated after 1905 when the government allowed Aleksei Suvorin's firm, one of the biggest publishing enterprises in

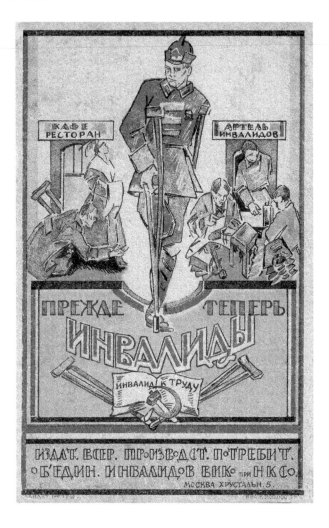

1.7 Fundraising postcard from the early Soviet period. Manufactured by Izdat. vser. proizvodst. potrebit. ob'edin. invalidov VIK pri NKFO, n.d.

the Russian Empire, to lease the book and newspaper kiosks in all of the country's railway stations. Suvorin's firm sold postcards alongside its other items.

Given how widely available postcards became, it is not surprising Russians quickly embraced their use in a variety of capacities. As we shall see, postcards facilitated the nature of business correspondence and provided another venue for advertising. They also fit well into the emerging tourist market, for postcards suggested what sites were remarkable in given locations and allowed tourists to send regular short communications home. Finally, collectors, too, found the market for picture postcards a heady one.

Business Uses of Postcards

Suvorin's agreement with the government should come as no surprise for the selling of books and postcards in turn-of-the-century Russia was extremely profitable. Businessmen across Europe and North America had quickly seen the advantages of postcards for all kinds of commercial activities. The mass production of postcards made them easy to obtain in bulk and, in all countries, postcards were cheaper to mail than other forms of business correspondence. Soon postcards were being used to set up appointments, confirm the receipt of goods, and send price lists to potential buyers.[47] Postcards were also employed in some communications between employers and employees. Russian writer Nikolai Teleshov remembered receiving a postcard from the editor of a journal suggesting what time he should come by the next day to be paid for the first verses he ever published.[48] He was not alone. Composer Sergei Prokofiev's diary is replete with references to postcards, including ones sent to confirm the dates when his works would be performed or published.[49] These usages contradict a commonly held perception that postcards were primarily associated with women.[50] While many women did avidly collect and send postcards, they were also widely employed by men.

For advertising purposes, firms sent out picture postcards showing their storefronts, factories, and even parts of the production process for their goods. Other postcards printed advertisements on the reverse side where senders would be forced to notice them as they wrote their messages. Figure 1.8 shows one such card – in this case advertising text providing the addresses for a number of shoe stores has been stamped onto the original postcard.

РЕКЛАМ КАРТОЧ. МОСКВА, ГАЗЕТН. 9 КР. 33, АВДЛОВА

ВСЕМІРНЫЙ ПОЧТОВЫЙ СОЮЗЪ. РОССІЯ.

Union Postale Universelle Russie.

Открытое письмо. — Carte Postale.

Собственные магазины:
въ Петрогр. Апраксинъ дворъ, 37 т. 589-40
„   „   Владимір. просп., 13 т. 232-40
„ Москвѣ, Срѣтенка, 27-29
„ Ростовѣ н/Д. Московская, 71
Кромѣ собствен. магазиновъ обувь Т-ва
можно получать въ лучшихъ магазинахъ
во всѣхъ городахъ Россіи и Сибири.

Петроградск. механ. произв. обуви
Т-ва Н. А. Столяровъ съ С-ми
Фабричн. марка „Якорь"

1.8 Back of postcard showing a ship in the Russian fleet. The text (stamped onto the postcard) provides the addresses for a number of shoe stores. Postcard manufactured by Sherer, Nabholzh & Co., 1904.

A more systematic campaign, involving a large number of postcards, was undertaken by the Singer Sewing Machine Company as it strove to corner the Russian market. When Singer first brought his machine to market, he quickly realized he had to find a way to create a demand for it. Massive advertising campaigns followed in each country where the firm set up a base of operations.[51] In Russia, the company logo showed a woman dressed in an elaborate traditional costume using a sewing machine. This emblem was reproduced in some form on all of Singer's advertising.[52] On postcards, which featured innocuous landscapes or patriotic paintings on the front (like a scene from Napoleon's failed invasion of Russia, see Figure 1.9), the logo was printed on the back where the message was written – in other words, where both the sender and recipient were likely to notice it. Postcards like these were undoubtedly a relatively cheap and efficient way of reaching out to new and existing customers.

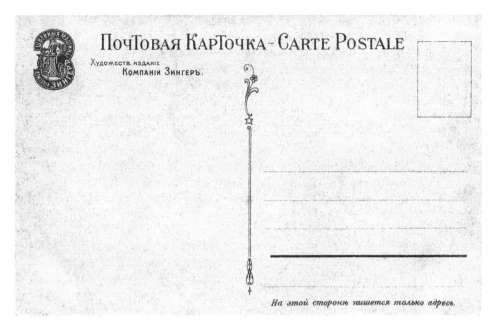

ПоЧТовая КарТочка - Carte Postale

Художеств. изданіе
Компаніи Зингеръ.

На этой сторонѣ пишется только адресъ.

1.9 Back of postcard showing a scene from Napoleon's invasion of Russia. The logo for the Singer Sewing Machine Company appears in the top corner. Manufactured by Khudozhestv izdanie kompanii Zinger', n.d.

Postcard Production after the Revolution

The Russian Revolution completely disrupted the market described in the last few pages. Most of the private firms were driven from it, although their remaining stock continued to be used until it was gone. The 1920s saw the establishment of a new postcard market – one that this time was dominated by state-affiliated agencies. The propaganda wing of the Red Army proved to be one of the earliest manufacturers of postcards since during the civil war it reprinted copies of political posters by the well-known graphic artists Viktor Deni and D.S. Moor in postcard form.[53] Doing so offered the possibility that they might penetrate into private spaces. While it is unlikely that many people decorated their homes with propaganda posters, they certainly would have kept postcards there. Moreover, their smaller size meant that postcards were much easier and cheaper to make which, given the paper shortages of the civil war period, undoubtedly increased their appeal. Museums, such as the Tretiakov Gallery and the Central Museum of the Revolution of the USSR, soon cornered certain niches of the market as did the Lenin Institute, which came to issue the majority of Lenin postcards. Other important producers included the Association of the Arts of Revolutionary Russia (AKhRR), founded in 1922. The Association, which was renamed the Association of Artists of the Revolution (AKhR) in 1928, produced postcards of about eight hundred different designs until it was absorbed by Izogiz (Gosudarstvennoe izdatel'stvo izobratizel'nogo iskusstva), at the end of 1931.[54] Among its subjects were scenes like lessons in workers' circles or the activities of Young Pioneers. An unusual, but memorable, feature of these postcards was the inclusion of the subjects' names, ages, addresses, and sometimes, even places of work, in the captions. Izogiz's emphasis on more educational-type postcards continued throughout the 1930s. As early as the mid-1920s, the Soviet government began to think of using postcards in the country's classrooms, since they were cheaper to produce than new textbooks. In 1932, it fell to Izogiz to create these materials. The designs included graphs and statistics that illustrated some of the social achievements of the new regime and complimented current propaganda campaigns. The titles of the postcards give some sense of their content: "The liquidation of illiteracy in the USSR," "Growth of the number of people starting school," "Growth of the number of people studying in higher schools in the USSR," and "Growth of book production in the USSR."[55]

Narkompochtel' got into the swing of postcard manufacturing just prior to the introduction of its "circular post" operations. In October 1923, it started to issue pre-stamped postcards with the worker image that was then also being used on Soviet postage stamps. Sviaz', a commercial arm of Narkompochtel', introduced the first Soviet postcards with advertisements in 1925, and advertising-agitational cards followed only a few years later.[56] These postcards had massive print runs of between one and four million copies each, and were meant for both domestic and international use. Some of them were part of multimedia advertising campaigns encouraging Soviet citizens to subscribe to magazines and government bonds or to buy life insurance. Others were more like the fundraising postcards described earlier in that they sought to encourage membership in voluntary associations or to raise money to build up the nation's defence capabilities (see Figure 1.10).

The most consistent producer of postcards in the early Soviet period, however, was the State Publishing House (Gosizdat'), which began its

1.10 Postcard encouraging Soviet citizens to join the paramilitary organization Osoaviakhim. Caption on the side reads, "Strengthen the defence of the USSR! Study military technology." Manufactured by Narkompochtel', 1932.

venture into the postcard market in 1919. It established a network of stores selling postcards and other printed items in urban areas across the country.[57] In 1924, Gosizdat' honoured its fifth anniversary by issuing a seventeen-postcard series illustrating aspects of its work as well as its first catalogue of postcards. The 504 items listed in the catalogue were divided into eleven groups, each with a number of individual series. Gosizdat' continued to issue this type of catalogue into the 1930s.

Postcards and Tourism

In July 1841, Thomas Cook led his first train excursion and the rest, as we say, is history. Cook's ever expanding network of tours ushered in the era of modern mass tourism. Within two decades, his firm offered trips to destinations on the continent (with more exotic locales coming in the final decades of the century), spurring the creation of new infrastructure to handle the flow of tourists. Across Europe, railways and hotels were built, and the number of tourists continued to grow. By 1880, Thomas Cook & Son had sixty offices worldwide, and its coupons were being accepted by five hundred hotels.[58] The firm's growth encouraged a number of competitors to join what was one of the nineteenth and twentieth centuries' most vibrant, and hotly contested, markets.

Although the history of tourism in Russia is still a relatively under-researched subject, some sources point to the way Russia was becoming part of the world tourist market at the end of the nineteenth century.[59] American Express, Thomas Cook's largest rival, opened an office in St. Petersburg, in 1916.[60] At about the same time, a handful of travel guides for, and traveller's accounts of, Russia were published in Europe. These works provided information about rail and steamer connections to Russia, in addition to price lists for food and transportation in some localities.[61] The language barrier was addressed by J.H. Wisdom's *The Briton in Russia*, which provided the English-speaking tourist with a pocket interpreter together with a phonetic pronunciation guide to standard Russian phrases.[62] Wisdom's guide included the expressions needed to purchase and mail postcards, while Baedaker's 1914 guide to Russia gave the prices of postal services as well as the hours of post office operations.[63] Both authors simply assumed that tourists would be sending postcards home.

Domestically, the Russian tourism industry expanded steadily at the end of the nineteenth century. The first local mountain climbing, hiking, and cyclist clubs were created. Organized outings and day trips, which were often partially subsidized by local zemstva or city governments, also began. In 1899, the Russian Society of Tourists (Rossiiskoe obshchestvo turistov) was founded. Membership remained small, never exceeding more than a few thousand people, and information about the Society's activities appeared in its journal, *Russian Tourist* (*Russkii turist*).[64] Three other travel publications were published in the first decade of the twentieth century: *Excursion Herald* (*Ekskursionnyi vestnik*), *Russkii ekskursant* (*Russian Excursionist*), and *Excursions and Museums for School-children* (*Shkol'nye ekskursii i shkol'nyi muzei*).

Despite these developments, tourism in Russia lacked a centralizing organization in the fin-de-siècle era. No firm emerged to occupy the role played elsewhere by Thomas Cook or American Express. Most tourists had to conceive of, plan, and execute their trips privately, at least until the end of the 1920s. In 1929, the Soviet government established the Society of Proletarian Tourism of the RSFSR (Obshchestvo proletarskogo turizma RSFSR). Branches were set up across the country and, within a year, the Society had fifty thousand members.[65] In 1936, the industry was reorganized, with oversight for tourism being granted to the All-Union Committee on Physical Culture and Sport (Vsesoiuznyi komitet po fizicheskoi kul'ture i sportu). By this time, tourism had become firmly linked with the physical culture movement, as well as with the installation of Soviet-style patriotism. The new Soviet constitution explicitly guaranteed people the right to take holidays.

The same years saw a renewed interest in developing foreign tourism. Beginning in the late 1920s, Thomas Cook added tours to the Soviet Union to its lineup, and American Express sponsored a number of trips for businessmen. The Soviets negotiated arrangements with foreign cruise lines like Cunard, Hamburg-American, and Holland-America. In April 1929, Intourist was established. Its mandate was to control every aspect of the foreign tourist market for the USSR. From the logistics of each individual trip to the development of modern tourist infrastructure to foreign marketing campaigns, seemingly nothing escaped its reach.[66] This type of centralization allowed a much larger market to develop. By the 1930s, one can speak of thousands of tourists visiting the Soviet Union every year.

From the beginning, the connections between tourism and picture postcards were strong. By the final decade of the nineteenth century, European tourists could seemingly find topographical picture postcards in every town and village.[67] Their very availability made them an attractive form of communication. Despite being mass-produced, postcards appeared more spontaneous than the traditional long-winded travel letter, and they promoted the notion that the recipient could somehow share the sights depicted with the sender.[68] Moreover, in the words of Steven Dotterer and Galen Cranz, the "postcard served as a symbol of status and the ability to travel."[69] Mailing someone a postcard proved the sender could afford to travel and was, indeed, visiting some interesting spot. Sergei Prokofiev, who admitted in his diary that he had "a great weakness" for postcards, delighted in sending them whenever he travelled abroad or even took day trips at home.[70] In June 1913, when he visited Paris, for instance, Prokofiev sent twenty-nine postcards to let his friends know he had ascended the Eiffel Tower.[71] Postcards, like those mailed by Prokofiev, came to signify what Louise McReynolds has termed "the commodification of adventures into souvenirs."[72]

Picture postcards proved vital to tourists visiting Russia. As Ruth Kedzie Wood outlined in the account of her Russian honeymoon, postcards helpfully bridged language barriers and ensured that tourists, like Wood and her husband, would see all of the main attractions. By buying postcards of what one wanted to see, and then showing them to cab drivers, the resourceful tourists did not even need a basic knowledge of Russian to navigate around their destinations.[73]

A second usage was described in Wood's later guidebook to Russia. As she noted, it was difficult for foreigners to take private photographs in Russia since permits were required – often separate ones for each town and sometimes even for individual attractions such as the Kremlin, a church, or a museum. Tourists were also forbidden to take photographs from the train along the Trans-Siberian Railway or at any of its stations.[74] Wood advised keen photographers either to join the Russian Photographic Society prior to their journey, or to buy postcards in lieu of taking their own holiday snaps.[75] Postcards were the cheaper option. While membership in the Photographic Society cost 5 roubles, postcards varied in price from only 1 kopeck for the very cheapest to 10 kopecks each for picture postcards in colour.[76] Postcards could be mailed abroad for an additional 4 kopecks.

The problem of securing permission to photograph sites continued to plague tourists in the Soviet era. When Owen Tweedy wrote of his brief visit to the Soviet Union in 1930, he noted with some frustration the restrictions on photography. Tweedy was told by his tour guide that he could not photograph military subjects or bridges. However, in his words, "The last-named restriction is ludicrous. In every hotel and museum we entered, there were postcards galore for sale, depicting bridges both on the Neva and the Moskwa [Moscow] river. They are taken by Government, sold by Government, and the proceeds go to Government."[77]

The connection between the Soviet government monopoly on tourism and picture postcards was also reflected in a number of other ways. Cruise ship passengers who disembarked in Leningrad found a kiosk in the docking area that had propaganda posters and postcards available for sale. Since passengers changed money on their ships, they were immediately able to purchase these items. Moreover, those who opted not to take excursions into the city were restricted to only this dock, making them a captive audience for the kiosk's souvenirs.[78]

In the early 1930s, half a dozen travel-related advertising-agitational postcards were issued by Narkompochtel'. Each design appeared in several languages and millions of copies were made. One postcard

1.11 Postcard encouraging Soviet citizens to save money for summer vacations. Manufactured by Narkompochtel', 1929.

encouraged Soviet citizens to subscribe to travel magazines such as *Around the World* (*Vokrug sveta*) or *International Tourist* (*Vsemirnyi turist*). A second presented tourism as a normal, expected part of life for the ideal Soviet family (see Figure 1.11). Nor were foreign audiences ignored, since four of the Narkompochtel' postcards, with their designs printed in English, advertised the services of Intourist and presented the Soviet landscape as a desirable one to visit (see Figure 1.12).[79]

In addition to businessmen and tourists, postcard collectors were instrumental in the growth of the international postcard market. Manufacturers encouraged the passion for collecting by issuing postcards in numbered series, assuming that collectors would be driven to obtain every postcard and avoid gaps in their collections.[80] By the 1890s, postcard collecting, termed "cartophilia" by its practitioners, was a firmly established pastime. In Britain, postcard collecting clubs formed, and they

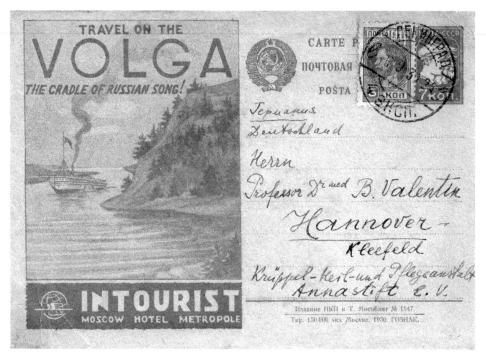

1.12 Postcard promoting the services of Intourist. Manufactured by Narkompochtel', 1930.

were aided by the establishment of no fewer than six specialist maga-zines.[81] Similar developments occurred on the continent, where clubs and periodicals also proliferated. Richard Carline's research on post-cards, for instance, mentions the existence of postcard collector jour-nals in Germany, France, Italy, Switzerland, Spain, and Hungary.[82] Clubs quickly established connections with one another so that their members could exchange postcards. The most important international association was Kosmopolit, headquartered in Nuremburg, but with branches in most European countries and in the United States. Collectors frequently used their membership numbers when trading cards, and serious collec-tors even had special hand stamps made showing their membership affiliations.[83]

Richard Bartmann suggests that by the end of 1897 Russian collectors, at least in St. Petersburg, were actively engaged in the trading networks that criss-crossed Europe, and that eventually collectors could be found throughout the empire's vast expanses. His own collection contained examples bearing postcard club membership numbers from people in Moscow, Reval, Kiev, Tambov, Ekaterinodar, and Vladivostok. Occasional postcard exhibitions also began to be held in these years.[84] Nevertheless, the growth of postcard collecting in Russia is an area we know frustratingly little about. Many collections were, undoubtedly, scattered or destroyed as war and revolution swept across the country in the first quarter of the twentieth century.[85] Existing information supports the conclusion that the number of Russian collectors grew until the Russo-Japanese War (1904–05) interrupted the flow of exchanges between collectors. Hostility towards Russia, not to say support for the Japanese underdog, may have played a role in rupturing the relationships between collectors. The situation did not improve until 1909 by which time Kosmopolit, and a rival collecting association Globus, had established branches in Russia. Collecting continued to thrive for the next few years, apparently even in the initial years of the First World War and despite changes to the Russian postcard market.

In the Soviet era, postcard collecting revived but did not apparently receive the same attention from the authorities as stamp collecting.[86] The journal *Among Collectors* (*Sredi kollektsionerov*), published by the Society of Lovers of Books (Obshchestvo liubitelei knigi) between 1921 and 1924, included articles touching on a number of different areas of collecting. Apart from its obvious focus on books, *Among Collectors* printed articles for collectors of porcelain, coins, stamps, and posters, although not a single item relating to postcards appeared within its pages.[87] A small section of *Soviet Collector* (*Sovetskii kollektsioner*), the journal for collectors established in 1963, printed information about postcards, but the short articles were subject to the dictates of Soviet political correctness. Hence, the focus of these journals never strayed into prerevolutionary postcards, apart from one article examining the illegal postcards produced by the Bolsheviks in 1905. The most serious object of study seems to have been the way in which the life of Lenin was depicted in postcards. A more positive development came in 1935 when Nikolai Tagrin joined the postcard section of the Leningrad branch of the All-Union Society of Collectors (Vsesoiuznoe obshchestvo kollektsionerov or VOK). The section had only eighteen members at the time, and while its activities never rivalled the clubs of the postcard's golden age, Tagrin was able through its auspices to become the most visible collector in the USSR. He donated all 143,000 postcards of his collection to the

Geographical Society of the USSR on the eve of the Second World War, continuing as the collection's archivist, exhibit organizer, and purchaser for the rest of his life.[88]

Censorship

Finally, this introductory survey of the history of Russian postcards would not be complete if it did not include a few words about censorship. From the moment they first appeared, picture postcards provoked concerns about politeness and morality. Some middle-class Europeans felt that sending postcards gave an impression of miserliness, believing that since postcards cost less to send, they implied that the recipients were not worth the added expense of a letter. Others initially worried about their privacy, fearing that servants, among others, would read their correspondence. In Britain, it was even suggested that postcards made it easier for people to libel and defame one another.[89] These fears prompted governments across Europe to establish some limits on the ways postcards could be used. In Russia, an 1873 addendum to the 1868 temporary decrees concerning the postal administration prohibited anyone from writing anything contrary to the law, public order, morals, or decency on a postcard. Apparently, a Third Section report had revealed some off-colour remarks about women and government officials written on postcards, hence the introduction of the new instructions.[90] Initially, all postcards were to be read by postal censors, but as the number of postcards sent grew to massive proportions, it proved impossible to do so. Therefore, postal authorities began to target specific groups for special attention (such as suspected revolutionaries and prisoners of war), and they devoted less time to the correspondence of everyday individuals.

Producers, too, were subject to various forms of censorship. M. Eager, an Irish nanny who worked for the royal family for six years, recorded in her memoirs what happened when it was discovered postcards lacking the censor's permit were for sale in St. Petersburg. Although their designs were perfectly innocuous, featuring pictures of the Winter Palace and St. Isaac's Cathedral, storeowners were forbidden to sell them. Eager found the situation incomprehensible, particularly since "frightfully indecent pictures and cards are openly shown in the windows and shops."[91] In other instances, some subjects would simply be declared beyond acceptable boundaries; sellers and manufacturers alike were then forced to remove the offending postcards from circulation. Such a furor arose, for example, over a series of postcards issued to commemorate the seventieth birthday of Lev Tolstoi. In the eyes of the authorities, the post-cards, which showed Tolstoi in peasant dress working in the fields or at home with his wife, were thought to encourage the spread of his radical opinions, and they had to be pulled from the market.[92] Additional censorship, in the form of special approval from court censors, was applied to any postcards depicting members of the royal family or even their emblems.

The situation in Russia was further complicated by the rise of an active revolutionary movement seeking to overthrow the existing regime. Mail to and from suspected revolutionaries had been perlustrated by black chambers since the 1860s. Moreover, people under arrest, in prison, or in exile in Siberia automatically had their mail censored. By law, those in exile were required to use postcards to correspond with relatives. Nor were revolutionaries abroad exempt from this kind of supervision. The Russian government paid undercover agents in foreign post offices to provide it with any suspicious items. There were, for example, agents in Romania, Bulgaria, Serbia, Austria, Germany, and France.[93] Revolutionaries responded in the 1880s by attempting to bypass the official postal system, especially for correspondence between those in Russia and their counterparts living abroad. A network of couriers developed to smuggle mail. The repeal of censorship laws at the time of the 1905 Revolution allowed revolutionary organizations to become more public in their activities, particularly in the publishing sphere.[94] Alongside the pamphlets and books, revolutionary postcards were issued in sizeable numbers, although the most overtly political images remained illegal to mail and black chambers continued their work unabated. It is believed the latter even expanded their activities in this era since the correspondence of all candidates for election to the Duma was being opened.[95]

Censorship was especially important in times of war. During both the Russo-Japanese War and the First World War, the Russian government issued special instructions restricting what types of mail could go into and out of war zones. Moreover, letters and postcards were subject to several layers of scrutiny from military censors. Despite government and military concern, the censorship network did not function perfectly because the authorities had not planned for the millions of prisoners of war who flooded the Russian postal system with postcards sent from their places of detention. By the time the tsarist regime collapsed, taking with it the existing censorship apparatus, millions of unread postcards were still waiting for approval from the censors.

Conclusion

"When the archaeologists of the thirtieth century begin to excavate the ruins of London, they will fasten upon the Picture Postcard as the best guide to the spirit of the Edwardian era. They will collect and collate thousands of these pieces of pasteboard and they will reconstruct our age from the strange hieroglyphs and pictures that time has spared. For the Picture Postcard is a candid revelation of our pursuits and pastimes, our customs and costumes, our morals and manners."[96] These words, written by journalist James Douglas in 1907, are just as applicable to fin-de-siècle Russia as they are to Edwardian Britain. This chapter began by outlining the growth of the Russian postal system and the technological changes that led to a booming market for cheap paper products, picture postcards among them. By focusing on the development of infrastructure and marketing practices, it has been shown how and why postcards were produced and consumed in such vast quantities. Postcards were useful to businessmen and tourists. They sparked the passions of collectors and the fears of government and social conservatives. In the end, their presence became ubiquitous, blanketing the globe in cheap visual images for the first time. But, just knowing postcards were popular does not explain the deeper significance of this revolution in visual mass culture. Instead, one must scrutinize the images on the postcards – the way Douglas suggests future historians will do – to look at how they presented Russian subjects with new conceptions of their country and with new social identities. It is to these subjects that the following chapters now turn.

Chapter Two

The Landscapes of Russian Imperialism

The words hung in the air. "Wow, that is so postcard!" This was the first thought of a rather jaded tourist looking at Victoria Falls for the first time.[1] Despite the banality of the comment, it does suggest that an irrevocable bond was established between picture postcards and visions of landscapes over the century separating the first purchasers of postcards from this modern tourist. In this chapter, we return to when postcards were new and the images they presented could still provoke a sense of wonder. By offering images of territories absorbed over the course of the nineteenth century, picture postcards allowed Russian subjects to watch the consolidation of the state, but in a sanitized fashion. Notably, most landscape postcards were devoid of people. Their absence negated the ethnic diversity of frontier regions and, instead, let Russians imagine peripheral regions as empty spaces, just primed for takeover and economic development. Similarly, because the images reproduced on picture postcards fixed boundaries in a variety of ways, they negated the fluidity of actual borders. Through these omissions, picture postcards were instrumental in constructing imaginary geographies of the Russian Empire in the fin-de-siècle period.

The discussion begins with an examination of picture postcards expressing "official nationalism" in Benedict Anderson's use of the term. Used by the autocratic state to counter challenges from emerging class-based and ethnically based nationalisms, these postcards firmly anchored the Russian nation to the existing political system and conflated nation with empire. Postcards featuring maps and coats of arms marked the limits of imperial control and legitimized the political status quo, while postcards of statues, which offer an expanded interpretation of landscape, suggested ways the Russian government imposed a uniform cultural and historical narrative on the country. Postcards of royal celebrations, notably, those that used electric light to manipulate nighttime landscapes, tried to instil a sense of awe and pride by connecting the dynasty to modernity and its technological innovations.

A second kind of landscape postcard evoked questions of imperial power and control by presenting images of formal gardens. The manipulation of plants for political purposes had long roots in Russia, as in the rest of Europe, but what may have been done for decades on imperial and gentry estates burst into public spaces in the nineteenth century as cities and towns built public gardens. As picture postcards reveal, gardens across the empire imposed a standardized, European-inspired ideal on public spaces. They presented scenes of social harmony that thereby implied Russian presence met no resistance and that a homogenized culture could be created.

Other postcards catalogued the progress of the nation by commemorating infrastructure developments. As an expression of economic nationalism, they reflected popular notions about Russia's status as a modern nation as well as the commodification of the landscape. As we will see, while postcards of the Caucasus region, where military engagements persisted past the mid-nineteenth century, mingled traces of the sublime with images of economic domination, postcards of Siberia offered a less threatening vision of territorial expansion. In both instances, however, postcards showed the government – as opposed to the tsar or the Orthodox Church – actively engaged in the economic development of frontier regions and, hence, occupying a place at the forefront of empire building.

Finally, the discussion of picture postcards and economic nationalism moves to the subject of tourism. Here, I do not come to the same conclusions as Christopher Ely in *This Meager Nature*. Ely argues that "the image of rural space was constructed very differently in Russia than it was in Europe" and that "provincial Russia was never successfully designated a scenic space for tourism because the Russian landscape came to acquire a special significance resistant to scenic interpretations."[2] Picture postcards often tell a slightly different story – one where Europeanized features (in the form of hotels, spas, and resorts) were imposed on the landscape, in a way that was consistent with tourist infrastructure across the Western world. Other postcards, particularly those showing Russian waterways like the Volga River, which celebrated the open spaces of the Russian heartland more closely approximate Ely's findings, but they still appealed to tourists who, seemingly, could embrace both Russian and Western notions about what constituted an attractive landscape. Either way, the strong connection between tourism, economic development, and imperial control is at the centre of this chapter's final section.

Postcards and Landscapes of Autocratic Power

The picture postcards described in this section are representative of a Russian "official nationalism" that emerged at the end of the nineteenth century. The analysis relies on Benedict Anderson's formulation of the term, which he defines as the "willed merger of nation and dynastic empire."[3] Anderson portrays official nationalism as a kind of rear-guard action devised by established power elites as they attempted to confront the strength of developing popular conceptions of the nation; in this case, elites worried about class-based and ethnically based nationalisms. He maintains that the rise of print capitalism played an instrumental role in this process since it provided "for a new way of linking fraternity, power and time meaningfully together."[4] It can be argued that the rise of cheap visual images – like picture postcards – took over some of the functions of print capitalism and became a significant component in creating official nationalism. Certain kinds of landscape postcards marked an effort to define the Russian nation within the framework of an autocratic state. These included postcards that incorporated symbols of state, like maps or official crests. Maps, in particular, relied on linear boundaries, often those artificially imposed by a central authority, to delimit territoriality and sovereignty.[5] They are a form of political and social control that offers clues to the imperial spatial imagination. Valerie Kivelson's insightful study of seventeenth-century Russian maps outlines how this process works. She explains that "maps visually codified the local into a system of signs and signifiers of importance to the central state, reifying that state's concerns and signifying the triviality, even the erasure of local particularism."[6] Kivelson goes on to say, "Maps served centralizing regimes not through crushing opposition but by involving varied interest groups in a single discussion, by standardizing the terms of the conversation, and by building a uniform framework in which disputes could be conducted."[7]

But, whereas the maps studied by Kivelson were produced for, and seen by, society's elites, the creation of picture postcard versions of maps allowed for their mass dissemination for the first time. As a result, imperial configurations of space, ones that reinforced the connections between landscape and the Russian autocracy, spread into popular culture. Figure 2.1 provides an example.

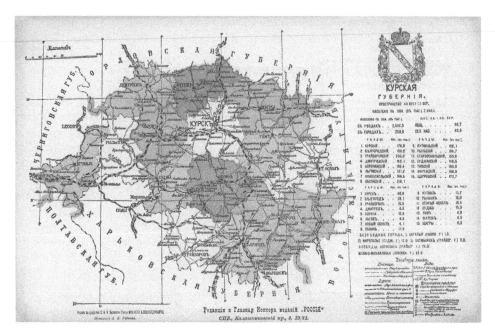

2.1 Map of Kurskaia guberniia. Izdanie "Rossiia," n.d.

A map of Kurskaia guberniia, the picture postcard gives a wealth of information about that region. The statistics placed off to one side list the population of each town and uezd in the guberniia. The map itself shows various kinds of roads and waterways. By using different colours for each uezd, the postcard map reflects the centralized state administrative divisions of the territory rather than boundaries that local inhabitants may have employed. The connection to official nationalism is reinforced by two additional elements. At the bottom of the postcard, it clearly states that His Imperial Highness the Grand Duke Mikhail Aleksandrovich, the tsar's younger brother, funded its publication. It is not much of a stretch, therefore, to call this postcard a piece of official tsarist propaganda. Imperial control over the locality was further denoted by the inclusion of the official crest of the guberniia, which includes a crown, in the design. Crests and coats of arms become, in the words of J.B. Harley, "badges of territorial possession," when they are used on maps.[8]

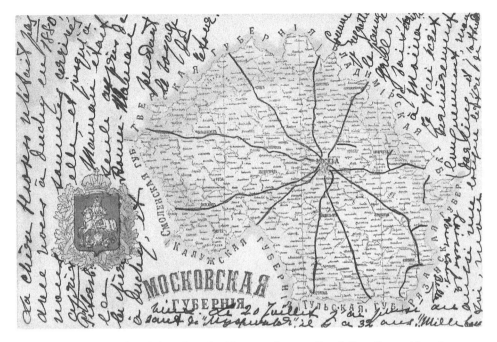

2.2 Map of Moskovskaia guberniia. No manufacturer listed. Postally used but the date has been obliterated by the removal of the postage stamp.

A second map – this time of Moscow guberniia – is striking in its use of colour (see Figure 2.2). The main roads converging on Russia's ancient capital are delimited in red, like blood flowing through the arteries of a living body to its heart. The crest of the city, a representation of St. George slaying the dragon, is placed off to one side.[9] The postcard is also noteworthy for the clues it provides about the mentality of the sender. Unsigned, but with text written in both French and Russian, the postcard suggests the sender was from the higher ranks in society and assumed the recipient would know who the postcard was from. (The recipient was a countess staying at a hotel in Lucerne, Switzerland.) The sender took the time to very carefully cover the front of the postcard with writing in several directions, but without touching the map or the main components of the crest. A respect for the image pervades the postcard as if it was unthinkable for the sender to desecrate the symbols of state represented there by writing on them.

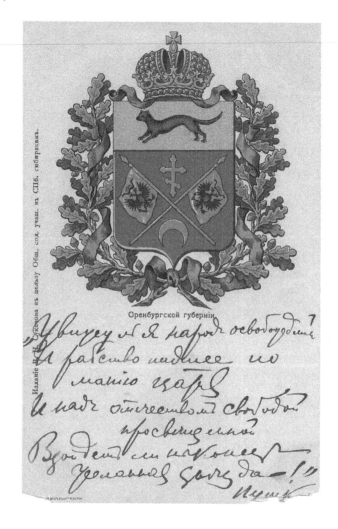

2.3 Coat of arms for Orenburgskaia guberniia. Izdanie V.P. Sukachova.

The use of crests as a kind of imperial shorthand on picture postcards was common. Indeed, one postcard reproduced in the album *Privet iz Moskvy* showed the entire country expressed in this symbolic fashion: the imperial double-headed eagle (the symbol of the Romanov dynasty) was surrounded by the coats of arms of the regional capitals of the empire.[10] Here, the imperial spatial imagination omitted any tangible reference to the physical landscape at all. Nor was this an isolated example. Several postcard series separated crests and reprinted them as individual picture postcards, like Figure 2.3. This postcard was sold to raise funds for Siberian students attending St. Petersburg University.[11] Likely the students in question came from Orenburgskaia guberniia, an area on the western edge of Siberia, since that would explain the use of this particular crest. On the postcard, Orenburgskaia guberniia as a place is conceived of solely by its official crest. No local divisions of territory are even suggested, and there are no statistics to connect the space with the people who reside there. The crest incorporates both an Orthodox cross and two standards bearing the imperial double-headed eagle. A large crown again sits atop the rest of the design. Through these elements, the designers of the crest imply the territory is firmly under central imperial control and its inhabitants are uniformly Orthodox in terms of their religion. The postcard manufacturers, by uncritically appropriating the crest, evoke the same ideas.

A second category of picture postcard evoked expressions of state power by showing statues erected across Russia by the tsarist authorities. Statues are, in the words of June Hargrove, "weapons of advocacy," meant to provide viewers with models to emulate, and they contribute to the establishment of a uniform historical narrative.[12] Statues symbolize the authority of the monarch or state that decided what would be erected and where.[13] Ceremonies unveiling the statues to the public are demonstrations of state power, particularly when they are held in regions only recently subdued or where the presence of the statue may have been particularly anachronistic, as in Figure 2.4, where a statue commemorating a Russian military leader is being unveiled in Central Asia.

That people understood such monuments to be symbols of imperial power is revealed in moments of political turmoil, when these statues were targeted and had their meanings deliberately subverted. Two examples – both discussing the fate of statues of Catherine the Great – are telling. Tatiana Alexinsky, who worked as a nurse on a Russian hospital train during the First World War, arrived in Vilna (today Vilnius, the capital of Lithuania) just as orders to evacuate the city were announced.

Открытіе памятника К. П. фонъ Кауфману и войск. покор. Среди. Азію.

2.4 Unveiling of a monument to K.P. von Kaufman in Central Asia. Izd. I.A. Bek-Nazarova, n.d.

Despite the ensuing chaos, some residents of the city saw an opportunity to remove a hated symbol of Russian domination. They erected a crane, used it to hang a rope around the statue's neck, and lifted it from its pedestal. Alexinsky, whose husband was a political opponent of the tsarist regime, was discomforted by what she witnessed. "Never surely was the Great Empress treated with so little respect," she wrote.[14] Members of the social elite who were closer to the centres of power were similarly disturbed when such episodes spread in the wake of the revolution and the collapse of the monarchy. Despite being highly critical of the last empress in her memoirs, Princess Julia Cantacuzene "didn't want to see the beautiful statue of the Empress Catherine in front of the Imperial theater [in St. Petersburg] with a red flag pushed into her hand."[15] She, too, understood that such behaviour implied a rejection of the imperial structure that things like statues (and the postcards of them) had worked so hard to create.

Picture postcards were part of the empire-building process since they allowed people who lived elsewhere to not only see the statues placed in distant landscapes, but also, it was believed, to become part of an imagined community. Quite deliberately, anything that would detract from the idealized identity was excised from these images. To begin with, there was the choice of subject. Local residents were seldom chosen. Instead, statues commemorated the activities of figures deemed to have national importance by imperial authority. Figure 2.5 shows a monument dedicated to Admiral V.A. Kornilov in Sevastopol.[16] Although here the subject did have some connection to the city, he was nonetheless a representative of official power rather than a native-born son. The postcard was to some extent disconnected from the local environment by the fact that it was produced by Scherer, Nabholz & Co., a large Moscow-based firm, rather than by a local manufacturer. Hence, one gets the sense of how outsiders conceived of Sevastopol and how their views determined what was of interest in the city's history and landscape. The postcard fits well with Serhii Plokhy's description of Sevastopol as a "city of Russian glory." Plokhy shows how the Russian public interpreted the Siege of Sevastopol during the Crimean War (1853–56) as an expression of popular heroism. He notes the government was initially reluctant to embrace the Sevastopol myth. Not until the end of the 1870s did the notion find official favour, and even then, the government wished to commemorate different actors from those celebrated by the public. Still the Siege of Sevastopol became an important component in official memory, for it "justified and glorified the defence of new imperial possessions acquired by the tsars during the eighteenth and nineteenth centuries."[17]

In addition to this control over the subject matter, it was standard practice for postcard makers to crop local geographical features out of their designs. Figure 2.6, which shows a statue of Catherine the Great erected in Odessa, is an extreme example since here nothing at all, other than the caption on the postcard, would indicate the statue is located in Odessa. Images such as these erased both local history and local identity via a double form of cultural imperialism. Power over public spaces lay in the hands of central authorities who used statues, among other things, to imply there was a standard, largely Russocentric, historical narrative that was believed to be applicable to all of the empire's inhabitants. Postcard manufacturers absorbed these ideas uncritically; hence, their products replicated the narrative coming from above. Picture postcards like the

2.5 Monument to Admiral Kornilov in Sevastopol. Scherer, Nabholz & Co., 1902. Postally used in 1904.

2.6 Statue of Catherine the Great in Odessa. Izdanie fototipii Otto Renar', n.d.

ones included in this book not only legitimized the prevailing political system, but also the belief that officials in St. Petersburg controlled the empire's hinterlands.

A final form of autocratic control over landscape was suggested by some picture postcards depicting royal celebrations, especially the ones that involved manipulating nighttime landscapes. Owing to the technical difficulties of producing them, picture postcards of nighttime landscapes were rare, particularly prior to the First World War.[18] However, artificial light played an important part in Romanov celebrations. Electric light had the power to awe the masses – both with the wonder of novelty and the sheer extravagance of the cost entailed. The most noteworthy instance of royal officials manipulating light came during Nicholas II's coronation festivities, when the newly crowned Empress Alexandra was given the task of switching on the illuminations that lit up the Kremlin.[19] The rest of the city was also awash with artificial light for a period of three nights. One visitor remarked that false facades of electric bulbs were placed in front of significant landmarks and public buildings. He

РИГА,   ИЛЛЮМИНАЦІЯ
Ц ГОРОДСКОГО ТЕАТРА 27/ІІ 1913

2.7 Illuminations of the City Theatre in Riga in 1913. No manufacturer listed. Postally used in 1915 but the writing in pencil on the back is now too
faint to read.

went on to describe how "colored glass bowls in the forms of gigantic
stars and crowns and crosses, or in letters that spelled the names of the
young Czar and Czarina were reared high in the air, so that they burned
against the darkness like pieces of stationary fireworks."[20] Nor were just
foreigners impressed by these spectacles of light. Well-known Russian
publisher Aleksei Suvorin's diary entries from the coronation reveal that
he, too, thought the "splendid" illuminations worthy of comment.[21]
Subsequent entries still mention the lighting, even after the public's
(and Suvorin's) primary focus shifted to the Khodynka massacre.
Commemorative picture postcards of the illuminations extended their
reach well beyond the revellers in the ancient capital to encompass purchasers across the empire.

Since artificial lighting had such a profound effect in 1896, it was used
again during the celebrations for the three-hundredth anniversary of the
Romanov dynasty. The image in Figure 2.7 gives an impression of what

such arrangements looked like and of the specific iconography invoked. By choosing to outline large public buildings that were typically situated in city centres, tsarist officials were staking a claim to those loci of power.[22]

Here, the postcard shows the City Theatre in Riga, in other words, a key cultural space, lit up to honour the anniversary. But, the Romanov celebrations were also trying to create among the viewers what Jakle describes as a "collective sense of community belonging, of individuals being part of an evolving city."[23] Despite this sense of evolution, on the one hand, the imagery also, on the other, sought to convey a sense of permanence, at least politically speaking. The inclusion of the dates 1613 and 1913 into the overall design underscored the longevity of the dynasty, even if that necessitated manipulating the historical record. Riga was not part of Russia in 1613. The postcard does not reveal that fact but, rather, alters history to conform to the needs of the dynasty. Should anyone not comprehend the meaning of the dates, the large crown placed between them, and squarely in the middle of the design, provided clarification. For those not present at the actual festivities, picture postcards like this one allowed them to feel part of the larger community. To quote John Jakle, "Not only was surrogate experience offered but a kind of surrogate ownership as well."[24] The nighttime illuminations employed by tsarist officials at significant imperial events, and the picture postcards showing them, served a number of purposes. First, the tsar's power to light the night and to create a fairytale landscape of wonder was reinforced. The darkness feared throughout history was overcome, significantly through the intervention of the tsar and those under his direction. Second, the use of electricity, then a very new technology, spoke to Russia's place as a modern nation. The point was that Russian cities were illuminated at times like these in just the same way as other European cities when their respective countries had something to celebrate. Finally, these images tried to rally a sense of national belonging around the figure of the tsar, even though, ultimately, it would prove to be impossible to meld modern nationalism with a pre-modern autocratic form of government.

Plants and Power: Picture Postcards of Formal Gardens

As far back as the seventeenth century, Russian rulers expressed an interest in landscape design. Here, as in so many other facets of social and political life, Peter the Great accelerated the adoption of Western trends. He viewed the manipulation of the physical environment as a mechanism of state building, and thus, he began the practice whereby gardens were laid out around imperial residences and in public spaces. In 1711, for example, work began on the Summer Garden in St. Petersburg, his new capital city. The Summer Garden replicated the Dutch baroque style. The statues placed throughout the garden were meant, according to Andreas Schönle, "to shock Orthodox sensibilities," for "not only did the statuary signal the Westernization of the nobility's lifestyle, it also served as a primer for antique mythology and a didactic tool."[25] At Peterhof, too, Western styles were in evidence. Meant to serve as a Russian Versailles, its gardens offered "a completely different ideal of public space and 'monumentality' from Muscovite palaces."[26]

The use of landscape to shape the thinking and behaviour of others, as well as to convey impressions of power, continued to interest Peter I's successors, most notably his daughter Elizabeth and Catherine the Great. They, too, had lavish gardens constructed around their palaces and used them to present the Russian state to visitors in particular ways. In eighteenth-century odes, the garden served as a metaphor for the state, with the tsar presented as its gardener. Catherine the Great demonstrably embraced this metaphor as a way of justifying the expansion of the Russian Empire. To quote Schönle, "The garden trope, with its subtext of benevolent civilizational project, thus could dress up in naturalizing metaphors a naked power grab and a brutal war of civilizations."[27] The orderly image of the formal garden rode roughshod over the animosity Russian territorial expansion had frequently generated. Moreover, the garden represented a kind of barrier – a "final frontier to the surrounding threatening and encroaching foreign beyond," in the words of one historian – that delimited the extent of the safety guaranteed by the Russian state.[28]

The structure of the formal garden came from its manipulation of plants. Imperial powers (and aristocratic elites) have long exploited plants to increase their status and wealth. They have shown no hesitation in moving them from habitat to habitat for their own benefit.[29] By the end of the eighteenth century, Russia was involved in this international exchange of plants, spurred in part by Peter the Great's impatience. His desire to have parks and gardens constructed quickly led to large-scale imports of mature trees and plants. His successors, together with members of the Russian nobility, continued in the same vein. Formal gardens displayed the power of their creators over specific territorial areas as well as over the natural world in a more general sense. Formal gardens (both public and private) created artificial layouts, often with the plants arranged in precise geometrical patterns never found in the wild. They frequently used plants not native to the given region.[30] The inclusion of footpaths and seating areas suggested ways in which the behaviour of those who now used the piece of land was controlled by invisible authorities.

By the nineteenth century, the planting of formal gardens expanded well beyond imperial residences or private gentry estates. Public gardens were created in urban centres across the empire. As we shall see in the figures discussed here, what the postcards of such places revealed were not necessarily local or even native Russian landscapes. Instead, the images conformed to a Europeanized ideal. Just as Russian social elites expressed Westernized identities by wearing Western clothing, so too did Russian authorities impose a Westernized conception of landscape on local terrains when they came to plan the layouts of public gardens. The uniformity of public spaces, as demonstrated by picture postcards, fostered another kind of imperialism, for it mapped only a centralized, Europeanized vision onto the diverse Russian landscape.

Gary Sampson's article in the collection *Colonialist Photography* is helpful here. Although his attention is fixed on "English" images of Indian landscapes, Sampson's ideas resonate in other contexts, too. They provide a useful starting point when considering picture postcard images of peripheral regions of the Russian Empire. Sampson notes that colonialist photographs "tend to favor elements that are culturally and geographically amenable to the intellectual concerns and aesthetic sensibilities of the photographers and their projected viewing audience."[31] They omit elements that would cause the viewer to pause or question the idyll presented. In particular, hints of social conflict or troubled political realities were deliberately avoided in this type of image, thereby suggesting the peaceful integration of the pictured place into the empire. Given the political upheavals and social turmoil that afflicted fin-de-siècle Russia, these omissions are noteworthy.

The very interchangeability of the images is striking. Figures 2.8, 2.9, and 2.10 show three public gardens from different parts of the Russian Empire: Stavropol', Smolensk, and Kazan'. There is little to distinguish these spaces from one another. On all three postcards, we find similar elements, most notably the geometrical layout of plants and the introduction of walkways and benches. The first of these postcards was produced in Moscow by Scherer, Nabholz & Co., a firm whose wares found favour in official circles.[32] It demonstrates how people in the centre of the country understood peripheral regions through the lens of the familiar rather than the exotic. However, the story does not stop there. The second postcard was manufactured by a local, Smolensk-based,

Ставрополь-Губернскій.

Цвѣтникъ въ городскомъ саду.

2.8 City garden in Stavropol'. Scherer, Nabholz & Co., 1902.

music store called Ranft and Gartvan. It is, therefore, indicative of the extent to which this aspect of official nationalism may have been internalized at the local level and become the norm for interpreting the Russian landscape. The third image illustrates the point concerning the absence of social conflict in these images. The only postcard among our examples to include people, the picture in Figure 2.10 gives no hint of the social turmoil, often class-based, in Russia in the decade prior to the February Revolution. Nor would one expect it to do so since to produce such a postcard would certainly have incurred the wrath of the Russian censors. While most of the people shown here appear to be middle or upper class and wear Western clothing, two of the men wear traditional Russian outfits. One is of particular interest because he is walking with a Western-dressed man, apparently engaged in conversation. The social harmony of the scene suggests no one was excluded from using these spaces, just as everyone was meant to feel included in the Russian Empire.

2.9 Garden in Smolensk. Izd. muzyk. magaz. Ranft' i Gartvan', n.d. Postally used in 1904.

Infrastructure and Empire Building

Picture postcards of regions along Russia's frontiers exemplify what Thomas Barrett refers to as the "constructive aspects of Russian colonization."[33] By focusing on infrastructure and economic development, the images on picture postcards reflected European perceptions that the land was a commodity to be exploited. They also provide a different way of envisioning the Russian Empire: whereas historians and literary figures have produced many works describing the military history of Russia's territorial expansion, studies that focus on its economic aspects are fewer in number. Owing perhaps to the technological constraints on photography, which made photographing battles and skirmishes impossible until much of the serious fighting on Russian frontiers was done, picture postcards expressed the growth of the Russian Empire in economic terms. By drawing on images, first of the Caucasus and then of Siberia,

2.10 Garden in Kazan'. Izd. V.I. Breeva, n.d. Mailed to Petrograd but the date is unclear.

we can gain a sense of how this popular medium presented the empire for mass consumption.

Despite growing scholarly interest in the Caucasus dating from the mid-nineteenth century as well as the appearance of a steady stream of military memoirs describing its conquest, popular impressions of that region were shaped, in large part, by earlier Romantic interpretations. As Susan Layton outlines, in the second half of the nineteenth century, "Russian visitors to the southern borderland continued to view things with eyes trained by the poetic representations of Pushkin, Marlinskii, and Lermontov – enthusiastically citing literary texts as 'accurate' renderings of the landscape."[34] These texts created an imaginary geography whose wild and rocky landscapes offered a vision of the natural sublime – one meant to trigger awe and enthusiasm in those who encountered it.

Traces of this vision are still evident on the Russian picture postcards of the fin-de-siècle era, particularly those like Figure 2.11, a photograph

КАВКАЗЪ. — CAUCASE. № 14.
Военно-Груз. дор. Скала „Пронеси Господи".

2.11 Georgian military road. Scherer, Nabholz & Co., 1902. Mailed from Odessa to Belgium in February 1904.

Воен. Гр. Дор.   Дарьяльское Ущелье
Route milit géorg, Détroit Darial

2.12 Georgian military road. No manufacturer or date listed.

of the Georgian military road. Here, the road cuts through a mountain-side, but the severed rock face seems to hover over it as if threatening to reclaim the space now taken up by the road. The bend in the road only deepens the mystery since curious viewers are left to speculate about what lies beyond the curve. Other postcards of military roads such as Figure 2.12 offer tension-filled images that continued to invoke the sublime, but also showed how modern technology was being used to overcome it. There are no signs of imminent conflict; nevertheless, the captions on the postcards remind viewers that these are military roads. In other words, they are part of an infrastructure developed to expand the borders of the Russian Empire by military means. Now that the areas have been at least partially tamed, roads, bridges, and eventually railway tracks become symbols of nation building and economic development. They mark the territorial limits of the Russian Empire that, unlike the empires forged by other European powers, possessed no overseas colonies. Moreover, the emphasis on technology assigned an active role to the state – as opposed to the tsar or the Church – in the expansion and solidification of the empire. Picture postcards showed the achievements of a government that was directing, sponsoring, and planning the economic development of the Caucasus, Siberia, and other border regions.

Mastery over the landscape was even more total on picture postcards that reproduced aerial views. Through the use of this camera angle, photographs were instrumental in claiming control over the places they showed. In this, they were reminiscent of travel literature. Like the common moment where an explorer stands on a promontory and describes all he sees below – what Mary Louise Pratt refers to as the "monarch-of-all-I-survey" scene – the postcards allowed for a measuring of the landscape and a resulting claim to dominate it.[35] They belie the difficulties of actual colonization since they offer no sense of the struggles to establish permanent settlements.

In the case of Figure 2.13, a view of Zlatoust', a city in the Ural Mountains on the border between European Russia and Siberia, the picture was taken from a nearby mountaintop.

By the early nineteenth century, Siberia was conceived of as an ideal mercantile colony, whose natural resources were ripe for exploitation. While other views of the region developed as the century progressed, the tantalizing promise of material riches never disappeared.[36] Moreover, the absorption of Siberia by the Russian Empire was depicted as somehow safer than imperial expansion along other frontiers. "The simple circumstance of territorial contiguity with the metropolis," writes Mark

2.13 Aerial view of Zlatoust'. Izd. kontragentstva A.S. Suvorina i ko., 1917.

Bassin, "together with Siberia's large and long-established Russian population made it possible to see the territories beyond the Urals as a con-
tinuation or extension of the zone of Russian culture and society."[37]
Simply put, Siberia did not require military conquest like the Caucasus;
instead, it could be absorbed and assimilated. Hence, the traces of the
sublime that marked the photographs on picture postcards of the
Caucasus did not make their way onto postcards of Siberian landscapes
like the illustration presented here.

A second aerial view shows the track of the Trans-Siberian Railroad as
it runs along the banks of the Ingoda River, near Chita, east of Lake
Baikal (see Figure 2.14). The precision of the postcard's caption, which
indicates that this section of track lies at the 832 verst mark, demonstrates how photographs fixed space (and it should be remembered that
the growth of empires entailed movement through space) so that it became a defined place. Moreover, the subject of the postcard points to a
key aspect of the integration of Siberia into the Russian Empire – the
development of a rail network linking the centre to the periphery.
Serving as symbols of human domination of the landscape, railways were

Забайкальская жел. дор.

Полотно жел. дор. и почтовый трактъ на берегу р. Ингоды на 832 верстѣ.

2.14 Aerial view of the Trans-Siberian Railroad. Izd. D.P. Efimova, n.d.

a vital component in nineteenth-century nation building, particularly in countries that covered large contiguous land masses.

In Russia, the construction of the Trans-Siberian Railroad, that signature project of the fin-de-siècle period, was motivated as much by economic desires as by dreams of expanding Russia's position as a power in Asia. Development would come via construction and colonization. To quote Sergei Witte, the government minister most closely associated with the project, "To connect Siberia by means of the railroad with the European Russian rail network, in such a way as to bring it closer to European Russia – this is to give it access to Russian life and to bring about those very conditions of existence and development that are prevalent in the other parts of Russia, which are linked among themselves by the railroads, as well as with the vital centers of the country."[38] The belief was that the settlers, who numbered about five million between 1891 and 1914, would assist in the construction and continued operation of the railway as well as, gradually, Russify the areas they occupied.[39]

A final feature suggesting mastery over the far reaches of the empire was the absence of people – particularly indigenous people – from the images reprinted on picture postcards. All of the examples reproduced here, for instance, are devoid of people, and these postcards are typical rather than unique. They reflect a way of seeing that was common to instruments of imperialism. Postcards, like maps, "gave a one-sided view of ethnic encounters and supported Europe's God-given right to territorial appropriation."[40] By construing the landscapes as empty, the images imply they are primed for economic development. It would have been particularly anachronistic to include indigenous people in the photographs since that would have indicated they had some kind of right to be there. For the Russian imperial landscape to appear modern and natural, many of its original inhabitants had to be removed from images signalling progress.

Packaging Empire:
Picture Postcards and the Landscapes of Tourism

In 1911, composer Sergei Prokofiev, then still a conservatory student, took a day trip to the island of Kronstadt' near St. Petersburg. He was disappointed by what he found, noting, "Kronstadt turned out to be a horrible little place, bare and dusty."[41] That did not stop him from finding a hotel where he could have lunch and pass the time writing postcards to his friends. It is likely that Prokofiev sent postcards like the one shown in Figure 2.15. A montage of sights in Kronstadt', it conforms to the stylistic norms of the "Greetings from" genre. Readily available even in small towns across Europe by the last decade of the nineteenth century, "Greetings from" postcards firmly anchored picture postcards to the tourist trade.

The pictorial montages of such postcards defined given locations by offering a visual shorthand of what a manufacturer thought were the most significant features of a city or town. They pointed out the landmarks all tourists ought to make a point of visiting and, consequently, simplified decision making. As Joan Schwartz notes, in this way, "countries were reduced to a litany of great cities, and great cities were reduced to a checklist of prominent buildings, historic monuments and scenic viewpoints ... Following itineraries orchestrated by photographic pre-texts, visits were acts of confirmation."[42] As a result, picture postcards, not surprisingly, affected how tourists framed what they saw by creating expectations for the landscapes being reproduced. "In the

2.15 Views of Kronstadt'. Izdan. knizh. mag. V. Gadaliniia. Mailed from Kronstadt'
to Narva in December 1904.

evening we arrived at Corfu," Prokofiev wrote in his diary a few years
after his disappointing trip to Kronstadt', "but we rode at anchor some
way offshore. I should have liked to go ashore, as to judge from the postcards it was a beautiful place, but it was too far."[43] In Prokofiev's case,
which surely cannot be unique in the annals of tourism history, Corfu
was destined to remain only a landscape constructed in his mind by picture postcards.

Even though "Greetings from" postcards supposedly identified
unique points of interest, they imposed commonalities on the tourist
experience, for such postcards did not encourage tourists to venture
beyond the suggested items. There was a similar uniformity in the kinds
of things included in the montages. "Greetings from" postcards celebrated modernity and the infrastructure of capitalist development
alongside older historical monuments. This is why one can find a picture of the stock exchange and the Nikolaevskii train station on a postcard of Petrograd (see Figure 1.2), a photograph of the arsenal on the

2.16 Views of the Nizhnii-Novgorod Fair. Izd. V.I. Breeva, n.d.

postcard of Kronstadt' (see Figure 2.15), and a view of Aleksandr Nevskii street – prominently displaying its street lamps – on a postcard of views of the Nizhnii-Novgorod Fair (see Figure 2.16). Such things connected tourism with technological change and offered a form of economic nationalism noticeable on the postcards which, judging by the use of Russian in their captions, were aimed at Russian consumers or at least at people residing in the Russian Empire.[44]

The celebration of economic development was reflected in two other kinds of postcards connected to tourism: those showing its expansion on Russian waterways and those advertising hotels and spas built at the edges of the Russian Empire. Passenger cruises, particularly along the Volga River, began in the second half of the nineteenth century. Traffic grew more rapidly from the 1870s when the first American-style paddle-wheel steamer was introduced to the trade. Christopher Ely's research has shown how this flourishing of tourism changed Russian perceptions of the Volga region. It turned the river into a "scenic location" to be celebrated in books, pamphlets, and articles.[45] Picture postcards were part of

Пароходъ „Князь" „О-ва по Волгѣ".

2.17 Cruise ship *Kniaz'* on the Volga. No manufacturer listed. Written 4 December 1913 but not mailed.

that process. By the 1890s, Ely remarks, "the shift to a scenic representation of the Volga was complete: almost every guidebook represented the river as a uniquely Russian and especially picturesque, natural space."[46] Foreigners, too, came to see the landscape in this way, spurred in part by the picture postcards made available to them as they relaxed on Volga River cruises. "Dear Earl, This is the boat we were on during our trip on the river Volga," reads the message on the back of the picture postcard in Figure 2.17, "You cant [sic] imagine how big and beautiful [the] Volga is. The scenery all the time was just grand." Even if the writer had not chosen to extol the scenery, the postcard still portrayed Russia, and its tourist infrastructure, in a positive light by focusing on one of the up-to-date vessels used to convey visitors along the river.

A final feature of the tourism landscape consisted of those European fortresses – hotels, resorts, and spas – built to accommodate tourists as they ventured to the Russian Empire's peripheries. The infrastructure that tourism created was itself another form of imperialism, for the most popular tourist destinations in Russia were not found in the country's traditional Slavic heartland, but in areas incorporated into the empire by Catherine the Great (the Crimean Peninsula) and her grandson, Nicholas I (the Caucasus). In the case of the Caucasus, military campaigns were still being fought in the mid-nineteenth century so the region continued to be a volatile one. The spa culture that developed there, so famously described in the literary works of Mikhail Lermontov, first catered to Russian soldiers recuperating from their wounds. Other visitors soon followed, usually reaching the region via the same roads the military had relied upon to conquer it.

As the number of tourists grew, imperial domination became more visible. First, the names of some particularly popular destinations (for instance, Tiflis and Piatigorsk) were Russianized. These new names were the ones eventually used in the captions of picture postcards. Then, the physical alteration of the landscape began. It behooved entrepreneurs and state officials interested in developing the Russian tourist trade to impose a uniform and overwhelmingly European architectural style onto the localities they were seeking to promote. The buildings were meant to impress. "When our motorboat reached Sochi," wrote Paul Grabbe in his memoirs as he remembered his family's flight from the revolution, "it docked at the Caucasian Riviera Hotel, where we planned to stay. Although the name of the hotel is pretentious, the group of white buildings that made up the complex was fittingly imposing. Beyond the hotel we could see a distant chain of snowcapped mountains: the main Caucasus Range."[47] For a brief instant, politics were forgotten and the young Grabbe indulged in a tourist-style moment by enjoying the scenery. No doubt the "imposing buildings" also offered reassurance as they were meant to do. While tourists may have appreciated a few distinct local features and a bit of local colour in their environment, they also liked the familiar to anchor their experience. Hence, there is a sameness to the hotels that were built and whose facades can still be seen on the era's picture postcards.

The postcards were a form of advertising that seemingly every hotel engaged in. As is clear from the three illustrations that follow, there were certain standardized conventions to this kind of postcard. Captions not only indicated the location of the hotel but, to make sure it was not confused with a rival establishment, the caption tended to include its name or the name of its proprietor. Occasionally, as in the case of Figure 2.18, where the caption states that the postcard shows the middle terrace of the pension, some distinguishing feature of the hotel was singled out. In

Симеизъ. Пансiонъ Л. Е. Александровой-Дольникъ. Средняя терраса.

2.18 Middle terrace of L.E. Aleksandrova-Dol'nik's Pension. No manufacturer or date listed.

other instances, the postcard's manufacturer aimed for a wider audience by printing the captions in more than one language.

Visually, the postcards showed landscapes that had been safely tamed and organized. Anything that might negatively affect the impression of the viewer – from dirt to litter to signs of neglect – was deliberately omitted, as were references to service sections of hotels. In many instances, including two of the examples shown here, even people disappeared. That allowed postcard manufacturers and hotel owners to avoid potentially troubling issues of race, social class, and gender as they sought to promote their regions. Instead, they emphasized the grandeur of the buildings in a number of ways. Yalta's Pension Iauzlar' (see Figure 2.19) was photographed from below – a camera angle that made the building appear more impressive. By carefully cropping an image – for example, cutting off part of the building in the photograph

2.19. Pension Iauzlar' in Yalta. Granberg, n.d.

of L.E. Aleksandrova-Dol'nik's Pension (see Figure 2.18) – a postcard could imply that the hotel was simply too large to capture in one image. And, in other instances, like Sochi's Hotel Kavkazskaia Riv'era, the building was shown to simply dominate the entire setting (see Figure 2.20). Notably, as an article by John Jakle and Keith Sculle demonstrates, all of the conventions that have just been described applied to picture postcards of hotels throughout the Western world.[48] The uniformity suggests just how deeply Russians absorbed the common tropes of tourist landscapes and their imperialistic underpinnings.

Conclusion

The title of this chapter quite deliberately refers to the *landscapes* of Russian imperialism. As an examination of picture postcards from the twilight years of the tsarist period reveals, there was no single, totalizing discourse. Instead, overlapping visions of the empire coincided. Images

СОЧИ. · Видъ на Гостинницу „Кавказская Ривьера".

2.20. Hotel Kavkazskaia Riv'era in Sochi. Izd. Br. Borisobykh. Mailed in July 1916.

of "official nationalism," in the form of maps, crests, and statues, made a claim for the continued relevance of, and control by, the tsar. Postcards of the formal gardens that sprang up in Russian cities and towns as the nineteenth century progressed spoke to the role of local urban planners in spreading a standardized, Western-inspired landscape across the empire. But, they were not alone. Military officials interested in the conquest of the Caucasus, as well as government bureaucrats keen to exploit the economic wealth of Siberia and other frontier regions, constructed other visions of the imperial landscape. They were expressed in the multitudes of picture postcards showing military roads, waterways, bridges, and of course, railways. A similar economic nationalism lay at the heart of Russia's emerging tourist industry, which created the "tourist landscape" – one that imposed Western structures such as hotels and resorts wherever tourists might reasonably be encouraged to visit. What these visions had in common was a desire to see the regions being targeted for imperial development as empty but ready for Russian control.

Chapter Three

Gender and Celebrity Culture via the Lens of the Picture Postcard: The Case of Vera Kholodnaia, the "Queen of the Russian Screen"

"I remember," wrote Nina Berberova, "covers of magazines with whiskered men, and the expanded nostrils of Vera Kholodnaya, snake-woman, bird-woman, fairy-woman, lioness-woman, into whom some of my classmates dreamt of transforming themselves but who only threw me into a state of panic."[1] Berberova's repulsion is not the subject of this chapter; the dreams of her school classmates are. The following pages explore the rise of celebrity culture in late Imperial Russia. The emphasis is on visual materials featuring images of performers, images that showed bodies defying traditional norms of representation, although not in such an explicit way as the erotic postcards to be discussed later.[2] Performers were chameleons that changed identities seemingly as regularly as they did their costumes. Moreover, the line separating life and performance was frequently deliberately blurred by them in visual materials, since performers were photographed in both costumes and street clothes. Despite this manipulation, celebrity images were seen by the public as windows into the essential personalities of popular cultural figures. A study of Vera Kholodnaia, one of Russia's first film celebrities, demonstrates how popular visual media played a role in encouraging consumption and in destabilizing conventional ideas about femininity and gender. The end of the nineteenth century saw the blurring of social boundaries and changing definitions of what constituted acceptable behaviour for Russian women as well as for their European counterparts. New ideas about consumption were literally embodied by actresses and other performers, whose sense of aesthetic selfhood was expressed by their clothes and public behaviour. Picture postcards of actresses, such as Vera Kholodnaia, catered to women looking to fashion their own identities rather than to men looking for titillation, which could more readily be obtained from pornographic picture postcards and cartes-de-visite.[3] Avidly consumed, series of celebrity picture postcards also fed into the compulsive behaviour of collectors, who were driven to acquire every possible image of their icons.

Actresses are at the forefront of this chapter because they offer an interesting window into larger questions of gender identity and celebrity culture at the end of the nineteenth and the start of the twentieth centuries. The very fact that they performed in front of others outside of the confines of the home meant actresses publicly exemplified gender identities, both acceptable and threatening, to the rest of society. In the mid-nineteenth century, actresses were thought to enjoy independence, wealth, and fame even if they continued to be shunned by respectable society.[4] Their exploits, both on and off the stage, were publicized in the press, and actresses were among the most popular subjects for the era's new visual media. In fact, the pull of the stage was so strong that the number of actresses grew rapidly. In England and Wales, for instance, there were 3,696 actresses by 1891 – up from only 891 in 1861.[5] Although such a precise tally cannot be given, it is true that in Russia, too, women flocked to the world of the theatre, particularly since starring actresses dominated the stage between 1870 and 1910. From 1895 to 1906, the courses offered by Moscow's Malyi Theatre graduated ninety-nine actors: forty-seven women and fifty-two men.[6] If we assume a similar percentage of women were members of the Russian Theatre Society, then, in 1917, an estimated 2,790 of its 6,000 members were women.[7] Economically, acting appeared to offer women a way to support themselves at a time when their educational opportunities were still very limited.[8] Their prospects for employment were further restricted by the fact that most employers did not recognize the few university degrees Russian women could earn. Hence, acting came to be seen as an attractive alternative. After all, as Catherine Schuler notes, "A starring actress like Maria Savina, whose salary in 1882 for an eight-month season was 12,000 rubles, earned more in a year than most women, even those with university educations or a skilled craft, could hope to earn in twenty."[9] Opportunities for women expanded at just this time, too, since the imperial theatre monopoly ended in 1882, thereby allowing for the establishment of a network of private commercial and art theatres for the first time. Life on the stage received added publicity when both Sarah Bernhardt and Eleonora Duse toured Russia in the 1880s and 1890s. These international superstars became the standard by which native talent was evaluated.[10] Soon the fame of Maria Savina and Vera Komissarzhevskaia came to rival that of Duse and Bernhardt in Russia, ushering in an era of celebrity cults that shifted to film actresses after 1910, when theatre began to take second place to film.

Part of this process must be linked to the popularity of women's themes in late nineteenth-century drama and literature, as well as to more general debates concerning the position of women in society. Roles with more complexity and psychological depth were created for women, most notably by Henrik Ibsen, whose works attracted attention across the continent. The first decade of the twentieth century also saw issues of sexual identity, gender construction, and legal rights for women hotly debated in Russia as in the rest of Europe. Whereas earlier generations had concerned themselves with securing access to universities and with greater employment opportunities for women, during the 1905 Revolution, the issue of women's political participation began to be raised by Russia's first feminists.[11] This was also a time when physicians and other public opinion leaders vigorously discussed the decriminalization of abortion and forms of contraception. Underlying these debates was the question of individualism and the limits the state could, or should, have over personal autonomy. Nowhere was this more apparent than in media treatments of the "New Woman." The defining characteristics of this "type," which was most notably associated with the heroines of novels by E. Nagrodskaia and A. Verbitskaia, were independence (legal, financial, and behavioural), assertiveness, and public visibility. The "New Woman" did not confine herself to domestic spaces; instead, she was often shown enjoying new urban spaces, like department stores, or partaking of emerging forms of leisure. Because of the rise of commercial publishing, and later movies, this "type" of woman was splashed across all forms of Russian popular culture and a wider audience than ever before was exposed to arguments over the proper behaviour for women. The postcards featured in this chapter form part of that debate.

Visual Celebrity and the Picture Postcard

As will be the case with the images of royalty to be discussed in a later chapter, cartes-de-visite played a key role in creating celebrity culture and paved the way for the later use of picture postcards. Alongside the cartes-de-visite of political and literary giants were those featuring all kinds of urban performers. Already by 1860, hundreds of portraits of actresses and vaudeville stars were on sale in Paris.[12] Similar wares were

А. П. Чеховъ.   „Дядя Ваня". д. IV.   М. Х. Т.

Войницкій. Прощайте. ..., Простите. .... Никогда больше не увидимся.

3.1 Moscow Art Theatre production of *Uncle Vanya*. Postcard manufactured by Scherer, Nabholz & Co., 1904.

rapidly available across the continent. Notably, this new form of publicity was quickly adopted by theatre managers and actors themselves who realized that name recognition sold tickets and filled seats. Visual forms of advertising reminded audiences of cast members and the costumes worn. It also became commonplace to use group photographs to highlight a particular production or theatre troupe.

The same techniques were employed on celebrity picture postcards once the craze for cartes-de-visite had waned. For instance, Figure 3.1 publicizes a Moscow Art Theatre production of Chekhov's *Uncle Vanya* The photograph, taken during an actual performance of the play, captures the action as one of its scenes progresses. Rather than single out an individual performer, the emphasis noticeably lies on the group. The postcard includes the well-known actress Olga Knipper. As Chekhov's wife, and a leading performer of the Moscow Art Theatre, she surely would have been singled out by name had that been the purpose of the postcard's maker. Instead, the caption provides only the name of the play, a snippet of dialogue from it, and the initials of the theatre. In this

Гр. Л. Н. Толстой.   Д. В. Григоровичъ.

И. А. Гончаровъ.   А. В. Дружининъ.

И. С. Тургеневъ.   А. Н. Островскій.

Въ мартѣ 1856 г. въ С.-Петербургѣ.

3.2 Group portrait of Russian writers. St. Eugenia Society, n.d.

instance, the purpose of the postcard was to emphasize both the particular production and the Moscow Art Theatre more generally. Other picture postcards celebrated Russia's literary heritage by making the portraits of leading writers available. Figure 3.2, for example, reprints an 1856 photograph of some of the country's best-known writers, including Lev Tolstoi, Ivan Goncharov, and Ivan Turgenev. .

This kind of postcard proved to be popular with the public. Samuil Marshak, for example, remembers how excited he was the first time he saw a portrait of Maksim Gorky, in this passage in his memoirs: "I was thirteen or fourteen when the older boys showed me a photograph which was being handed round from one person to the next, and avidly examined, of a young man with broad cheek-bones and a face at once dreamy and sullen, a vertical shock of straight hair falling back on to this [sic] temples."[13] When group photographs of literary figures and other celebrities were not available, they could be created through a variety of montage techniques as is the case in Figure 3.3, which shows an ensemble of Russian women writers. In these instances, names are included in the captions but the focus, again, remains on the larger group or the shared identity that allows these individuals to be grouped together. It is most obvious here where the caption "Women Writers Russian Series III" (*Russkaia pisatelnitsy seriia III*) is written in larger font than the names of the women themselves.

These group depictions are only part of the story, though, for the picture postcards of the late nineteenth and early twentieth centuries also actively promoted individualized identities. Louise McReynolds, in her excellent study of late imperial Russian culture, terms such postcards "icons of the secular age," and she notes how they were used to commodify the identities of actresses like Maria Savina as well as a number of male wrestlers.[14] Distinctive identities allowed the audience to distinguish between performers and provided the context for building fan support and, ultimately, a star system. Stars themselves clearly understood the power of items such as publicity postcards, and they were actively involved in their distribution. That could be done privately as was the case, for instance, when the tenor I.V. Yershov visited some acquaintances at their home. He graciously autographed postcards bearing his picture for a cluster of young girls who were friends of his hosts' daughters.[15] In other instances, more public venues were used. When A.P. Vygodskaia was a student in the Bestuzhev Courses for women, in the late 1880s, she volunteered to help with a benefit concert to raise money to support needy students. The highlight of the evening was a

3.3 Montage of Russian women writers. No manufacturer or date listed.

performance by Maria Savina. "I recall that after the concert," wrote Vygodskaia, "Savina sold autographed picture postcards of herself to benefit the Courses."[16] The postcards no doubt raised a tidy sum since they were being sold for 25 roubles each – at a time when most students lived on 10 to 15 roubles per month. But, they also benefited Savina. The postcards marked her as a celebrity whose photograph was worth purchasing and keeping. They constructed an image of Savina as a caring performer, whose philanthropic work aided the less fortunate and, hence, was worthy of the adulation she might receive. Nor was Savina alone in this kind of publicity.

Figure 3.4 singles out the singer M.A. Karinskaia. It is quite typical in how the subject is portrayed: she wears a richly ornamented dress, most likely one of her costumes, and holds some papers rolled in her hand – thereby connecting her with sheet music. There is only a minimal amount of detail in the rest of the image. Most notable is the vase of flowers that is perhaps meant to remind the viewer of similar bouquets that were given to her by admirers after performances. What makes the card noteworthy, though, is the text included on the far right-hand side of the

3.4 Portrait of M.A. Karinskaia. St. Eugenia Society, n.d.

postcard. The French part reads, "Russian singer M.A. Karinskaia," but the Russian adds the word "well-known" (*izvestnaia*). Hence, the adjective serves to separate Karinskaia from the mass of other singers of the era, and obviously implies that she is superior to them.

Another more elaborate form of picture postcard publicity can be seen in Figure 3.5. Here, the singer, who is identified only by her last name as Plemanova, occupies roughly one-third of the image. The remaining two-thirds are given over to song lyrics and the accompanying music. This technique, of printing the words and music to a popular tune on a postcard, was common across Europe at the time, and meant that popular songs circulated well beyond the audience that would have heard them in nightclubs and other such venues.[17] Presumably, Plemanova's best number was the slow waltz "Dear One, I Wait for You" (*Milyi, ia zhdu tebia*) since this is what the postcard connects her to. However, rather than emphasize singing talent, the postcard instead connected the singer to a distinctive commodity much as other picture postcards would do when they showed a still from a film rather than a studio-taken portrait of an actor or actress. But, the process of

3.5 Plemanova and the music for "Dear One, I Wait for You." No manufacturer or date listed.

commodification does not end there, for the back of the postcard shows marks from either the tape or glue used to fix it into an album. These residual traces point to the fact that most surviving postcards of Russian celebrities were never mailed. They were collected in order to be looked at and admired over and over again.

The Rise of the Russian Film Industry

It did not take long for the first films to reach Russia. Within months of first exhibiting their work in Paris, the Lumiere brothers opened a movie theatre on Nevskii Prospekt in St. Petersburg. For the next decade, they and other foreign firms dominated the market and foreign stars, like Asta Nielsen and Max Linder, captured the imagination of Russian audiences. It was not until the autumn of 1907 that the first native film company was formed by Aleksandr Drankov. Competitors soon emerged, but financial viability proved to be a constant concern for most of them.

Bankruptcies and mergers were commonplace. Still, the number of Russian producers, as well as the number of films they made, continued to grow, and the industry as a whole received a boost from the outbreak of the First World War. As was the case for postcard manufacturers, the war eliminated foreign firms from the market but did not decrease demand for the product. Russian producers simply stepped in to fill the gap: by 1916, there were forty-seven film studios, up from eighteen on the eve of the war.[18] Moreover, Russian filmmakers released five hundred movies in 1916 – quite a dramatic increase from the nineteen made only seven years earlier.[19] The network of theatres showing movies also saw spectacular expansion in these years. In the capital, by 1916, there were 229 movie theatres, with fifteen of them on Nevskii Prospekt alone.[20] Across the country, in 1910, there were 120 movie theatres and 108 million tickets were sold. By 1916, these figures had jumped to four thousand theatres and 180 million tickets sold.[21] To put the numbers in perspective, one film scholar has noted that, in 1916, movies sold ten times more tickets than Russia's live theatres.[22] Moviegoing continued to be a popular activity even after the country collapsed into revolutionary turmoil. Films were screened as gunshots rang out on nearby streets, and they allowed people to escape from the uncertain reality – if only for a few short moments. To give but two examples from opposite ends of the political spectrum: In his memoirs, Prince Lobanov-Rostovsky reminisced about being caught up in a street demonstration in St. Petersburg in 1917. When the crowd was fired upon, he helped some nearby people into the safety of a side street and then searched for a friend, whom he eventually found standing outside the entrance of a movie theatre. The man said, "Let's go to the movies and let them murder each other." Lobanov-Rostovsky summed up the experience by saying, "There was no revolution in the cool darkness of the half-filled house."[23] The movies featured in an equally memorable instance in the life of Anna Andzhievskaia. In 1918, Andzhievskaia, a Bolshevik party activist, found herself in occupied Baku and was briefly reunited with her husband, a fellow party member. One day, the pair took time out from their underground activities and went to the movies. When they came out of the theatre, Andzhievskii was seized by British policemen. Two weeks later he was hanged.[24]

The popularity of films meant the emergence of new celebrities in Russian popular culture. Very quickly, the film studios themselves engaged in active, multifaceted publicity campaigns. Louise McReynolds notes, "At least twenty-seven specialized journals and forty-one cinema-oriented newspapers were published empirewide in pre-Revolutionary Russia, several of which enjoyed circulations in the tens of thousands."[25] Nor were visual materials neglected. A vast array of publicity posters was created, and it should come as no surprise that picture postcards were immediately embraced by Russia's film industry.[26] Their usage, by and large, followed the same trends that scholars have described vis-à-vis other movie markets.[27] They were what one historian has referred to as "geographically penetrative instrument[s]," meaning postcards "freed the cultural image of the performer from the constraints of locality, gender, class, and social capital which limit live theatre [or film] attendance, to disperse images of glamour and celebrity into many new reception contexts and across the widest possible territory."[28] Notoriety could be achieved in a number of ways. For example, Figure 3.6 shows how a picture postcard publicized Russia's first full-length feature film. *The Defence of Sevastopol* (*Oborona Sevastopolia*) was made in 1911 by the Khanzhonkov studio. Featuring one of the Russian box office's biggest stars, Ivan Mozzhukin, in the role of Napoleon III, the film aroused much excitement, particularly since its predistribution publicity boldly trumpeted to the public that the film was made with the approval of members of the royal family.[29] Indeed, no form of publicity was neglected – as we see in Figure 3.6 – for it was vital to the continued financial health of the new industry that producers publicize their latest releases as widely as possible. For an industry plagued by financial risk, any advantage that led to more tickets being sold was readily applied. For the Russian population, the creation of secondary visual materials meant that film publicity and celebrity culture in general spread across the country.

The Case of Vera Kholodnaia

Vera Kholodnaia (née Levchenko), the "Queen" of Russia's silent film screens, was born in Poltava on 5 August 1893.[30] She was the eldest of three sisters and received some training in ballet in her childhood. The family's fortunes were affected when Kholodnaia's father died soon after the birth of her sister Sofiia, in 1905. Kholodnaia graduated from gymnasium in 1910, and shortly afterwards married Moscow lawyer Vladimir Grigor'evich Kholodnyi. Two years later, the couple's first daughter, Evgeniia was born. The birth was a difficult one and doctors told Kholodnaia not to have any more children. A second daughter, Nonna, was adopted the following year. In 1914, when the First World

На перевязочномъ пунктѣ

3.6 Film still from *The Defence of Sevastopol*. Society for Publicizing Historical Events in Russia (Obshchestvo oznakomaenim s istoricheskimi sobytiiami Rossii), n.d.

War began, Vladimir Kholodnyi was quickly drafted into the Russian Army. The material circumstances of the family worsened, and Kholodnaia became largely responsible for providing for its members, which included her mother and sisters. She did so by starting a career in Russian cinema.

Kholodnaia herself traced her interest in film back to 1910 when she saw Asta Nielsen on a Moscow screen for the first time. Nielsen's films had a profound impact on the course of Russian cinema, since they were among the first star-driven productions to be screened, and they encouraged Russian filmmakers to also orient films around star performers. Four years later, Kholodnaia sought to emulate Nielsen and act in films herself. Kholodnaia's first film role was a small part in a 1914 film adaptation of *Anna Karenina*. Her first real success came in *Fire of Heaven* (*Plamia neba*), which was released in August 1915. Both the public and film critics took notice of her performance, with the review in *Teatral'naia gazeta* stating, "In the central female role, Mrs. Kholodnaia. The actress is extraordinarily effective, the camera does not disturb her, and she maintains a good statuesque tension of gesture and movement."[31] Once she moved into leading roles, Kholodnaia appeared in more and more films, averaging ten or more a year for the next several years. In total, it is estimated she made fifty films or so, although copies of most of them have not survived. She achieved particular success with Evgenii Bauer's 1916 film *A Life for a Life* (*Zhizn' za zhizn'*), which in some theatres ran for two straight months and which continued to be screened occasionally in the Soviet Union until the start of the 1930s.[32] At least one film scholar has stated it was in this film that Kholodnaia formed the character type she would play over and over again, and that would make her famous: the weak-willed and suffering woman.[33] *By the Fireside* (*U Kamina*), made in 1917, was another box office smash and marked the zenith of her fame. It ran for ninety straight days in Odessa and a hundred days in Khar'kov. This film, too, continued to be screened in the Soviet era.[34] Despite performing in hundreds of benefit events during the war years, Kholodnaia was not taken seriously as a potential stage actress by the theatre establishment until she appeared in a film version of Tolstoi's *A Living Corpse* (*Zhivoi trup*) in 1918. That performance led to an invitation from Konstantin Stanislavskii to appear, with his theatre, in the role of Katerina in a production of Ostrovsky's *The Storm*. Despite serious negotiations and a flurry of letters back and forth, Kholodnaia ultimately did not accept the offer. Instead, at the end of June 1918, she moved with Dmitrii Kharitonov's film studio to Odessa, where it was believed producers would be able to avoid new Bolshevik restrictions on the film industry.[35] Around the same time, a number of well-known Russian actors began to get offers to join foreign film companies and, thereby, escape the turmoil of Russia in the middle of its civil war. Kholodnaia received an offer from Berlin, but refused to leave her country. Instead, in early 1919, she fell ill. A victim of the worldwide flu epidemic, Kholodnaia died on 16 February 1919. She was only twenty-six years old.

Kholodnaia's rise to fame was rapid. Once she began to garner glowing reviews, her name received greater billing on publicity materials. For instance, a few days after the release of *A Life for a Life*, when it became clear audiences and critics were far more intrigued by her performance than by anyone else's, Kholodnaia's name was moved from second place to top billing on the posters and advertisements for the movie.[36] The amounts she earned escalated quickly. It is said that she was eventually paid as much as 25,000 roubles per film.[37] Her photograph began to be printed in newspapers and film journals, and a popular waltz was named for her. Soon, advertisements for films began to refer to Kholodnaia as the "Queen of the Screen" (*Koroleva ekrana*). She was the subject of a May 1918 special issue of *Kinogazeta*, which celebrated her three years in cinema with a series of commemorative articles, more than forty photographs of her, and her only interview. And, finally, even in death, Kholodnaia continued to fascinate. Her funeral was filmed, and within three days of the event, *The Funeral of Vera Kholodnaia* was being screened in theatres.[38]

Kholodnaia's image was such that she became an instantly recognizable figure of reference in Russian popular culture. The writer Konstantin Paustovsky's memoirs give us some sense of her place as such. A scene in the volume devoted to the First World War captures the gossiping of two women in a market in Odessa: "Well, there was this woman, Tamara, she was the cymbalist [in an orchestra in Odessa] – true, she was beautiful and striking, and I suppose he was dazzled by the sequins and the velvets, the cymbals and the waltzes ... 'I'll make her so happy, I'll give her such a life,' he said, 'that Vera Kholodnaya herself will be green with envy.'"[39] The passage demonstrates the assumptions about Kholodnaia's lifestyle that must have been current at the time. During the civil war, Kholodnaia's fame persisted. Paustovsky records one rumour that circulated in Kiev: "the cinema star Vera Kholodnaya had recruited her own army like Joan of Arc and, riding a white charger at the head of her victorious troops, had entered the town of Priluki and proclaimed herself Empress of Ukraine."[40] Later, as he describes the White forces on the eve of their departure from Odessa, Paustovsky notices that some of them "crowded the night-clubs, singing the heart-rending lay of Vera Kholodnaya's death."[41] There is a poignancy to the moment, as if the soldiers were not just singing a popular song but, instead, were using its words to mourn their own fate and the death of the old regime.

These three anecdotes show how successfully Vera Kholodnaia, and the owners of the studios that employed her, were in fashioning her celebrity status and in creating a star system for the Russian film industry. To date, most film scholars have focused their attention on the content and themes of Kholodnaia's movies, particularly those she made for the Khanzhonkov studio and with director Evgenii Bauer. That has left the business side of her career out of the picture, so to speak. When we go beyond aesthetics to look at the economics of the film industry, Kholodnaia's 1916 move to the studio of Dmitrii Kharitonov becomes paramount. Kharitonov, who was nicknamed the "Russian American," instituted a number of Hollywood-style business practices, such as fining

ВѢРА ХОЛОДНАЯ

3.7 Vera Kholodnaia with Kharitonov's studio logo at the bottom of the postcard. No manufacturer or date listed.

actors for lateness, which changed the nature of the industry.[42] For instance, he branded stars by linking his studio logo with publicity stills of them, as shown on a postcard shown as Figure 3.7. Such images allowed Kharitonov to connect the star power of his actors directly to his studio and its productions.

Kharitonov was also the first Russian film producer to cast several big stars in the same picture and to match them with the talents of a well-known director. Specifically, he grouped Kholodnaia with Vitold Polonskii and Vladimir Maksimov under the direction of Petr Chardynin. At the time, Kharitonov's rivals expected this act to spell financial ruin for his company since combining the large salaries paid to stars added greatly to the cost of making a film. However, the critics were proved wrong. The first movie with Kholodnaia, Polonskii, and Maksimov, *By the Fireside*, was a triumphant success. A new era in Russian film production had begun. As the work of Richard de Cordova and Paul McDonald vis-à-vis the emergence of the star system in the United States at roughly the same time has shown, stars were instrumental in producers' and distributors' efforts to control the demand for movies and minimize financial risk.[43] From this perspective, the film star is a capital asset, whose name and image are used to garner an advantage in the film market. For the system to function, distinct identities have to be created for a select group of stars, who are frequently typecast into playing similar parts over and over again. This way of assigning roles allowed for what de Cordova has referred to as "picture personalities" to evolve over a number of films. In Kholodnaia's case, beginning with Bauer's *A Life for a Life* and continuing through her films for Kharitonov, she became known for playing weak-willed and suffering women. Her heroines were frequently victimized by men of higher socio-economic standing, but the suffering they endured took place amid a backdrop of conspicuous consumption and a more freely expressed sexuality.

Typecasting was bolstered by forms of film publicity such as picture postcards, in particular, by those that were produced using film stills. These allowed viewers to simultaneously imagine Kholodnaia as both her true self and as the characters she played on screen. In other words, they blurred the line between her real identity and her picture personality.[44] Any confusion in the minds of viewers was, at least in part, deliberately orchestrated by the captions used for this kind of postcard. The postcard in Figure 3.8 is a typical example. It is a still taken from *By the Fireside*, Kholodnaia's first movie for Kharitonov. In addition to giving the title of the film, the caption makes sure to give the names of the three

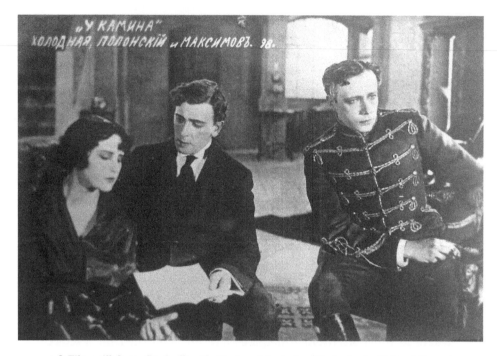

3.8 Film still from *By the Fireside*. Postcard includes Kholodnaia, Polonskii, and Maksimov. No manufacturer or date listed.

major performers enlisted to star in it. However, the names of the characters they are playing are omitted. Typecasting, in fact, made the names quite superfluous since parts did not vary dramatically from one movie to the next.

In addition to typecasting, the creation of a star system was aided by evolving filming techniques. As McDonald describes, in the 1910s, "an increased use of close-ups, patterns of shot/reverse-shot cutting, and eyeline matching, were all used to bring further emphasis to the actor's face as a source of meaning."[45] In Kholodnaia's case, these techniques allowed directors to focus on her most memorable feature: her eyes. Film scholars, together with her contemporaries, all agree that the Russian public was taken by Kholodnaia's striking beauty and captivating eyes. In the words of fellow actress G.S. Kravchenko, "Vera Kholodnaia had her own unique charm and such expressive, mournful, penetrating eyes that once you saw them, you would remember them your whole life.

Her eyes disturbed and agitated people."[46] It is not surprising that people took note of Kholodnaia's eyes since she was apparently filmed in close-up more often than other actresses of the day. As Yuri Tsivian notes, when one of her films contained fewer close-ups than usual, critics tended to give it less glowing reviews.[47] Moreover, the actress further accentuated her eyes through her choice of costume. Often appearing in black or white, Kholodnaia's black hair and white face made her green eyes even more conspicuous.

When we turn to the picture postcards created of her, we again find that a large number of them showed Kholodnaia in close-up, with her eyes singled out to the viewer. In other words, the postcards upheld the image the studio created for her. Figure 3.9 is a typical example. Here, the darkness of Kholodnaia's hair, as well as the shadowing that obscures her neck and parts of her face, lends greater emphasis to her eyes. The positioning of her head further introduces an enigmatic and vulnerable element to the image. Although no particular film is mentioned in the postcard's caption, the photograph clearly fits the picture personality that Kholodnaia developed.

Picture postcards revealed more than just Kholodnaia's memorable eyes and beautiful face. They also allowed viewers to gaze at her body outside of the confines of the movie theatre. While not falling into the category of outright pornography, these postcards did make Kholodnaia's body, often posed in an intimate setting, an object of public display, and many of the photographs are tinged with eroticism. For example, Figure 3.10 shows Kholodnaia in a reclined position, with dishevelled hair and a shirt partially open at the neck.

A second postcard (see Figure 3.11) presents Kholodnaia with one of her frequent co-stars, Osip Runin. Here, Kholodnaia's bare arms, legs, and shoulders stand in marked contrast with the relatively well-covered body of Runin. Moreover, her choice of pose can also be read as a provocative one, since sitting with one's legs crossed was still considered impermissible for women in polite society.[48]

In a final example (see Figure 3.12), Kholodnaia appears in a white diaphanous dress against a solid-black background. Much of her upper body is again bare, and the cut of dress suggests quite openly the contours of her bust and hips. Although there is no indication this was deliberate on the part of the photographer, shadowing lower down on the image draws the eye to the area of Kholodnaia's genitals, possibly intimating that Kholodnaia is not wearing anything under the dress and that the camera has, in a fashion, penetrated the material of it.

ВѢРА ХОЛОДНАЯ.

3.9 Close-up of Kholodnaia, emphasizing her eyes. No manufacturer or date listed. Postally used in Estonia in 1926.

3.10 Kholodnaia in *A Tale of Dear Love* (*Skazka liubvi dorogoi*). No manufacturer or date listed.

3.11 Kholodnaia and Osip Runin. No manufacturer or date listed.

3.12 Kholodnaia. No manufacturer or date listed.

While no doubt sexually charged, these images of Kholodnaia differ, however, from the cartes-de-visite of actresses and other performers that were produced fifty years earlier and that have been so aptly analysed by Laurence Senelick. According to his research, "Photography ... reinforced the traditional division of female sexuality into respectable woman and woman devoted to man's enjoyment, and the wide diffusion of images contributed to the regulation of female behavior."[49] By the time picture postcards replaced cartes-de-visite in the market for cheap visual images, this binary opposition was in the process of being challenged by new conceptions of acceptable femininity and sexual expression. Women had also become an important component of the consuming public for visual materials and, most likely, bought more postcards of Kholodnaia than men did. As such, it can be suggested that, for Russian women, the example of Kholodnaia offered a daring new way of seeing themselves as women and as consumers.

A final part in the evolution in the star system involved growing attention devoted to the personal lives of actors and actresses. It is here, however, that the Russian context deviates from the American model. By 1913–14, it was common for the American media to discuss the marriages and family life of actors and to provide information about their hobbies and various likes and dislikes. Photographs of stars with their spouses and children abounded. In Russia, on the other hand, this aspect of the star system was underdeveloped, with stars continuing to keep their personal lives out of the spotlight. As mentioned above, it was not until May 1918 that Kholodnaia's only interview was published. It is also noteworthy that among the hundreds of picture postcards of Vera Kholodnaia, I have found only one that strayed into her personal life. Figure 3.13 shows Kholodnaia with one of her daughters. Even here the postcard reveals relatively little information about its subjects. The caption merely says, "Vera Kholodnaia with her daughter." It gives no indication of where the photograph was taken or under what circumstances. And, most importantly, it does not give the girl's name, thereby allowing the family to still possess a modicum of privacy and anonymity.

Kholodnaia Fashions the Russian Woman

Kholodnaia's rise to stardom coincided with an era of great social and economic change in Russia. Minister of Finance Sergei Witte's reforms led to rapid industrialization and an alteration of the country's landscape.

Вера Холодная с дочерью.

3.13 Kholodnaia with her daughter. No manufacturer or date listed.

The number of factories rose by more than 25 per cent and the urban population more than doubled between 1856 and 1897.[50] By the turn of the twentieth century, three of the cities in the Russian Empire, St. Petersburg, Moscow, and Warsaw, were among the ten largest in Europe, and nearly three dozen others approached the 100,000 mark in terms of population.[51] Urbanization on this scale meant millions of peasants had to adjust to city living.

Changing attitudes towards clothing and self-presentation were part of the process of fashioning new urban identities. As the empire's cities, too, became home to brightly lit department stores, its subjects adjusted their notions about fashion and consumption.[52] They received information about fashion from a number of popular cultural media, including magazines, movies, and picture postcards. The fin-de-siècle saw the blossoming of the fashion press as well as the women's press more generally. Between 1870 and 1917, the market for fashion magazines grew to include middle-class, and even lower-class, readers. The content of fashion magazines also evolved. Coverage of Russian fashion was dropped in favour of reporting only the latest trends in Paris.[53] This development meant Russia was now part of a pan-European fashion continuum. Moreover, as Christine Ruane has described, the "construction of shopping into 'Western' and 'Russian' meant that clothes shopping became part of the larger cultural debate about the meaning of westernization in Russia."[54]

A similarly important shift took place vis-à-vis ideas about taste. What was once thought of as something an individual was born with now came to be seen as something that could be acquired provided an individual had access to the right advice and role models.[55] And role models were readily available since, beginning in the late 1880s, French fashion magazines began the practice of using portraits of society beauties as illustrations. As the century ended, society beauties came to be joined by others, like actresses, as arbiters of good taste in the minds of the public.

Their impact cut across class lines. A particularly noteworthy aspect of Russia's urbanization was how quickly lower-class migrants to the cities abandoned traditional dress in order to carve out what they saw as more modern identities for themselves. The adoption of Western-style clothing allowed individuals to assert their individuality and, thereby, turn their backs on what they perceived as the conservatism and conformism controlling village life.[56] Clothes were visual markers of class, identities, and aspirations. For instance, Semen Kanatchikov recorded in detail and with obvious pride the fashion transformation that accompanied his rise to the status of skilled worker: "I had bought myself a holiday 'outfit,' a watch, and, for the summer, a wide belt, grey trousers, a straw hat, and a pair of fancy shoes. In a word, I dressed myself up in the manner of those young urban metalworkers of that period who earned an independent living and didn't ruin themselves with vodka."[57] Migrant women were equally affected by this desire to reshape their identities, and they spent a considerable amount of their income – especially if they were single – on clothes. One historian puts the figure at around 20 per cent of their income.[58] The taste of Russian women was influenced by the fashions they saw not only in shop windows, but on the pages of cheap fashion magazines, on the nation's movie screens, and on picture postcards. By adopting these clothes, Russian working women co-opted the visual markers of middle-class urban life.

The emphasis on Vera Kholodnaia's clothes, in both her films and the picture postcards issued with her photograph, points to this intersection of new media, changes in dress, and ideas about modernity in fin-de-siècle Russia. Kholodnaia's status as a film star meant that she served as a fashion icon, a woman who set the tone for others and encouraged the spread of a new consumer culture. It is worth remembering that most of Kholodnaia's movies were made while the First World War cut Russia off from the world of European fashion. It was a time when fashion magazines closed owing to shortages of paper and to declining subscription rates.[59] These economic changes only made pictures postcards all the more important as purveyors of information concerning fashion and taste. While many women were forced to give up their subscriptions as their economic woes mounted, they could still usually afford to buy a cheap postcard or two. Moreover, this was the exact moment when the number of Kholodnaia postcards on the market burgeoned, thereby, making her an icon of the new consumer culture. This culture, in the words of Lisa Tiersten, "offered a whole new range of possibilities for theatrical self-display and feminine posing."[60] Jane Gaines' analysis of costume in silent-era American films offers an interesting framework with which to consider the role clothes played in Kholodnaia's celebrity status. Gaines argues that costumes were central to the presentation of female actors, with a distinction being drawn between everyday clothing and more elaborate film costumes as true movie stars began to emerge. Certain film techniques, such as concentrating on a specific or particularly noteworthy detail on a costume, or moving the camera so that an entire costume was visible, were also used to enhance the attention paid to the clothes worn by actresses. Gaines even suggests, "Not only did costume, like décor, provide iconographic cues related to typage and narrative conventions; in the absence of sound it was seen as a substitute for speech."[61] Indeed, costumes soon transcended the movies themselves, becoming an increasingly important component in the publicity materials released by both film studios and the performers themselves. Here the connection with picture postcards should be evident. Items like these allowed fans to construct an identity for the star even if they did not see the films the star appeared in. In the case of Vera Kholodnaia, many of the picture postcards of her emphasized her clothing in the same way the camera did in her films. They provided viewers with the fantasy of dressing like her should their life circumstances permit. In these images, Kholodnaia was never portrayed as someone who worked in a factory or as a domestic. Instead, they associated Kholodnaia with femininity, luxury, and leisure. Figure 3.14 shows Kholodnaia wrapped in lush, elegant fabric. On a second postcard (see Figure 3.15), Kholodnaia is photographed wearing an elaborate hat.

3.14 Kholodnaia. No manufacturer listed, 1917.

3.15 Kholodnaia in fancy hat. No manufacturer or date listed.

And, to return to Figure 3.12, the postcard shows Kholodnaia in a dress that would have been completely unsuitable for work, and with a long string of pearls draped around her neck. It must be noted that in none of these cases was Kholodnaia dressed in traditional Russian clothing. Instead, she served as a role model for women drawn to dress in a Western, middle- or even upper-class fashion.

Conclusion

In *The Naked Year*, Boris Pil'niak's satirical look at the October Revolution and the civil war, the reader is briefly introduced to Olenka Kuntz, a Bolshevik supporter who spends her day copying and signing police arrest warrants. In the evening, she goes to the cinema and meets one of her co-workers there. In Pil'niak's words, "The day had faded into yellow dusk, and at dusk Olenka Kuntz went to the 'Venice' cinema; there Vera Kholodnaya 'was playing.' In the 'Venice' the Head of the People's Police Department, Comrade Jan Laitis, approached Olenka Kuntz, – in the darkness, when Kholodnaya 'was playing,' Comrade Laitis squeezed

Olenka's hand."[62] Two things stand out in this passage. First, both characters are employed by the new Soviet regime as police officials, and yet, they still go to see pre-revolutionary melodramas in their free time. They prove Anthony Swift's point that "it was possible to be both a Bolshevik and a fan of melodrama."[63] In other words, they demonstrate the continuing appeal of Vera Kholodnaia as a celebrity despite the ruptures caused by the revolution. The second point concerns the language used by Pil'niak since he does not feel the need to name which of Kholodnaia's movies is being screened, nor does he offer any information about its storyline. It is merely enough to say that Kholodnaia was playing for the reader to infer what the film was about.

Vera Kholodnaia's status as one of Russia's first picture personalities, and as an influential popular cultural figure, was engineered by exposing her image in a number of media. Picture postcards were an important part of this process. But, the images they provided to the public also had connections to larger debates within Imperial Russian society at the turn of the twentieth century. Photographs of Kholodnaia contained messages about femininity and the power of individualism. They encouraged new forms of consumption and the shaping of explicitly Western conceptions of identity. They speak to the continuing power of the celebrity, as well, since Kholodnaia served as a powerful example when picture personalities were created around Soviet actresses in the 1930s.

Chapter Four

Bodies on Display:
Romantic and Erotic Postcards
in Fin-de-Siècle Russia

When discussing the postcards of chorus girls that he used to buy as a teenager, Soviet writer Ilya Ehrenburg singled out one in particular. "I remember a photograph of Natasha Trukhanova, a famous beauty who drove me wild." Imagine Ehrenburg's surprise when "a quarter of a century later, in Paris, I met A.A. Ignatyev, formerly military attaché in France, then a member of the staff of our trade delegation. His wife turned out to be the Natasha who had enchanted me in my adolescence. I told her about the old picture postcard and my story made her laugh."[1] Ehrenburg's honesty about his boyhood consumption of revealing photographs of women is rare, for Russian memoirs are seldom that candid about sexual matters or even about the wide array of romantic and erotic postcards that were available to boys like him.

Their silence is matched by the discomfort of generations of Russian and Soviet historians when it comes to the subject of sex. Going back to the fin-de-siècle period, many social commentators in Russia wanted to believe in the relative "sexual innocence" of their compatriots, particularly the peasants, and thereby underscore what they perceived to be a major difference between their country and the rest of Europe. They argued that the majority of Russians had no contact with pornographic literature or images; hence, they were not infected by the social ills plaguing modern urban life. The small minority that did use pornography, it was emphasized, did so to make political or social statements. As literary critic and author Kornei Chukhovskii put it in his review of Mikhail Artsybashev's novel *Sanin*, "Russian pornography is not plain pornography such as the French or Germans produce, but pornography with ideas."[2] Western historians, too, are often more comfortable writing about pornography when it can be treated as a form of protest. They follow the approach of Lynn Hunt whose pioneering studies have done much to make pornography a serious and acceptable subject for historical analysis. To Hunt's way of thinking, pornography in the early modern period was used primarily for its shock value when someone wanted to attack political or religious authorities.[3] It was not until the end of the Terror in the French Revolution, Hunt argues, that "French pornographers' attention shifted almost exclusively to the depiction of sexual pleasure as an end in itself."[4]

Even Hunt admits, however, that a small number of works, created solely to arouse, had been in circulation for hundreds of years. The advent of printing made it easier to publish such works; the rise of the novel did much to structure them; and the rediscovery of classical learning stimulated their subject matter.[5] Russians joined the fray in the eighteenth century when a protégé of Mikhail Lomonosov, Ivan Barkov (1732–68), began to produce pornographic writings like his collection *The Maiden's Plaything*. *Barkovshchina* soon became a code word for pornography in Russian. Apart from Barkov, some of Russia's most beloved literary heroes – including Pushkin and Lermontov – wrote erotic poems. These works were later suppressed, excluded from anthologies and collected editions, or otherwise excised from public discussion even among scholars. Erotic poems by less known figures were occasionally gathered into collections and published in Geneva in very limited numbers, most notably in the 1870s. Two of the best known were *Russian Folk Tales* (*Russkie narodnyi skazki*) and *Eros Russe: Russian Erotica Not for Ladies* (*Russkii erot ne dlia dam*).

In terms of visual materials, erotic drawings by artists Aleksandr Orlovskii and Mikhail Zichy circulated privately. The latter moved in exalted circles after his arrival in St. Petersburg in 1847. He was appointed court painter in 1856. Many of his erotic drawings were eventually gathered into a privately printed volume published in Leipzig in 1911.[6] Zichy is also noteworthy because he taught Emperor Alexander II, who went on to make several erotic pictures of his second wife, Ekaterina Dolgorukaia. These were discovered (along with Nicholas I's collection of antique phalluses) when the Bolsheviks seized the Winter Palace in 1917.[7] Obviously, such items remained hidden away and the public knew nothing of the tastes of Russia's royals or famous writers. A similar veil was cast over the leading figures of the Silver Age. For instance, the letters describing his sexual conquests that famed Russian philosopher Vladimir Soloviev sent in the 1890s to his friend Sergei Trubetskoi were ignored by scholars. The examples cited in Olga Matich's *Erotic Utopia* are more than explicit enough to be labelled pornography.[8] Moreover, this silence continued throughout the Soviet era when the existence of pre-revolutionary pornography was denied and the subject was certainly not deemed worthy of academic study.

In this chapter, I want to show how deeply Russia was, in fact, embedded in the European market for erotic materials, of which picture postcards were an important component. The kinds of images produced stretched from romantic or humorous postcards that could be read in a suggestive manner to full-blown pornography according to anyone's definition. Among the subjects this chapter considers are the alternative readings possible for postcards reproducing works of art (meant to enlighten or publicize, they could also arouse) and the connection between nudity and social protest. All too often it is assumed that picture postcards only displayed the bodies of ethnic minorities or of the colonized. Certainly, these images have received the most scholarly attention, with works such as Malek Alloula's *The Colonial Harem* being quoted far and wide.[9] This chapter should remind readers that other bodies were also commodified. Some studies of pornography in Britain and France have raised the question of social class, positing that pornography made the bodies of working-class people available for a kind of consumption by others. They note that actresses and prostitutes supplemented their incomes by posing nude or in more sexually explicit scenes.[10] The booming market for cartes-de-visite and later picture postcards – both so cheap and easy to produce – made erotic and pornographic images available to a mass audience for the first time. As Lisa Sigel has described, working-class subjects, by the 1880s and 1890s, could be objectified by their social peers as well as by those higher up the economic ladder.[11] Pornography became part of mass consumption.

Russian materials fit into this second model. Irrespective of whether we talk of domestically produced images or foreign imports, the bodies on display were all white and probably from the lower classes. Existing studies of prostitution in Russia, such as Laurie Bernstein's *Sonia's Daughters*, do not connect it with pornography. What Bernstein's book does do is introduce the notion of "public women." She argues that the government's decision in the mid-nineteenth century to regulate commercial sex made possible a category of women "whose bodies were supposed to be available to clients, doctors, and policemen on demand."[12] Pornography did the same thing by making their bodies available over and over again.

Methodology and the Market

In a little more than forty years, the British Society for the Suppression of Vice was responsible for the seizure by the police of 385,000 prints and photographs, 28,000 sheets of song lyrics, and 80,000 books and pamphlets.[13] All had been labelled obscene and, hence, a threat to public morality. Indeed, historians of Britain have a wealth of information about the spread of pornographic materials in that country. The *Vigilance Record*, the organ of the National Vigilance Association, dutifully recorded each instance when a postcard vendor, travelling salesman, tobacconist, or newsagent had his goods seized because they were deemed obscene.[14] Historians of Russia, on the other hand, do not have this luxury. Instead, evidence on the production and distribution of erotic and pornographic materials is slim, fragmented, and anecdotal.

By the 1890s, the main manufacturing centres for erotic and pornographic images in Europe were Paris, Amsterdam, and Rotterdam. Evidence shows smaller producers in Antwerp, Budapest, Barcelona, Berlin, and Geneva.[15] Budapest was apparently the main centre of production for European stag films in the first decade of the twentieth century.[16] Within the borders of the Russian Empire, references have been made to two manufacturers of printed materials. In 1913, the right-wing, antisemitic press made much of the seizure of a printing press in Warsaw, owned by, as they put it, "a certain Zimmerman." Judging by the fact that the article in *Przeglad Katolicki* referred to it as a "filthy" press, one can assume it was involved in the production of obscene materials.[17] Information about a second publisher, Renesans, is more solid. Also based out of Warsaw, Renesans published a variety of items from 1906 to 1912. Examples of more than thirty of its postcards were included in the scholarly volume *Eros i pornografiia v russkoi kul'ture*.[18] That both of these enterprises were based in Warsaw should not be surprising since the city was a major centre of publishing, and items printed there were distributed and sold throughout the rest of the Russian Empire.[19]

Of course, Russians travelling abroad had easy access to pornographic materials in any European city and did not have to rely on domestic manufacturers. In France, for instance, erotic postcards could be bought in brothels, stationery stores, bookstores, hotels, and cafés.[20] Their prevalence is suggested by the following story. On his first trip abroad, young composer Sergei Prokofiev was shocked at how quickly he was approached by someone selling pornographic postcards. He arrived in Paris in the afternoon of 2 June 1913 and, after leaving his luggage at the hotel, went to find a café. In the first one, "I was immediately approached by a Frenchman who sold me a plan of the city, a dozen postcards with views of Paris, and offered me from under the counter a packet of indecent pictures." Although his diary was filled with references to youthful courtships, Prokofiev recorded that "somewhat embarrassed I said that I was in no need of the last of these, and going off into a quiet corner unfolded my map."[21] His experience cannot have been unique. Many Russians when travelling must have been similarly accosted, while others undoubtedly actively sought out suppliers of pornography.

For those who could not go abroad, imported materials, however, were easily obtained, and European postcard makers were adept at modifying the language of captions to fit local markets. (They already did so with postcards of scenic views, for instance.) Advertisements in mainstream periodicals like *Novoe Vremia, Niva, Satirikon,* and *Solntse Rossii* informed readers how to purchase naughty postcards from France as well as where they could buy similar items in St. Petersburg.[22] An outraged article on fighting pornography appeared in *Peterburgskaia gazeta,* in 1906, describing how pornographic postcards and alphabet cards were being sold openly on the streets of the capital and noting that similar wares were available in taverns and at book stalls.[23] Little had changed more than a decade later. The writer Ivan Bunin noted in his diary, in April 1917, that obscene postcards were still for sale on Nevskii Prospekt, St. Petersburg's main thoroughfare.[24] Apparently the Russian government's decision, in May 1910, to join with thirteen others and sign an agreement on the suppression of pornography had little effect. Entitled the "Paris Convention on the Suppression of the Traffic in Obscene Publications," the agreement called for the establishment of an international organization to facilitate the sharing of information between members, who would then prosecute offenders according to the laws of their own countries. In Russia, that meant a charge of "corrupting morals," which could be punished by a fine or a custodial sentence of up to three months. However, prosecutions in Russia were few.[25]

Finally, the annual Nizhnii-Novgorod Fair was another point of entry. John Foster Fraser visited the fair in the first decade of the twentieth century and found there "literally billions of postcards" for sale, a large number of them pornographic. "I am too seasoned a man of the world to be affected by such things," he reasoned before going on to express his outrage in no uncertain terms: "But when I have seen thousands of the vilest photographs openly on sale and being turned over by boys of fifteen and sixteen, and when a dozen times in a single day I have in cafés been approached by youngsters of nine and ten years of age, and they have grinningly produced abominable pictures from their pockets, I am quite certain there is some official in Nizhni-Novgorod who ought to be tied to a post and publicly flogged."[26]

Despite the vast array of postcards described by Foster, finding sources for this chapter has been difficult. Pornographic postcards clearly intended for the Russian market – I use the inclusion of Russian words somewhere on the postcard, including the back, as my standard here – are seldom included in institutional collections like those of the Kinsey Institute or the Victoria and Albert Museum. They also do not figure among the illustrations in published collections, with the sole exception of the thirty or so mentioned above that were reprinted in *Eros i pornografiia v russkoi kul'ture.*[27] As a result, the examples analysed and reproduced here have been gathered by combing the storefronts of postcard dealers and online auctions. In addition, I consulted a collection of twenty-eight postcards held by the New York Public Library.[28] Ultimately, there is no way of knowing exactly how many erotic picture postcards were ever made, nor how many may have survived the upheavals of the twentieth century. So, rather than apply a quantitative approach, I want to explore these picture postcards qualitatively by focusing on what they can tell us about depictions of the body and Russian participation in some European artistic and social movements in the fin-de-siècle period.

Romance and Sexual Comedy

One day, in the winter of 1922, a bored Niura Lurye rummaged through a dresser drawer and stumbled upon a collection of picture postcards. The young girl soon had them spread across the floor of her apartment much to the irritation of her father when he arrived home from work. Adolf Luyre's anger stemmed from the fact that these postcards were particularly treasured items, precious reminders of the days, before war and revolution, when he had courted his wife. Adolf and Olga sent each other postcards regularly. If he went away on business, the frequency of the correspondence increased. Daily, sometimes even more often, Adolf used his free moments to write to the woman he loved. The postcards, to quote Esther Milne's recent book on technologies of presence, came "to stand in for the corporeal presence of their author."[29] When the Bolshevik seizure of power forced him to flee to Manchuria, Adolf took these postcards with him, believing they brought him closer to his wife and child. It was four years before he saw them in person again.[30]

In their use of picture postcards, the Luryes were like thousands of couples across Europe and North America. Despite the rather public nature of this new form of communication, couples used them to share the intimacies of courtship. Postcard manufacturers, quick to recognize the money-making possibilities of this segment of the market, moved rapidly to produce items appealing to those in the midst of a romance. Russian romantic postcards were quite interchangeable with their European counterparts, and typically featured scenes of courting couples, like in Figure 4.1.

Most such cards culminated, at most, with a kiss so it is safe to assume their intended audience included women (unlike the pornographic images to be discussed later). They provided a lighthearted means of communication between lovers, although their usage was not confined to this group. Sergei Prokofiev's diaries from his student days show how such postcards – often modified in some way by the sender – could be used to tease or annoy his female friends.[31] In terms of imagery, flirtation scenes were common and, in them, gestures were often as deliberately exaggerated as they were in turn-of-the-century melodramatic films (see Figure 4.2).

Other picture postcards dovetailed with the nineteenth-century predilection for secret codes to be used between lovers. Even the suggestion of such codes added hints of forbidden excitement to ordinary correspondence. The language of flowers is the most frequently referred to of these. Beverly Seaton, whose *The Language of Flowers: A History* is the most comprehensive study of it, argues that there were enormous obstacles for anyone wanting to use the code.[32] Hence, she concludes that while it captured many imaginations, it was seldom employed. There are some suggestions, however, that Seaton's conclusions may not be as definitive as she makes them out to be. At least one French postcard provided a key to the code, and the Russian postcard in Figure 4.3 explains how particular bouquets of flowers are connected to women's first names and traits like elegance or intelligence.[33]

Nor was this the only floral code circulating in Russia in the early twentieth century. Valentin Berezhkov, who is best known as one of Stalin's interpreters in the Second World War, included an interesting tidbit in his memoirs. When recalling the party games he played as a teenager in the 1920s, he included one called "the flirtation of flowers" which, according to him, dated from the pre-revolutionary era but remained

4.1 Courting couple. Trisa, n.d.

4.2 Romantic postcard. No manufacturer listed. Postally used in 1912.

4.3 Postcard with floral code. Manufactured by NGZ & Co. Mailed from Petrograd in 1915.

popular. In the game, "every player got a card in which the name of a flower was used to invoke a passage from a [literary] classic. By calling out the name of the flower and addressing it to a fellow player of the opposite sex, messages were exchanged without anything being said out loud."[34]

Figures 4.4 and 4.5 refer to two other codes. The former features the language of postage stamps, where their placement on letters indicated hidden meanings to the recipient. The latter explains the romantic messages that could be given by wax seals.

Figure 4.5 is particularly interesting since it harkens back to St. Valentine's Day celebrations in Western Europe rather than to any kind of native Russian tradition, thereby demonstrating that manufacturers were not always concerned about the cultural particularities of each country or that Russia was conceived of as part of a pan-European culture. In the early nineteenth century, it became fashionable in the West

4.4 "The language of postage stamps." Izdanie "KaRe," n.d.

to write a keepsake letter on richly ornamented paper and give it to a loved one in honour of St. Valentine's Day. Prior to the establishment of state-run postal systems and the development of cheap paper, which made the use of envelopes widespread, such Valentine letters were fold-ed and sealed with wax in just the way the postcard shows.

Another frequently used device was seriality, whereby a series of post-cards was produced which, when viewed in order, provided a longer nar-rative to the images displayed. The narratives could show the progress of a rendezvous and end with a clinch, kiss, or proposal. More explicit post-cards used series to show people undressing or to chronicle the progress of a sexual encounter. Postcard manufacturers liked series because they induced customers to buy more, given that all of the instalments were needed in order for the story to make sense and reach a logical conclu-sion. Series were also geared towards collectors who it was known disliked having gaps in their collections. The postcards in a series were usually

4.5 "Stamps and their secrets." NGZ & Co., n.d.

numbered in some way so buyers could know if their set was complete. Unfortunately for historians, a century separates their manufacture from our scholarly studies and few series have survived intact, so any analysis of them often contains an element of ambiguity.

Many postcard series approached the question of sexual relations from the most graphic of perspectives, while sometimes drawing on Russian popular culture's bawdy strain.[35] As the examples in *Eros i pornografiia* and the postcards held by the New York Public Library show, seriality was an important convention of the genre.[36] By attempting to describe a sexual encounter in its entirety – often from dressed beginning through obvious climax – the postcards offered a complete story. Postcards 23–28 in the New York Library collection are a good example. The story they tell begins with a young man and woman sitting at a piano under the watchful eye of an older female chaperone, most likely intended to be interpreted as the young woman's mother. Once she leaves the room, the couple's behaviour – as expressed on subsequent postcards – becomes ever more explicit. It moves from dancing to the fondling of the woman's breasts and genitals to full-fledged intercourse. In the final postcard, the chaperone returns to discover the pair in flagrante delicto – on top of the piano.

These postcards fit into the patterns demarcated by Steven Marcus in *The Other Victorians*. Marcus' "pornotopia" involves endless variations of positions and partners. As he writes, "For though repetition is a central formal attribute of pornography, this repetition is set within a context which also demands that it be accompanied by minute, mechanical variations in both general arrangement and language – thereby delivering it from the onus of 'mere' repetition."[37] While the changing of partners was less obvious on picture postcards, the changing of positions was frequently invoked. It not only added a forbidden tinge to the images since they showed positions forbidden by Orthodox religious teachings (and for which practitioners would be assigned lengthy penances), but allowed for different perspectives on the bodies involved to be presented to the viewers, thereby making the most secret recesses of the body human knowable and visible.

In contrast to the dominant culture of the era, which by and large, accorded no sexual impulses to women, erotic picture postcards followed the line of pornographic novels. Here, all women were insatiable and constantly ready for sex. Figure 26 in *Eros i pornografiia* is a good example for it shows an unsatisfied woman begging for more sex but the flaccid penis of her partner is clearly not up to the job. The woman's desire becomes the butt of the joke. The availability of women – as well as another comedic twist – is offered by the carte-de-visite in Figure 4.6. It suggests a woman just had to fall over in order to be ready for sex. The very faint caption, "Dangerous place," gives an obvious double entendre.

The structure of pornographic novels lends itself to exhaustively listing the sexual conquests of the hero or heroine. It should be noted, however, that even when the narrator is female, the authorial voice is usually male so the narrator becomes a reflection of male sexuality.[38] The emphasis is on quantity and variety – simply put, the more partners, the more virile the man. This notion could be rendered in visual form, as Figure 4.7 demonstrates. On this postcard, the letters of the man's name – Sergei – are composed from a montage of photographs of women, some featuring décolletage and others knowing looks. The inclusion of flowers and stems in the design suggests fertility and sexual reproduction. Moreover, the image gives a kind of instant sexual history since it certainly implies "Sergei" has possessed all of these women.

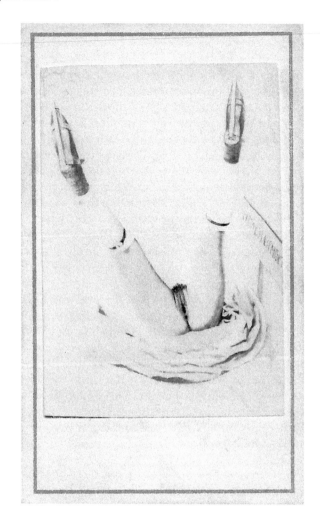

4.6 "Dangerous place" carte-de-visite. No manufacturer or date listed.

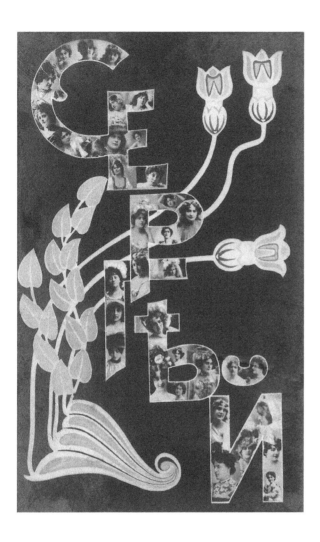

4.7. "Sergei." No manufacturer or date listed.

This last example is a play on another frequently used device in pornographic postcards: references to letters or alphabet cards. It will be remembered that alphabet cards were one of the items explicitly mentioned in a contemporary newspaper article decrying the prevalence of pornography in St. Petersburg, in 1906. Apart from Figure 4.8, another example of such an image is included in *Eros i pornografiia* where the first three letters of the Russian alphabet are spelled out by bodies of people engaged in a variety of sexual activities.[39] As items used to teach children to read, alphabet cards are a symbol of innocence and lack of knowledge. Hence, to create pornographic ones is perhaps the ultimate inversion of innocence. The postcards may also be referring obliquely to the common narrative in pornographic novels whereby a young innocent gains sexual knowledge as the story progresses. Again, it is worth quoting Marcus, who writes, "In pornography, however, life or existence in time does not begin with birth; it begins with one's first sexual impulse or experience, and one is said to be born in pornotopia only after one has experienced his first erection or witnessed his first primal scene."[40] Figure 4.8, an alphabet card for the letter "F," apart from making a witty comment about the French, provides a kind of sexual primer to the viewer, suggesting new variations or positions to be tried. Other postcards in the same series make no comment about the nationality of the subjects. The postcard for the letter "Shch" (Щ), for instance, plays on the verb "schipat'" (to pinch or tweak) by showing a man pinching a woman's nipple.

Arousal and Enlightenment

In the nineteenth century, nudes became increasingly prevalent subjects in the European art world, and statues in the classical style were fashionable ornaments for public places. Aesthetic theories, like Joshua Reynolds's theory of ideal beauty, provided ways of seeing the nude with studied detachment, ways that de-eroticized it by emphasizing characteristics like balance and symmetry rather than its potential to arouse.[41] Travelling exhibitions exposed Russian audiences to these latest artistic trends. In 1888, an exhibition of French paintings was staged in St. Petersburg, and another followed three years later. This second event featured works by 150 artists, covering all of the major movements in the second half of the nineteenth century. The exhibition eventually travelled to Moscow.[42] In one of his essays, modernist writer Vasilii Rozanov recorded Tsar Alexander III's reaction to the exhibition: he made it only

4.8. Pornographic alphabet postcard for letter "F." No manufacturer or date listed.

to the doorway, where a quick glance at the nudity on display convinced the tsar he had seen enough, and he quickly left.[43]

Despite reactions like that of the tsar, picture postcard manufacturers often defended themselves by arguing that they were providing people with images that served an educational or culturally edifying purpose.[44] Such picture postcards were supposedly justified on the grounds that they informed an audience unable to travel to see the originals of the latest artistic movements, particularly in Europe. In most cases involving nudes, the postcard manufacturer attached a caption in Russian indicating that the image showed a work from the annual Paris Salon – it is not without reason that many commentators referred to erotic postcards as French postcards for the Lapin firm in Paris produced a series entitled "Paris Salon" especially for the Russian market.[45] Such items frequently equated "Frenchness" with sexuality and offered some of the most erotically charged images to circulate in postcard form.

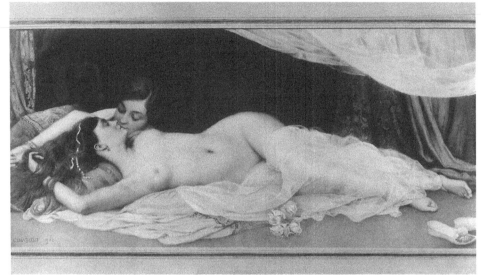

5434   *Парижъ. Салонъ.* — Забытіе — Ж. Корабэйфъ

4.9 "Forgetting" by Jean Coraboeuf. Glavnyi sklad dlia vsei Rossii, n.d.

The postcard in Figure 4.9 presents one such work, a 1908 painting by French artist Jean Coraboeuf (1870–1947). It shows two women on the verge of kissing. Because the central figure's nude body extends the length of the image, the eyes of the viewer are eventually led across her entire body after first being drawn to her pelvic region, which is slightly shaded in a fashion that suggests pubic hair. The image also contains a number of details that are familiar sexual fetishes: the nude woman's hair is draped across a cushion, a bouquet of flowers lies on the floor near her pelvic region, and a pair of discarded shoes lies at the far side of the postcard so her naked feet (complete with toe rings) are fully revealed. Nothing about this picture postcard is truly innocent; indeed, every component of the image is so sexually charged that one is hardpressed to believe this postcard ever served an educational or artistic purpose.

Both the acts of working with nude models, and observing nude statues (the end products of such labours) were popular subjects for erotic postcards (see Figures 4.10 and 4.11). They create triangular relationships where the viewer looks at the clothed men who, in turn, gaze at the

4.10 "Critics" by Jose Bellon. Glavnyi sklad' dlia vsei Rossii, n.d.

nude female figures. These images confront viewers in a way other images do not. They make viewers evaluate not only their own responses to the nudes, but also those of the men depicted. They also offer a kind of standard, for if the men appear dispassionate in the face of the body, then viewers may be discomforted by their own, potentially more aroused, responses to the scenes. The images further suggest the power involved in voyeurism, where stimulation comes from having the ability to manipulate and control the body of someone else, particularly if that person is forced into doing something that breaks social norms. That these images could be interpreted as pornography is evident in G. B-n's article in *Peterburgskaia gazeta* which ends with a couple of paragraphs connecting photography, nude modelling, and prostitution.[46]

Another tendency of art postcards was to rely on obscure subject matters and cultural references. Here, the argument about making artistic materials more accessible breaks down since the allusions were often so unknown they would have been unintelligible to the vast majority of potential viewers. At this point, artistic nudes that may have

5126. Парижскій Салонъ 1909 г. Р. Белижанъ.
Первый дебютъ натурщицы.

4.11 "Debut of a Nude Model" by Raoul Baligant. No manufacturer or date listed.

served some enlightening purpose, however much of a stretch that argument was to begin with, definitely descended to the level of pornographic images of naked bodies. A comment in a letter by Nadezhda Teffi to the writer Ivan Bunin shows the different ways in which art postcards were interpreted. "One time when I was visiting in the area around Novgorod, I came across a customs officer who was looking through an album," she wrote. "Suddenly he smirked and handed the album over to a friend of his. Both began looking ... at a picture of Canova's famous sculpture, 'Cupid Awakening Psyche.' When I approached, the officer said, 'Young ladies should not see such a thing!' and slammed the album shut."[47]

This trend in erotic materials has a long history since much early written pornography also relied on classical examples, particularly abundant references to Ancient Greece. By drawing on such stories, postcard makers increased the risqué factor of their images. They hinted at such taboos as lesbianism, bestiality, and sexual violence without accepting the label of pornography for their wares. In other words, they could maintain a sense of distance from the image that supposedly downplayed its potential to arouse. However, the postcards could be interpreted in other ways. Figure 4.12 shows a reproduction intended for the Russian market of a painting by French artist Joseph Aubert (1849–1924).

The image can be viewed as implying bestiality, given it shows a woman being bound to a bull by a naked man. Scientific discourse in the nineteenth century assumed women were ruled by their senses and emotions, like other seemingly "less evolved" species were. Hence, as Allison Pease remarks, "late nineteenth-century representations of women with animals began to take on a different overtone, a practical assimilation of erotic interests. Playing upon these associations, there was an entire subgenre of Victorian pornography featuring women in erotic poses with animals."[48] Here, the man's muscles bulge with the violence of his efforts. The woman's breasts, centred in the image and whose whiteness contrasts the dark hues of the bull's fur, draw the attention of the viewer. They are also on a visual level with what is likely to be a tuft of pubic hair on the man. Most picture postcards of works of art shied away from including pubic hair – as I mentioned above, they did sometimes use shading to imply its presence – possibly because it marked an unwritten line between art and pornography.

Sexual violence and death were frequently addressed by works of art that were then reproduced on picture postcards. The fin-de-siècle era was rife with references to such subjects. Studies of the sexual habits of

На арену 131

Ауберть

4.12 "In the Arena" by Joseph Aubert. No manufacturer listed. Postally used 1911.

university students done at the time revealed that a third read pornography while two-thirds read popular medical tracts.[49] Dead bodies were prominent in Russian fiction. Two of the most well-known novels in Russian literature contain moments that connect death and the display of a woman's body: Anna Karenina's body was put on display in a railway shed after her suicide, and Bazarov in Turgenev's *Fathers and Sons* envisions a woman's body in a dissecting room. This trend of anatomizing women's bodies but in a sexually charged way found further expression in popular visual media. A number of European artists, including Gabriel Max, J.H. Hasselhorst, and Enrique Simonet, painted images of women being dissected.[50] The paintings, which circulated widely in the form of picture postcards, contain similar elements that belie the horror and gruesome nature of an actual autopsy. Instead, the subjects, who appear in a type of peaceful repose, are all young and have beautiful long hair draped across the tables on which they lie. While artfully draped cloths cover parts of their bodies, the women's pert breasts are

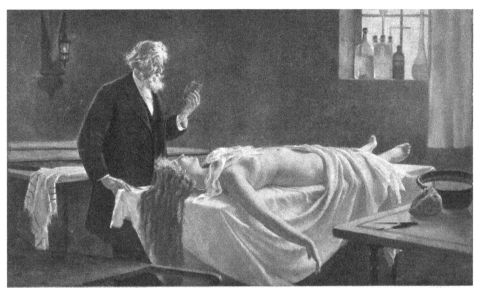

E. Зимонетъ. Анатомія сердца.　　　　　　　　　　E. Simonet. L'anatomie du cœur.

4.13 "The Anatomy of the Heart" by E. Simonet. Izdanie "Richard" (St. Petersburg), n.d.

usually exposed. A Russian postcard version of Simonet's "The Anatomy of the Heart," made by the St. Petersburg firm "Richard," is shown in Figure 4.13. On the one hand, the picture purportedly illustrates part of a dissection, the moment when the medical examiner removed the subject's heart. On the other, the image is loaded with details that lend themselves to sexualized readings. To begin with, the picture does not reveal the gaping hole through which the woman's heart must have been removed. Instead, the only visible part of her torso is her naked breast, situated right in the middle of the image where it can draw the eye of the viewer. No marks of violence appear on the body, and the position of the corpse's arm suggests a sensual languor rather than rigor mortis. This sensuality is reinforced by the positioning of the woman's hair and the draping of the sheets covering her legs. Nothing in the image suggests the blood and gore that would have accompanied a real dissection. It celebrates the beauty of a woman's body rather than its eventual putrefaction.

Pornography as Artistic Protest?

In the summer of 1908, English dancer Olga Desmond arrived in St. Petersburg intending to put on her "Evenings of Beauty" (*Schönheitsabende*) for a Russian audience. Given that these events involved actors posing nude or only in body paint on stage, they had a history of being banned across Europe. Local authorities were not usually interested in the purpose of the evenings, or in their stated connections to classical culture. To them, the actors who assumed positions similar to classical works of art were simply naked people defying social norms. Indeed, performances like the one Desmond wanted to give were hard to separate from the tableaux vivants that could be seen every night in Russian music halls. Russian officials, to no one's surprise except maybe Desmond herself, prevented her from performing.

Olga Desmond was only one of a number of dancers who made their reputations by appearing in the nude. Others included Adorée Villany, Nina Hard, and Gertrud Leistikow.[51] What separated Desmond for posterity was her use of other media besides the stage to publicize her ideas. She had strong connections to the German nudist movement. She was married for a time to Karl Vanselow, who founded the nudist magazine *Die Schönheit*, in 1903. The magazine promoted nudism as part of modernism in the arts.[52] This idea did find some echoes in fin-de-siècle Russia, although we know almost nothing about the history of nudism – naturism as it is referred to today – in the country since the subject has yet to capture the interest of Russian historians. Snippets of information reveal that some modernists were apparently interested in it: writers Leonid Andreev and Maximilian Voloshin participated in nudism while painter Ivan Miasoedov, who had himself photographed in the nude, published a "Manifesto on Nudity" in 1912.[53] Critics were scandalized by what they thought was a display of female nudity in Nikolai Evreinov's production of Fedor Sologub's play, *Nighttime Dances* (*Nochnye pliaski*), in 1911.[54]

Other plays by Valerii Briusov, Viacheslav Ivanov, Velimir Khlebnikov, and Innokentii Annenskii featured either statues coming to life or people being turned into statues. The fascination with women – particularly naked ones – posing as statues can be traced back to Russian serf theatre in the eighteenth century where it was a common occurrence.[55] As Katherine Lahti argues, this device is ideal for voyeurism since it "freezes a woman's body for the sake of erotic contemplation without any threat of interference."[56] In the nineteenth century, particularly in the era under discussion here, it helps to explain the popularity of the Pygmalion story, where the sculptor falls in love with his statue, Galatea, and wills her to life. This motif of a statue coming to life featured in the poetry of Alexander Pushkin and Evgeny Baratynsky, the philosophical works of Vladimir Solov'ev and Nikolai Fedorov, and the writings of Russian symbolists.[57] On a less exalted note, the story was also a popular one for erotic postcards, including some available in Russia.

To return to Desmond, the device of living statuary was reflected in her work both on stage and in other media. A book featuring nude photographs of her in classical Greek poses was published. Moreover, the publicity materials used for her visit to Russia included picture postcard versions of some of these photographs. Despite her protestations and artistic pretensions, the postcards blur the line between art and pornography. Given that her performances were cancelled, all Russians were left with were postcards, such as Figure 4.14, and their ambiguity.

Eroticism in the Eye of the Beholder

Historians and collectors agree that postcards can be read in more than one way. In the golden age of the picture postcard, double entendres abounded as things that appeared inconsequential or innocuous to one viewer held hidden meanings for others. Some of the most common fetish items or body parts were legs, buttocks, breasts, feet, mirrors, cigarettes, and musical instruments. As should be evident from the examples that follow, Russian postcards followed the same patterns as their European counterparts and offered a wide variety of implied meanings. To begin with, bared breasts, or at least deep cleavage, appeared with startling regularity, and in a gratuitous manner. The fascination with breasts also revealed itself in the sheer number of items compared to them. Everything from Easter eggs to melons to apples served as references to breasts on picture postcards (see Figure 4.15). Seemingly, any oversized rounded object would do to add a double entendre to the most innocent of postcards. That the objects were often edible underscored the notion that women's breasts were also objects to be bought and consumed orally.

All kinds of handheld objects lent themselves to other erotically charged categories of picture postcard. The inclusion of mirrors suggested pleasure could be derived from contemplation and voyeurism as well as the fantasy of interrupting a lady in the midst of her toilette. For educated Russians, mirrors may have had an additional connotation.

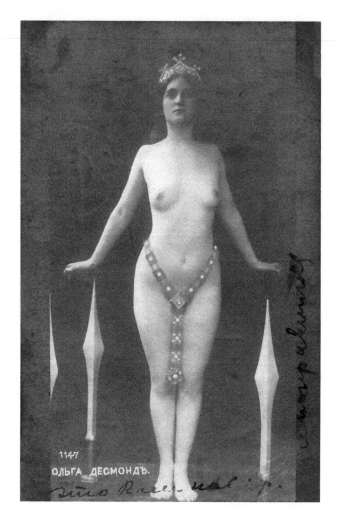

4.14 Olga Desmond. No manufacturer or date listed. Author's collection.

4.15 Easter greetings. No manufacturer listed. Mailed from Irkutsk in 1913.

Mirrors were symbols of Aphrodite, the goddess of love and the patron saint of prostitutes. Hence, while the women being photographed may never have known it, the mirrors they held implied, at least to some viewers, that they were prostitutes and sexually available.[58] In other instances, musical instruments, like the more obvious canes and whips, served as phallic substitutes when included in photographs with naked women. The woman with the guitar in Figure 4.16 connects picture postcards with Russia's long history of sexual exploitation of performers. In Western Europe, the theatre was a socially approved source of erotic sensations where spectators "in the know" could spot hidden messages. In Russia that was also true, but an additional frisson came from the theatre's connection to serfdom. Serfdom had allowed wealthy aristocrats to have their own private theatres, where they controlled every aspect of the performance as well as of the lives of the performers.[59] Stories of serf owners engaging in outrageous behaviour demonstrate to what extent the bodies of performers were eroticized and commodified. For instance, Nikolai Yusopov amused his friends with this trick: after a wave of his cane, the ballerinas in his troupe stripped naked on stage.[60] The powerlessness of the performers was obvious and their sexual availability clearly suggested by incidents like these. Even once the serfs had been emancipated and private gentry theatres closed, performers remained marginalized, tainted figures in the popular mind. This position was further reinforced by the lurid stories of dancers and actresses that featured quite prominently in tabloid newspaper articles and boulevard novels in the fin-de-siècle era.

Picture postcards added a different visual element to the subject of performers and their sexual availability. In these photographs, taboos were broken and it was not necessary for the viewer to even attend a performance in order to gaze upon the bodies of actresses and dancers. Figure 4.17 is a relatively understated example, but it still has suggestive elements. The postcard shows the well-known ballet dancer, and former mistress of the tsar, Mathilde Kshesinskaia, dressed for one of her performances. As Tracy Davis notes, in her work on actresses in Victorian Britain, "theatrical costume flagrantly violated the dress codes of the street and drawing room, flaunting the ankles, calves, knees, thighs, crotch, and upper torso."[61] Here, Kshesinskaia's costume does not cling tightly to her body, leaving little to the imagination, the way some postcards did. But, it still reveals more flesh than many women would have done in polite society and that she appeared in it on stage, a place where women from polite society did not go, added to the

4.16 "Mlle. Lo." No manufacturer or date listed.

4.17 Mathilde Kshesinskaia. No manufacturer listed. Postally used in 1903.

eroticism of the image. While little of her breasts or legs is visible, her arms and shoulders are bare, allowing viewers to fetishize these areas. Kshesinskaia's unbound hair is another violation of social norms, given that married women in Russia did not appear in public with their hair loose. Unbound hair would only have been seen in intimate settings such as the bedroom; hence, its use in an image automatically carries sexual connotations. Kshesinskaia's pose is also risqué. Although her foot is turned to imply that this is a proper ballet pose, it is still one that leaves Kshesinskaia in a frilly skirt with her legs spread.

Conclusion

When Kornei Chukovsky insisted Russia had only pornography with ideas, he was clearly seeing but part of the picture. As the examples in this chapter prove, by the end of the nineteenth century, Russia had the same kinds of erotica available as any Western country. Examining picture postcards reveals an erotic spectrum stretching from romantic images that could tastefully be used by courting couples to purely pornographic items that would have been hidden from public view. Postcards also give some idea of the extent to which female bodies were on display for consumption by the masses. While some manufacturers and consumers argued that these images served an edifying purpose by educating the public about art or that they protested against social restrictions concerning nudity and the body, the same postcards were interpreted by others as items meant solely to arouse. If anything, this chapter meant to show how slippery the lines were (and arguably still are) between romance and sex as well as between art and sexual exploitation.

Chapter Five

Monarchy and the Mundane: Picture Postcards and Images of the Romanovs

In mid-nineteenth century Europe, the emerging market for new paper products allowed for the widespread circulation of mass-produced depictions of royalty for the first time. This chapter uses picture postcards to examine this process of commodification as well as some of the implications of it. In particular, the focus is on the depiction of members of the Romanov dynasty and the unwitting desacralization that accompanied their efforts to employ a new form of mass media. From objects of awe, the Romanovs were transformed into something much more mundane: an ordinary bourgeois family. Existing scholarship has looked at this shift in terms of the impact of ceremonial occasions, of pornographic pamphlets, films, and rumours featuring the tsar, the tsarina, and Rasputin, and of such major events as Bloody Sunday or the Lena Goldfields massacre. The contribution, even if it is only a minor one, of such ephemeral items as picture postcards has so far been overlooked. Yet, the production of literally millions of such items, things that could be defaced or thrown in the garbage, did have ramifications on the popular perception of the tsar and point to how pervasively his image problems spread.

The story begins in 1854 when the process for making cartes-de-visite was patented. Avidly collected, cartes-de-visite laid the groundwork for the ways in which royalty would be presented for the remainder of the nineteenth and early twentieth centuries. Of great significance was Queen Victoria's decision to allow portraits of the British royal family to be published in this way. Gradually, members of her extended family all came to employ similar images to publicize their activities, and the commemorative picture postcard was born. However, what in the British context created a sense of attachment to the monarchy, proved to be detrimental in Russia where a greater sense of majesty was needed to justify the continuing existence of an autocratic form of government.

Soon picture postcards went beyond merely noting the public activities of monarchs and offered revealing glances into their private lives. It is worth remembering that in the wake of the executions of Louis XVI and Marie Antoinette during the French Revolution, "the question of how royals should behave had become a pertinent one."[1] In the case of the tsar, such private images did little to improve his standing with his subjects. They showed Nicholas II in a decidedly un-majestic fashion: more middle-class father than awe-inspiring autocrat. Picture postcards of the empress also failed to create an image of her as an ideal wife and mother in the minds of the Russian public. As we will see, they provoked satirical responses that mocked her relationship with Rasputin and her husband's masculinity.

The chapter ends with an examination of the connection between picture postcards and royal charity. Here, too, there are links to developments in the rest of Europe. Royal patronage of charities, as well as charitable activities directly undertaken by royalty, were supposed to enhance the prestige of monarchies. The start of the First World War provided Nicholas and Alexandra with new opportunities in this direction, as Alexandra, in particular, very publicly moved to assist the war wounded. But, once again, the picture postcards sometimes provoked an unexpected response. Far from invoking the medieval idea of the healing power of royal touch, or even nineteenth-century notions concerning the bonds between monarchs and individual subjects, the images further undermined the reputation of the empress by associating her with filth and damaged male bodies. In the end, picture postcards did not fulfil their potential to enhance the standing of the Romanovs. Instead, they point to how the tsar, by tolerating the production of royal kitsch, was himself implicated in undermining his position as a divine right monarch.

The Long Reach of Queen Victoria

When Prince Albert bought the couple's first photograph in 1840, he had no idea this invention would revolutionize the way the public conceived of his wife Queen Victoria and, through her example, Europe's other monarchs. Albert, as an active patron of scientific discoveries in general, found photography of great interest from its earliest days. In 1842, he was the first member of the royal family to sit for a photograph. Eleven years later, in 1853, the Royal Photographic Society was founded. Both Victoria and Albert were patrons of it. Apart from this very public endorsement of photography, the pair also retained a strong private interest in it. They arranged for daguerreotypes to be made on the occasion of their eldest daughter Vicky's wedding to the heir to the Prussian throne, and eventually a private darkroom was installed at Windsor Castle so that the family could be photographed regularly.[2] But, these early photographs remained singular, usually private, products. It was not until the 1850s that the images could be mass-produced and, hence, circulated beyond the confines of the royal family.

Before discussing this process, however, two digressions should be made. The first explains the emphasis placed on Britain's Queen Victoria in a chapter on visual popular culture and Russia's Romanov dynasty. Simply put, through Victoria, so many royal houses were related to one another, and her longevity, together with the image of stability she projected, influenced the behaviour of the other European monarchs. As mentioned above, Victoria's eldest daughter married into the Prussian royal family and was the mother of the last kaiser, Wilhelm II. Victoria was also grandmother to the Princesses of Hesse (their mother was Princess Alice). Alice's daughters both married into the Russian royal family: Ella married Grand Duke Sergei, the tsar's uncle, and Alix, of course, married Tsar Nicholas II. Nicholas had his own ties to the British royal family. His mother, Dowager Empress Maria Fedorovna, was the sister of Alexandra, the wife of Albert Edward, Queen Victoria's eldest son and heir. In the 1890s, in particular, relations between the British royal family and the Romanovs were very warm.[3] The families vacationed together in Copenhagen (the birthplace of Queen Alexandra and Dowager Empress Maria Fedorovna) and the death of Tsar Alexander III led to a visit by the then Prince and Princess of Wales to Russia. Ultimately, Albert Edward remained in Russia for a month in order to become well acquainted with Nicholas II.

Second, it is also important to show how picture postcards were used by European royalty in their own correspondence. Although diplomatic relations between the major European powers were often strained in the years leading up to the First World War, members of the various royal families continued to write to one another and to see themselves as members of a large extended family. It should be noted, incidentally, that sending picture postcards was a normal feature of this correspondence. Grand Duke Nikolai Mikhailovich, for instance, corresponded with friends using a specially produced picture postcard of his favourite house in Borjomi.[4] The photograph collection of the British royal family contains another interesting example: a postcard showing Russian Empress Alexandra and her five children. As the children, dressed in identical sailor-style costumes, play with a pony, Alexandra stands with her back to the viewer watching them. A camera is in her hand. This particular postcard was sent by Alexandra to her cousin George, Prince of Wales, as a Christmas/New Year card in 1906.[5] Even after the February Revolution had swept the Romanovs from the Russian throne, postcards continued to be used by them for private reasons. To give but two examples, Mark Steinberg and Vladimir Khrustalev's *The Fall of the Romanovs* reprints the messages found on a postcard of the baby Jesus and the Virgin Mary (where Grand Duchess Olga composed a poem for her mother), and a postcard from Alexandra to Aleksandr Syroboiarsky in 1918.[6]

Turning the focus back to the mass-produced images consumed by the public, in 1854, Andre Disderi patented the process for making cartes-de-visite, and this event marked a decisive shift in the way monarchs and their relations were seen. His invention allowed for multiple copies of photographs to be mounted onto heavy cardboard and used as calling cards. In addition to cards featuring private individuals, manufacturers were soon making special sets designed for collectors to keep in albums. Works of art, views, and pictures of royalty were among the most popular subjects. Queen Victoria gave a boost to the new industry in two ways. First, she allowed J.E. Mayall to publish a collection of cartes-de-visite photographs of the royal family, in August 1860. Sixty thousand sets were promptly sold and other sets followed in subsequent years.[7] When the Prince Consort died in 1861, seventy thousand cartes-de-visite bearing his portrait were sold in a week.[8] Queen Victoria herself proved to be a popular subject, and it is estimated that three to four million cartes with her portrait, like that in Figure 5.1, sold between 1860 and 1862.[9]

Second, Victoria let it be known that she herself was an avid collector of cartes-de-visite. She ultimately amassed a collection that filled thirty-six albums.[10] On the continent, Empress Elisabeth of Austria was also a passionate collector of cartes-de-visite, and their popularity in France rose after Napoleon III visited Disderi's studio. Russia, too, was affected by the craze and the country's leading manufacturers were Denier (St. Petersburg), Lorenz (Moscow), Panov (Moscow), and Posekin (Khar'kov).

Soon, across Europe, cartes-de-visite, and later picture postcards, brought likenesses of royalty into the mainstream of popular culture. This innovation marked a true democratization of the visual image since it allowed monarchs to be constantly visible, for the first time, in

5.1 Carte-de-visite of Queen Victoria. No manufacturer or date listed.

media that could be purchased by a mass audience. It turned them into tangible beings in the minds of their subjects as well as into articles of popular consumption. In the case of Queen Victoria, there was a deliberate attempt towards the end of her reign to turn her into the symbolic representation of first the nation state, and then the empire. In this way, Victoria was very effectively able to counter the republican criticism that had been a prevalent feature of the first decades of her reign.[11]

Republicans argued that the monarchy was an obstacle to popular sovereignty (and, implicitly, to what they saw as good government) and that its cost was a crippling burden to Britain's lower classes. By presenting herself as a symbol of stability and historical continuity, however, Victoria was able to become the embodiment of national prestige at just this moment when depictions of her were turned into articles of mass consumption. Her image was to serve as a type of individualized connection between the monarch and all her subjects. For instance, Alexis Schwarzenbach's research demonstrates how members of the British, Belgian, and Italian royal families cemented relations with members of the general public by sending copies of official photographs, or postcards displaying an official portrait, as responses to unsolicited correspondence.

The choice of official portraits was usually a sound one, for as Schwarzenbach notes, "on official photographs they are seldom doing anything specific. Usually immobile, either standing or seated, the royal sitters appear in front of artificial backgrounds, usually canvasses, sometimes monochrome, sometimes figuratively decorated, or in one of the royal residences."[12] There is nothing in these portraits to undermine the sense of majesty of the individual being photographed. Far from it, since it was normal for the subject to be lavishly dressed and, in the case of women, to be literally covered in extravagant jewelry. The portraits could serve an overt ideological purpose though and, in some instances, they presented what Richard Wortman has termed a ruler's "scenario of power." In the case of Nicholas II, for instance, picture postcards were made for both the domestic and wider European markets that showed him dressed in Tsar Aleksei Mikhailovich's clothes for a court ball held in February 1903 to commemorate the bicentennial of the founding of St. Petersburg (see Figure 5.2). A second postcard from the series showed him with the tsarina, who wore a costume owned by Aleksei Mikhailovich's first wife.[13]

The event was well publicized and photographs of Nicholas in his costume were frequently republished over the next decade. They are noteworthy because Nicholas is captured using one of the aspects of ritual identified by David Cannadine: anachronistic dress worn to enhance the majesty and mystery of the ruler.[14] Here, the Russian caftan, notably attacked by Peter the Great as part of his Westernizing agenda, has re-emerged as a royal symbol, and the props used in the photograph also recall items from pre-modern Russia. The postcard suggests "an idealised image of desired harmony and people was now seen in Muscovy rather

5.2 French postcard showing Nicholas II dressed as Aleksei Mikhailovich. No manufacturer listed. Postally used, date unclear.

than Petersburg."[15] This notion, as we will see below, was also prevalent in the materials created to celebrate the three-hundredth anniversary of the Romanov dynasty, in 1913. However, Nicholas's scenario did not necessarily resonate well with some members of the Russian general public who, because they did not attend the ball in person, could only have become acquainted with it via the visual materials circulated in the aftermath of the event. Nina Berberova, for one, was scathing in her rejection of it. She included the following passage in her memoirs: "He thought he was a second Tsar Alexis Mikhailovich and that Russia was that pre-Petrine country which needed anointed ones, synods, and gendarmes, when what Russia needed were quick steps through a parliamentary system and capitalism to planning, new taxes, freedom of speech and the press, and twentieth-century technology, civilization for all, universal education, self-respect for all."[16]

Other portraits linked members of royal families with the very cohesion of Europe's empires, suggesting it was they who held together the disparate territories and ethnic groups into single wholes, and they who provided a crucial symbol of loyalty to the armed forces. As such, picture postcards showing members of the royal family dressed in the costumes of various ethnic minorities wrote national difference and political turmoil out of the political and social story. Again, this type of imagery had a Victorian connection. Queen Victoria's acquisition of the title Empress of India, as well as the jubilee celebrations that brought representatives from the farthest reaches of the empire to London, established her as the political centre of the British Empire. In the Russian context, as early as the reign of Nicholas I, various ethnic-based military units had been established and used to accompany the emperor at public events. Thomas Barrett has noted that their presence, particularly since they wore traditional clothing, projected the very image of the Russian Empire.[17] By the end of the century, picture postcards of the Romanov children wearing ethnic and military clothing were commonly issued for both the foreign and domestic markets. For example, when Grand Duchess Olga Nikolaevna came of age, in November 1911, commemorative picture postcards were created, showing her outfitted both in traditional court dress and in the uniform of the 3rd Elizavetgradskii Life Guards Hussars regiment.[18] Such images visually underscored the unity of the empire with its political centre. Figure 5.3 provides an example. Here, two of Nicholas II's daughters, Olga and Tatiana, dress in the military uniforms of elite Guards regiments. At the time, it was assumed within the aristocracy that these regiments formed the backbone of support

5.3 Grand Duchesses Olga Nikolaevna and Tatiana Nikolaevna dressed in Guards regimental uniforms. Manufacturer "Ste Russie" in Paris, n.d.

for the dynasty. Hence, the tsar followed established tradition by connecting his family to them. Although his daughters could not serve in combat with these units, they did fulfil a variety of other public duties to reinforce the relationships. In 1909, for instance, Grand Duchess Olga Nikolaevna was appointed colonel-in-chief of the aforementioned 3rd Elizavetgradskii Life Guards Hussars regiment. In that capacity, she was able to take part in regimental dinners and military reviews.[19]

The Negative Image of Nicholas II
and the Use of Commemorative Postcards

Just as Queen Victoria faced challenges from republicans who argued that the monarchy was unnecessary, and possibly detrimental, to the country's development, so too, did Nicholas II have to counter the opinions of liberals and revolutionaries who stood in opposition to his regime. Nicholas II particularly needed to resort to drastic, unprecedented mass forms of publicity because his was a reign seemingly plagued by constant image problems. Long before Rasputin appeared on the scene to tarnish what remained of the imperial reputation, Nicholas II's reign had been characterized by ineptitude and bloodshed. In the words of General Denikin, "Everyone considered the tsar to be 'unfortunate' and an 'unlucky fellow.' They mentioned as evidence such things as Khodynka, the Japanese War, and the first revolution, as well as the incurable affliction of his only son the tsarevich."[20]

The problems began in 1891 when Nicholas, then still tsarevich, visited Japan. His trip to various parts of Asia was conceived of as a necessary part of his education, but it also provided an opportunity to connect him with larger concerns of empire building and the modernization of the country. One of the most publicized activities that had been scheduled for Nicholas had him laying the first stone of the Vladivostok-Khabarovsk segment of the future Trans-Siberian Railway. On 11 May, however, Nicholas visited Otsu, a resort near the Japanese city of Kyōto. There he was attacked by one of the guards who lined his route. The man's sword inflicted two deep cuts to Nicholas' head. Word of the attack was strictly censored in Russia with the Telegraph Department closely monitoring all official reports and foreign newspaper accounts. As a result, rumours began to swirl, each seemingly more fantastic than the last. Even though the immediate sensation wrought by the incident died down without any major repercussions for Russo-Japanese relations, it did have a lasting effect on Nicholas' public image. As George Lensen writes, "Years later

political opponents were to jeer at Nicholas's head injury as 'explana-
tion' of his shortcomings as tsar."[21] We can find just such a comment in
publisher Aleksei Suvorin's diary. Part of his entry for 2 October 1903
reads, "A Japanese hit the Tsar on the head with a saber when he was
[still] the heir to the throne. A Japanese beat him on the head, and that
head does not know what it must do and what it should do. In everything,
he waits for a successor, and until that 'joyful event' does nothing."[22]

This episode was followed by the tragic Khodynka coronation debacle,
in 1896. The coronation should have been an event that underscored
the majesty of the Russian throne and created a sense of national glory.[23]
Instead, more than thirteen hundred people attending a festival to celebrate the occasion were crushed or trampled to death. Nicholas compounded the disaster when, acting on the advice of his uncles and
Konstantin Pobedonostsev, he decided to go ahead and attend a ball
thrown by the French ambassador the same evening. Word of the debacle quickly spread throughout the country and seemed to portend an
ominous beginning to the new reign. Writer Samuil Marshak recorded
the reaction of Russians in his small town to the news. "A shadow was
soon cast over the festivities, however, by ominous new rumours," he
wrote. "From mouth to mouth spread the strange and terrible news of
something called 'Khodinka.' The word sounded terrible because it was
always uttered in a low voice or a whisper, accompanied by sighs and
shakes of the head."[24] Research by Helen Baker has revealed that, in the
wake of the incident, two images of the tsar were created in the minds of
the Russian public: one of an insecure man who was not forceful enough
to rule, and the second of a tsar who did not care about the welfare of his
subjects. In her words, the episode "undermined the traditional image of
the tsar as a benevolent protector of the people."[25]

This impression was compounded by two later incidents: Bloody
Sunday in January 1905 and the Lena Goldfields massacre in April 1912.
In the first instance, reaction to the shooting of unarmed workers and
their families as they attempted to bring a petition to the tsar was swift. A
wave of strikes spread, first throughout the capital and then, within days,
to other cities across the empire. Over half a million people went on
strike that month.[26] Indeed, the disturbances were not quelled until the
tsar issued his October Manifesto that autumn. The outrage that Bloody
Sunday provoked destroyed the belief held by many workers and peasants that the regime was interested in improving their living conditions.
Loyalty to the tsar, in particular, was undermined by the event. In the
words of one historian, "after Bloody Sunday even the most religious

monarchists among the workers tore portraits of the tsars from the walls of their homes. Some removed the icons also. The Tsar was no longer distinguished from the hated bureaucrats surrounding him; he was held personally responsible for the tragedy in front of his palace."[27]

A similarly strong reaction greeted the news of the Lena Goldfields massacre, seven years later, where more than 230 people were killed and another 540 wounded. Again, strikes and demonstrations were triggered across the country, newspapers devoted extensive coverage to the fallout from the massacre for weeks on end, and society in general was outraged. The speeches made in the Duma in response to the incident were so fiery that both the minister of the interior and the minister of trade and industry felt compelled to appear before the Duma to justify the government's action. Notably, the event was also a boon for the revolutionary movement since its propaganda turned the dead strikers into martyrs who had been killed for the sake of capitalists and their lust for gold. Both the number of recruits and contributions to revolutionary organizations increased. Michael Melancon's work on the event notes that it "shattered the last fragile remnants of Russia's post-1905 consensus."[28]

The four episodes described above worked together to undermine the naïve monarchism of the Russian masses. They demonstrated, time and again, that the tsar was inept and seemingly unconcerned about his subjects.[29] They also point to the widening gap between state and society that existed at the end of the imperial period.[30]

To counter the negative publicity, the tsar and court officials began to create a rival narrative, one that celebrated great ceremonials in the history of the dynasty or, in other words, instances when the tsar's majesty was not in question. In this, the Russians were not unique. By the 1890s, it was already clear to most European monarchs that photography could be used to generate a record of "great events" for mass popular consumption.[31] Commemorative picture postcards were part of this process, since they were issued to mark the movements and public activities of royalty. British postcards commemorated such major events as the death of Queen Victoria, in 1901, or more mundane royal visits like the one that celebrated the opening of a new building at Leeds University, in July 1908.[32] In Germany, the royal family also used this form of publicity. For example, when Kaiser Wilhelm II visited the Holy Land in 1890, he had the occasion recorded with a commemorative postcard. The card featured a view of Jerusalem with an inset of the kaiser's portrait in a top corner.[33] In terms of the Russian royal family, its movements, too, caught the attention of the European public. Several ornate postcards were

5.4 Postcard commemorating the tsar's visit to France in 1896. Manufactured by Seughol & Magdelin in Paris, n.d.

issued in France in the wake of an official visit of the tsar and the Russian fleet, in October 1893. Other postcards were created to honour a second visit three years later (see Figure 5.4).[34] "Such visits were," in the words of historian Roderick McLean, "the public face of royal diplomacy before the First World War."[35] They argued that monarchs still had a vital role and a great deal of influence on European political systems. To a young tsar keen to step out of his father's shadow and counteract the early missteps of his political life, the publicity invoked by commemorative postcards can only have been seen in a positive light.

Domestically, anniversary celebrations fulfilled a similar function and were the focus of much publicity. They, too, generated a vast array of kitsch.[36] Figure 5.5 shows a postcard created to mark the two-hundredth anniversary of the invasion of Riga by Russian forces during the Great Northern War. It is similar in composition to the more plentiful postcards issued in conjunction with the three-hundredth anniversary of the Romanov dynasty, three years later. In each case, portraits of Nicholas II,

5.5 Postcard commemorating the 200th anniversary of the capture of Riga by Russian forces in the Great Northern War. No manufacturer or date listed.

5.6 Postcard commemorating the 300th anniversary of the Romanov dynasty. Note the mark at the bottom indicating that it passed Russian censorship. Printed by Meisenbach Riffarth & Co. Postally used in 1913.

as well as other tsars, appear inset, thereby linking the figures together in a common historical narrative and creating a type of visual family tree (see Figure 5.6).

Figure 5.7, which includes an artistic rendition of Mikhail Fedorovich's coronation, goes even further by making the Tsarevich Aleksei the main focus of attention, thereby implying the dynasty will, of course, continue beyond the reign of Nicholas II. Aleksei's image was a good choice, for no matter how unpopular his father became, the small boy who embodied the dreams of Russian monarchists remained a popular figure whose portraits sold well. Princess Catherine Sayn-Wittgenstein, a self-described monarchist, remembered how she avidly collected pictures of the tsarevich. "J'honorais le petit Alexis de mon amour le plus fort et dévoué," she wrote, "je m'étais acheté tous ses portraits et dans ce but j'avais vidé tous les magasins de Petrograd et de Moscou. A Petrograd existe encore mon gros album de cartes postales de tous les membres de la famille impériale."[37]

The iconography used on these postcards would have been familiar to Russian Orthodox viewers. For hundreds of years, Russian icons had often included medallions with portraits of saints around their borders, thereby suggesting a kind of spiritual succession to the viewer. In others, such as Simeon Ushakov's 1668 icon *The Tree of the Russian Realm*, the smaller portraits included on the icon were linked together by leaves, grapes, and roses – in other words, by details that suggested fertility and continuity.[38] But unlike icons, these picture postcards were not venerated. There is evidence they were used, instead, like *lubki* – as decorative items that added a bit of colourful cheer in some lower-class homes and peasant huts.[39] Higher up the social ladder, picture postcards with portraits of the tsar were used in casual correspondence or as conversation pieces. For instance, an Englishman who moved in the highest social circles in pre-revolutionary Russia, informed a correspondent that "I sen[t] you a postcard of Syerov's wonderful portrait of the Emperor, which has all his charm."[40] Some portraits were also given out by monarchists during holiday celebrations. Henry Nevinson, who was in Moscow as a special correspondent for the *Daily Chronicle*, described how some members of the crowd distributed photographs of the tsar holding the tsarevich on his knee at the annual St. Nicholas Day festivities.[41] It is important to note that by the mid-nineteenth century, the visual family tree iconography had come into use across Europe, and it was widely employed in images of the various royal families, as the example in Figure 5.8 suggests.

5.7 Postcard celebrating the 300th anniversary of the Romanov dynasty. Izd. D. Khromov & M. Bakhre, 1913.

5.8 Carte-de-visite of the British royal family.

The anniversary celebrations, as was the case across Europe, were staged in the belief that impressive displays of state pageantry were reflective of national strength. By emphasizing lineage and the perpetuation of the dynasty, they were believed to provide evidence of political stability. In his impressive research on Russian royal ceremonials, Richard Wortman argues that Nicholas II was attracted to this kind of pageantry "as a partisan device to compete with the Duma and to show himself as sole focus of national sentiment. By appearing at the sacred sites of great national battles, he drew precedents for the resurgence of Russian monarchy from his forbearer's triumphs at moments of crisis."[42] Ceremonials, and the publicity given to them, undoubtedly were a way for Nicholas to continue claiming that autocracy was the correct form of government for Russia. Although he writes about the British royal family, Peter Baker's comments along this line are just as valid for the Russian context. He says, "the institution of the monarchy illustrated par excellence the virtues of continuity in government ... By an almost Darwinian line of argument, the prolonged survival of the institution was a testament to its vitality and its continued importance."[43] But, to return to the postcards, from what we can tell they apparently generated a mixed reception. On the right end of the political spectrum, not everyone greeted the kitsch created in connection with the events with enthusiasm. In the case of the special postage stamps made for the dynasty's three-hundredth anniversary, for instance, church officials disliked seeing the tsar associated with monetary values or having his likeness on items that would then be defaced by franking.[44] According to Wortman, at least one right-wing periodical criticized the stamps by noting that they contravened a law prohibiting the defacing of the imperial image.[45] Use of the stamps was even briefly suspended, in 1913. However, the anniversary picture postcards, which included the controversial stamps as part of their overall design, seem to have caught the fancy of at least postcard collectors. In the words of one, who judging by his title may have come from a family that sympathized with the monarchy: "Personally I recall how proud my younger brother, living in Russia in 1913, was of a series of postcards which he had, franked with a complete series of stamps marking the tercentenary of the Romanov dynasty, and including the celebrated five rouble stamp with the portrait of Tsar Nicholas II."[46]

Mobilizing Images of Family

By the last decade of the nineteenth century, the tsar's family life came to be subjected to the same kinds of scrutiny, and ultimately criticism, as his public activities. These activities gradually decreased in number as Nicholas, and to an even greater extent Alexandra, retreated from court life. Indeed, it can be argued that for most Russians the physical presence of the couple came to be replaced by photographic representations of them. Photographs, and picture postcards made from them, were now issued to mark moments in the family life of the Romanovs. As Simon Schama notes vis-à-vis nineteenth-century monarchies in general, "a whole calendar of domestic events – births, christenings, betrothals, weddings, and comings-of-age – was transferred to the public domain."[47] This outpouring of visual material implied that what was important to the royal family should also be somehow important to the nation. Richard Wortman argues that it is in just such materials that one finds the underlying message of Nicholas II's reign. He posits, "Nicholas II made his domestic virtues a public sign of his supreme humanity. From the beginning of his reign, Nicholas cultivated the image of himself as an ideal family man who doted on his children. Popular pictures show him and Alexandra in warm scenes with beautiful cherubic children, as exemplars of family happiness."[48] The French postcard in Figure 5.9, whose manufacturer reprinted a photograph taken in Russia, proves Wortman's point and how widely such images circulated in Europe. In the picture, Nicholas sits in close physical contact with his three eldest daughters while Alexandra holds the newest addition to the family. Since the setting has been cropped, few background details are in evidence and the focus remains on the family, instead.

In Figure 5.10, however, the viewer receives a much less formal impression of the royal family and a boundary seems to have been crossed. The tsar no longer appears majestic in any sense of the word. Instead, he appears bourgeois, with all the negative meanings that the word implies in Russian. Moreover, the long, impressive titles listed in the postcard's caption are particularly jarring when they are considered alongside the picture of the tsar rowing a boat with his wife and daughters.

On picture postcards like this one, the tsar became an ordinary man – obviously a wealthy one, but still an ordinary man. These images did not conform with popular expectations about the monarchy. The tsar does not appear as a figure of authority. Instead of commanding respect and exuding power, here Nicholas has been captured in the private sphere, surrounded by only female companions. Such picture postcards, along with others discussed below, called into question Nicholas's ability to rule as well as his manliness in the minds of some of his subjects.

Other picture postcards singled out royal women and their children for attention. Since women's roles as wives and mothers ensured the

5.9 French postcard of the Russian royal family. Manufacturer's name obscured by writing. Postally used 1901.

Их Императорскія Величества Государь Императоръ
и Государыня Императрица, Великія Княжны Ольга и
Таѣіана Николаевны
на прогулкѣ въ Финляндскихъ шхерахъ.

5.10. Tsar Nicholas II rowing with his wife and daughters. No manufacturer or date listed.

continuity of royal dynasties, it was this aspect of their lives that was often at the fore on picture postcards and other visual media. Again, Queen Victoria's example established the pattern followed by her many relatives. Over the course of her reign, many photographs (hence, cartes-de-visite and picture postcards, too) showed Victoria either surrounded by, or holding, her children (see Figure 5.11). Through these images, Victoria came to symbolize motherhood itself, and the European public clearly conceived of her as both monarch and mother. Figure 5.12 shows how similar dynastic tableaux spread into the depiction of monarchies across the continent, in this instance to the family of Kaiser Wilhelm II.

We can also see in Figure 5.13 a more obvious example of the connection made between royal women and maternity. Here, the German crown princess has been photographed with her two sons, and the picture is reminiscent of Figure 5.9 and other picture postcards that featured Russian Empress Alexandra alone with her children.

5.11 Carte-de-visite of the British royal family. No manufacturer or date listed.

The iconography of such poses has deep historical roots. In historical portraiture, such representations of women and their children were meant to suggest the Virgin and Child, in other words, the apex of maternal love and devotion in its purest form.[49]

It was this very notion of royal feminine purity, however, that was attacked in pornographic postcards of Alexandra. Typically the hand-drawn postcards showed a naked Alexandra being groped by Rasputin.[50] Viewers were meant to recognize the empress by markers such as her hairstyle, jewelry, or even a crown – the same items that were designed to emphasize her majesty on officially produced postcards. The caricatures vividly expressed the popular belief that the empress was engaged in a sexual relationship with the Siberian peasant. Even to those who knew otherwise, the connection was a damaging one that contributed to the desacralization of the monarchy. In the words of Dowager Empress Maria Fedorovna, "My unhappy daughter-in-law does not understand that she is ruining both the dynasty and herself. She sincerely believes in the holiness of some rogue and we are all helpless to avert misfortune."[51] Pornographic caricatures put forward the idea that Alexandra should not be conceptualized as an ideal wife and mother. Hence, they rejected the dynastic scenario offered

5.12 Postcard of the German royal family. Verlag von Gustav Liersch & Co., n.d.

by the tsar's supporters. Moreover, on these postcards, Alexandra's body could be made visible in ways that titillated the masses and suggested that it could also be sold on cheap pieces of cardboard.

Other satirical postcards, produced in Russia and across Europe, worked to undermine popular conceptions about the tsar's manliness as well as his fitness to rule. Nicholas's sex life, and his seeming inability to produce a male heir (Aleksei was not born until 1894, almost ten years after the marriage of his parents, and after four girls had already been born to them) had already been a source of ridicule for years. Although not an overtly pornographic drawing, the French postcard seen in Figure 5.14, for instance, mocks the tsar for not producing a male heir. Such images were widely seen by Russian tourists as they travelled on the continent, and some had to have been mailed or saved for postcard collections.

As Marie-Monique Huss notes, "in French popular culture baby boys came from cabbages, an association reinforced by countless postcards and posters of the period."[52] Here, although the tsar is shown watering a cabbage patch, the caption humorously says that his specialty as a

5.13 German crown princess with her children. Verlag von Gustav Liersch & Co. Postally used in 1912.

Au bon jardinier. - Spécialité de poires Duchesses

5.14 French postcard mocking the tsar's lack of a male heir. No manufacturer or date listed.

gardener lies in producing Duchess pears. Along with the postcards mentioned earlier, such images implied that the tsar's deficiencies as a man had driven his wife into the arms of another or that he was simply incapable of being a "real man." These postcards countered the officially produced ones that depicted Nicholas II as a father with offspring to prove his manhood. Instead, satirical and pornographic postcards made the tsar into a source of laughter, and contributed to the desacralization of the throne. Figes and Kolonitskii succinctly summarize the impact of this line of popular thought when they write, "A man who could not rule or satisfy his wife could not be taken seriously as a tsar."[53]

Royal Charity

In 1908, *Queen Alexandra's Christmas Gift Book*, a volume that contained more than 140 of the British queen's photographs (including, incidentally,

some that she took on a formal visit to Reval when King Edward VII met
with the tsar), went on sale to raise funds for charity. Very quickly more than
a hundred thousand copies were sold.[54] Avidly consumed by the British
public, copies of the book were also sought by people across the continent,
with many orders coming from the Scandinavian countries, Germany,
France, and even Russia.[55] More than just a mere collector like many of her
relations, Queen Alexandra was an avid photographer and, ultimately, saw
her work made available in a number of ways, including in picture postcard
form. Via her photographs, the public was able to enjoy images that sug-
gestively hinted they came from the private albums of the royal family.
When a touring exhibition of her photographs in 1904–05 proved to be
wildly popular, the idea for the charitable volume was born.

Queen Alexandra's charitable work, while different in its outward expression, was considered a normal part of royal behaviour at the time. By
the turn of the last century, charity had become an increasingly important and visible public function of European monarchies. Many monarchs had seen their participation in actual governance diminish in the
nineteenth century but charity, as David Cannadine points out, "enabled
them to reinvent themselves as anxious, concerned, generous, benevolent and public-spirited."[56]

In Russia, charity had been associated with the royal family for much
of the nineteenth century. In 1828, when Empress Maria Fedorovna,
wife of Emperor Paul and an ardent philanthropist in her own right,
died, the 4th Department of the emperor's own chancellery was established to run the institutions she had founded. By the early twentieth
century, the department had grown, via ongoing donations from the
government and members of the royal family, to massive proportions. It
encompassed 862 institutions and had expenditures approaching
23 million roubles in 1904.[57] By the time of the revolution, Dowager
Empress Maria Fedorovna, mother of the tsar, had been serving as its
patron for decades. She also headed the Russian Red Cross, an institution she had been affiliated with since the Russo-Turkish War of 1877–
78.[58] Her activities fit well with the growing fin-de-siècle interest in public
activism in Russia. This was a time when increasing middle-class involvement led to a mushrooming in the number of voluntary and philanthropic organizations.[59]

At the same time, charitable groups turned to new methods of fundraising, including the sale of specifically designed picture postcards. It is
worth remembering that the very first domestically produced Russian
picture postcards were created under the auspices of a charitable

organization. In 1898, the government granted the St. Eugenia Society (Obshchina sv. Evgenii krasnogo kresta) permission to issue picture postcards. As we have seen, the Society went on to become one of the most important suppliers to the Russian market, eventually producing roughly thirty million postcards over a twenty-year period.[60] One of its series was the "Romanov Gallery," which reproduced portraits of members of the royal family (see Figure 5.15).

These postcards established a tangible link between mass-produced images of royalty and charitable activities. Moreover, the success of the St. Eugenia Society spawned a number of imitators – groups that also used picture postcard sales as a source of revenue.[61] During the First World War, several of them, such as the Royal Philanthropic Association to Assist Wounded Soldiers of the Lower Ranks and Their Families, and the Special Petrograd Committee under the Auspices of H.M. Princess Olga Nikolaevna, enjoyed royal patronage. The First World War finally allowed Empress Alexandra to step out of her mother-in-law's shadow and try to claim some positive publicity for her own charitable endeavours.[62] Picture postcards, like the one in Figure 5.16, were sold to raise money on behalf of charitable groups that counted the empress as their official patron. While these images often had nothing to do with the Romanovs themselves per se, the postcards had special markings on the reverse side indicating which organization benefited from their purchase and explicitly connected the group with the empress.

In addition to serving as patrons, Alexandra and her daughters took a more active role in charitable activities. As Frank Prochaska's work suggests, this more hands-on approach was important for royal charity since "the face-to-face setting promoted deferential behavior" at the same time as it suggested that monarchs cared about the fate of individual subjects.[63] Alexandra and the grand duchesses trained to become certified Red Cross nurses by attending lectures on anatomy and internal medicine. By November 1914, the empress and her older daughters had completed a full surgical course. Alexandra moved quickly to convert royal residences and aristocratic palaces into hospitals. According to one of her biographers, "Within the first four months of the war, eighty-five such hospitals were operating in and around Petrograd, all under her patronage."[64] Most notably, the Catherine Palace at Tsarskoe Selo became a hospital for wounded officers. Here, Alexandra and her daughters assisted with the patients, bandaged wounds, and attended operations. They were frequently photographed in their nurses' uniforms. Picture postcards soon showcased them in this role (see Figure 5.17). Given the

Раб: В. Эриксень. 1762.   V. Eriksen pinx

Екатерина II.ая

Романовская галлерея.

5.15 Portrait of Catherine the Great. Part of the "Romanov Gallery." St. Eugenia
Society, n.d.

5.16 Charity postcard raising money for the St. Petersburg Society for Helping the Poor and Educating Orphans as well as the Society for Children of Those Killed and Wounded in the War. Izdanie Petergofskago O-va, n.d.

publication of such pictures required the permission of court officials and even the empress, it is not a stretch to say the photographs then showed Alexandra as she herself wished to be thought of in the popular imagination. Moreover, the postcards were reasonably priced – series were produced by both Suvorin's publishing house and the St. Eugenia Society with individual postcards selling for between 5 and 15 kopecks a piece.[65] In the case of Figure 5.17, the image also makes reference to the practice of giving Easter eggs. The tsar and tsarina had hundreds of porcelain eggs, bearing the imperial insignia, made each year. The eggs were distributed to court officials, military guards, and diplomats, among others, at special receptions.[66]

Postcards such as these moved beyond those merely associated with royal patronage. Now, the empress and her daughters were presented as active participants in nursing and charitable work, and their likenesses were widely distributed. The photographs may have been meant to

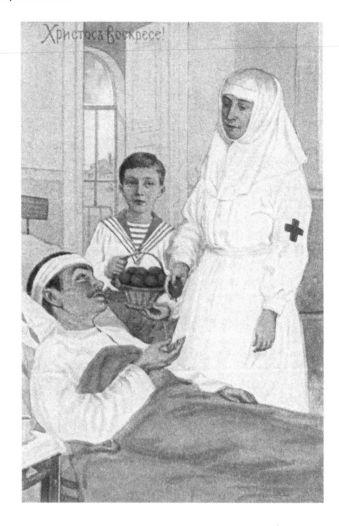

5.17 Postcard showing Empress Alexandra dressed as a nurse and giving an Easter egg to a wounded soldier. No manufacturer or date listed.

revive memories of the healing power of monarchs, a notion abandoned in Western Europe in the wake of the rise of Protestantism and political revolution, although there is no definite proof that was the case.[67] However, the images did not improve Alexandra's reputation for, like those of the tsar as an ordinary man and bourgeois father, the picture postcards and photographs eroded the sense of majesty that Alexandra was supposed to embody as tsarina. Projected as merely an ordinary nurse, she came to be associated with male bodies and bodily functions as well as undignified tasks, rather than with sacred healing. A passage in Countess Kleinmichel's memoirs, which shall be quoted at length, is indicative of these sentiments and demonstrates that images of Alexandra's war work failed to change people's minds about the Empress. She writes,

> When the war broke out, the Empress devoted herself entirely to hospital work, but here again she betrayed her lack of knowledge of human nature. Instead of managing the hospitals and remaining the benevolent Empress, she became the Sister of Charity, the nurse, who herself passed the dishes, washed the mutilated bodies, and even cut the nails of the patients. Now the people, a people as primitive as ours, love to picture their sovereign with all the pomp of the Caesars. In their childish dreams they imagine him with the Imperial crown on his head, and a purple cloak on his shoulders, and thus robed they love and venerate him. But when a soldier saw his Empress dressed in a nurse's uniform, just like any other nurse, he was disappointed. Looking at the Tsarina, whom he had pictured as a princess in a fairy tale, he thought:
> "And that is a Tsarina? But there is no difference between us."[68]

As Figes and Kolonitskii state, approval for the empress' nursing activities continued to decline as the war progressed and the postcards, in the end, did nothing to counteract her overall negative image with the Russian public.[69] The grand duchesses, too, were not spared from criticism. Again, to refer to Countess Kleinmichel's memoirs, she notes that photographs of the young women sitting on the beds of wounded soldiers gave rise to "unclean" thoughts in the imaginations of some people.[70] Even the transformation of royal residences into hospitals, a fact made plain in the settings of some of the postcards, was imbued with more selfish motives according to some rumours. In his memoirs, George Marye, who served as the American ambassador to Russia from 1914 to 1916, described a conversation he had in August 1915 regarding the possible use of the Winter Palace as a hospital for war wounded.

According to Marye, his Russian acquaintance responded, "That is what they say, but that isn't what they have in mind. They think the Germans will get here and they make the talk about the hospital a pretext for removing to a place of greater safety all the works of art and things of great value in the palace."[71]

Conclusion

More than ninety years after his death, the little boy, still in short trousers and with baby curls poking out from beneath his cap, continues to salute the modern viewer (see Figure 5.18). Indeed, it is highly likely that this postcard was produced after its subject had already been killed by the Bolsheviks. It is a telling example of failed visual propaganda. While the image may have resonated with confirmed monarchists like Catherine Sayn-Wittgenstein, whom I quoted earlier, it failed to strike a chord with the mass public. Made in France by a group calling itself the Comité anti-Bolcheviste, the postcard encapsulates the Romanov family's earlier inability to create a positive popular image with part of the Russian population, as well as the later failure of pro-monarchist forces in the Russian Civil War.

By focusing on the imagery of picture postcards produced over the final two decades of the imperial era, this chapter posits that the process of desacralization of the Russian monarchy was a gradual and often unintended one. This is not to discount the impact of such major incidents as the Khodynka catastrophe or Bloody Sunday. Instead, they were dramatic explosions that punctuated a more gradual evolution, one that picture postcards played a role in bringing about. Picture postcards of Russian royalty were seldom shocking, except for the overtly pornographic items analysed by Figes and Kolonitskii, but they were part of a more insidious phenomenon since their images penetrated popular consciousness over time. They showed the Russian public a monarch more comfortable in private life than in ruling the country and a man who seemingly lacked the qualities needed in an autocrat. All attempts on the part of the Romanovs to counter with positive images of themselves failed. The empress was not considered an ideal mother and wife. Instead, a rival visual narrative suggested she sought sexual satisfaction outside of her marriage, thereby undermining the position of her husband still further. And, as we have seen, even in the realm of charity, the Romanovs were incapable of presenting the right public impression. The story must end with this postscript though. Ironically, today it is

ЕГО ИМП.ВЫС. НАСЛ. ЦЕСАР. и ВЕЛ. КН. АЛЕКСѢЙ НИКОЛАЕВИЧЪ.

5.18 Postcard of Tsarevich Aleksei. Comité anti-Bolcheviste, n.d.

these postcards of Nicholas II and his family, of history's losers, that are the most highly prized. Modern reprints are sold to tourists in Russia and are widely available on the Internet. Original issues are hotly sought after by postcard collectors and can command prices in the hundreds of dollars each. By comparison, it is usually possible to buy original postcards of Lenin or other Soviet leaders for a fraction of that amount.

Chapter Six

Beyond Patriotic Discourse: Picture Postcards and Russia's First World War

In *Fighting Different Wars: Experience, Memory, and the First World War in Britain,* Janet Watson describes how the story of the disillusioned trench soldier eventually came to overwhelm all other perspectives on the war.[1] That process attempted to impose a uniformity on the wartime experience. It silenced and marginalized the stories of other groups, notably those of women who had served as nurses and of men who had found happiness in their new role as soldiers. Watson convincingly argues that by recovering their stories, we can see how different people fought what she terms "different wars" depending on their gender or social class. Watson's notion of "different wars" is a useful approach to the story, too, of picture postcards, Russia, and the First World War. It helps to separate the patriotic narrative of the war from other efforts to standardize its experience as well as more personal, private stories of those years.

The patriotic narrative, as it was reflected in picture postcards, had three main streams. One encouraged Russians to buy war bonds in order to provide desperately needed funds for the increasingly cash-strapped government. War bonds posters were reproduced in picture postcard form for mass distribution. Very brightly coloured, the postcards often printed some form of the word "patriotic" in their appeal and linked the bond purchases to the successful prosecution of the war, usually by including things like artillery shells in the image (see Figure 6.1). Other postcards in the same series appealed to patriotism by using historical figures in allegorical fashion. A second stream drew on Russia's history of political satire by presenting caricatures of the country's enemies, particularly the kaiser, or by drawing on well-established ethnic stereotypes of the Germans, the Austrians, and the Turks (see Figure 6.2). Finally, a third stream united the home front behind the war effort. These

6.1 War bond postcard. Izdanie upravleniia po delam melkago kredita, n.d.

6.2 "So, Willi, you have nowhere left to climb." No manufacturer or date listed.

6.3 Factory workers during the First World War. Skobelev Committee, 1916.

postcards suggested patriotism had over-ridden class-consciousness, and they hid the growing problem of labour unrest that plagued Russia as the war dragged on.[2] Images like Figure 6.3 showed workers surrounded by heaps of their output, testifying to their hard work. A slogan on the back of this particular postcard reads, "When the motherland needs guns, then factories work day and night." The postcard fails to speak, however, for the 880,000 workers who went on strike in 1916, the year when it was produced.[3]

Emphasis solely on these patriotic narratives has drowned out competing stories, particularly since it is patriotic culture that historians such as Aaron Cohen, Hubertus Jahn, Stephen Norris, and Richard Stites have focused their attention on.[4] Their works largely overlook both other attempts to construct universalizing narratives of the war and private initiatives that captured the war as lived experience for individual soldiers. The purpose of this chapter is twofold: to describe the picture postcards produced by the Russian government and charitable organizations that fixed identities on prisoners of war and refugees; and then to discuss how picture postcards were, in fact, used by soldiers and their families during the conflict. It is important to note right away that in some places in this chapter I use references to picture postcards rather interchangeably with others discussing photographs in general. This is a deliberate choice on my part since it reflects practices of the era rather than the hardened categories of our times. While today it is quite clear what is a photograph and what is a postcard, the distinction was rather fuzzy in the first two decades of the twentieth century. It is worth remembering that many photographs, particularly those termed "photo postcards" by collectors, were printed on photo stock also meant for postcards, meaning the same sizes and cardboard were used for both.[5] This was especially true for privately produced images, in other words, ones that feature prominently in the pages that follow. Hence, when contemporaries discussed the power of pictures in the First World War, they could technically be referring to either postcards or photographs. Finally, the chapter shows how picture postcards often contradicted the patriotic discourse so carefully crafted by the Russian government and various social organizations, thereby, in their own way, undermining the war effort.

Photography and War

The first mass-produced photographs of war emerged with the cartes-de-visite and stereograph crazes of the mid-nineteenth century. Both media drew on the work of hundreds of photographers who followed first the armies in the U.S. Civil War, and then took to photographing European conflicts, such as the Franco-Prussian War (1870–71). In Russia, well-known photographer D.A. Nikitin was attached to the Russian forces during the Russo-Turkish War (1877–78). Nor was he alone. Eight other photographers were sent to cover the fighting by *World-wide Illustration* (*Vsemirnaia illiustratsiia*). Other illustrated periodicals, such as *Grain Field* (*Niva*) and *Illustrated Journal* (*Illiustrirovannaia gazeta*) also included photographs in their war coverage.[6] By 1900, the market was saturated with illustrated publications as all of the major Russian daily newspapers published illustrated weekly supplements.[7] Not surprisingly, the interest these periodicals generated spilled over into other markets, notably merging with the craze for collecting postcards and thereby ensuring that photographic postcards found ready consumers. In some cases, the same pictures were used in both media, as in the postcard in Figure 6.4, which was a reprint of a picture from *Niva*.

Тяжело-раненые 3-го октября въ дер. Шихученъ. По фот. авт. «Нивы»

6.4 Postcard reprint of an image from *Niva*. Trinks & Co. Mailed to Moscow from Leipzig in 1912.

Over the same period, the work of war photographers made warfare a visual event in new ways; more realistic portrayals of combat and combatants became the order of the day after 1900. Battlefields came to be shown while still littered with the contorted bodies of the dead. Such photographs offered a striking contrast to traditional ways that battles were represented in painting, where the focus was either on commanders (who were often safely removed from the actual fighting) or on stock figures whose poses were meant to suggest heroic behaviour.[8] Now the gruesome, yet often also banal, nature of death in battle was on display for all to see.

However, the vast majority of war photographs did not focus on its casualties since they were taken while the guns were silent. In these instances, the greater realism that photography seemed to provide replaced the heroic with the mundane. "Endless columns of marching men, soldiers eating, cleaning guns, or merely posing for the camera," wrote one scholar when discussing First World War photographs. He concluded, "It is unusual to be able to pick out from the early records a picture that stands out either for its visual beauty or for the sheer poignancy of its subject matter."9 His remarks miss the point of these images. As we shall see, they were not meant to serve as great works of art, but as reminders of the war as lived experience for everyday soldiers and their families. They were what Ester Milne terms "a technology of presence," where the materiality of the picture was intended to suggest the corporeal presence of absent loved ones.[10]

The market for cheap, widely reproduced images changed when the Boer War (now also called the South African War) broke out in 1899. Although cartes-de-visite and stereographs, which had been dominant in the nineteenth century, continued to be manufactured until well into the first decades of the twentieth century, they were eclipsed at this point by picture postcards.[11] The Boer War was the first to see a large number of propaganda postcards issued in both countries at war as well as by interested bystanders in other nations. Ian McDonald's lavishly illustrated work, *The Boer War in Postcards*, gives some sense of the sheer number of picture postcards – most of them overtly partisan in nature – created in response to the war.[12] Indeed, it is possible to follow the entire course of that war in postcards.

The same could be said about the Russo-Japanese War (1904–05), although no scholar has as yet organized and published such a systematic collection. In countries across Europe, political satirists, postcard manufacturers, and ordinary photographers rushed to produce postcards commenting on seemingly every event as the Russian conflict with Japan progressed. Their expressions typically reflected the loyalties of existing diplomatic alliances. In other words, British postcards sympathized with the Japanese, whereas French ones championed the Russian cause until the Bloody Sunday massacre so tarnished the tsar's reputation that even the French came to favour the Japanese.[13] Like the racialized cartoons mocking the enemy that appeared in illustrated periodicals and newspapers in both countries during the war, some postcards resorted to crude jokes and racialized stereotypes to inspire patriotism.[14] Russian picture postcards of the conflict were dominated by informative images, particularly those conveyed by documentary-style postcards commonly referred to in Russian as "*sobytiinie otrkrytki.*"[15] Like much war photography from the first two decades of the new century, the postcards of the Russo-Japanese War presented the mundane, everyday face of war: soldiers stood for inspection or went about their daily routines. Figure 6.5 is a typical example.

Осмотръ ген. Соболевымъ передовыхъ позицiй по р. Шахэ у д. Сахэпу. № 69.

6.5 Soldiers reviewing their position. Izd. D.P. Efimova, 1905.

When the postcards ventured into documenting the progress of the fighting, manufacturers were hampered by a sizeable time lag. It took at least six weeks for the work of photographers such as V. Bulla and V. Taburin to arrive from the front in the Far East.[16] The delay did not stop at least some people from using picture postcards to establish a narrative of the war. For example, Figure 6.6 is a postcard of the Russian gunboat *Bobr'*. At some point, its owner neatly recorded in English, "Blown up at Newetwang July 1904," beneath the Russian caption. Frustratingly, the postcard was never mailed, so we have no way of knowing who added that information or when that person may have done so.

In the end, the images that eventually found their way onto picture postcards included battle scenes, pictures of the ships in the Russian Navy, and portraits of both soldiers and commanders. These postcards set the stage for the way in which the First World War was presented in Russia.

Мореходная канонерская лодка „Бобр". 1,187 тоннъ.   Изданіе Н. Апостоли. 117.

Blown up at Newchwang July 1904.

6.6 The *Bobr'*. Izdanie N. Apostoli, 1904.

Imposing Uniformity: Picture Postcards and Prisoners of War

Prisoners of war do not fit neatly into the categories used by social historians. In their own time, they raise difficult questions for all combatant nations. It is frequently assumed that prisoners become captives owing to some unheroic behaviour on their part – in other words, they themselves are responsible for their situations. People then have to decide if prisoners should be pitied or scorned. Either way, the removal of prisoners from active roles on the battlefield in the First World War created questions about their identities, particularly in gendered terms, and on a massive scale. From the beginning of the war until the start of January 1918, a total of 3,395,105 Russian soldiers as well as 14,323 officers spent some time as POWs – or 21.2 per cent of the men mobilized by the Russian Army.[17] The figures for other combatant nations on the eastern front were similarly staggering.

The huge number of POWs meant they remained in the public eye. The millions of postcards and letters they mailed offered an image of the war that was in direct contradiction to the patriotisms so carefully crafted by their governments and various social organizations. Hence, there was deep concern about prisoners and the impact of their mail on morale. The Russian government had been sufficiently worried in the aftermath of the Russo-Japanese War that it tightened military censorship. New regulations were enacted by the government in 1906 and later supplemented by the "Temporary Decree on War Censorship," signed by the tsar on 20 July 1914. These measures ensured mail to and from a war zone passed through several layers of military censorship. Each army group and each front had a censorship office that screened the mail before it arrived at individual units. Officers were also instructed to read and censor the mail of the soldiers under their command.

Mail from prisoners of war proved especially problematic because their correspondence frequently contradicted government propaganda and the lurid stories found in the popular press concerning the cruel mistreatment of those same prisoners. Realizing the propaganda value of such accounts, the German government, for instance, had a Russian-language collection of letters – all raving about the treatment of Russian POWs by the Germans – printed in Berlin.[18] Military leaders were keen to keep such items out of the hands of soldiers serving at the front since the fear that soldiers would voluntarily surrender to the enemy remained a constant throughout the war. The commander of the Russian 41st Infantry Division issued this order, for example, on 24 December 1914:

> Letters have been received lately from our prisoners of war in enemy countries. In some of those letters the writers describe life in captivity in a very favourable light. The spreading of such news among the troops and recruits in undesirable. The military censors are therefore to be instructed that such letters of our prisoners of war as may, by their contents, exercise an injurious influence, are to be confiscated and not to be delivered to the addressees.[19]

In the eyes of government and military officials, there was clearly an urgent need to control what prisoners were reading and writing.

On paper, prisoners were guaranteed certain rights. According to Article 16 of the Hague Convention on the treatment of prisoners of war (adopted in October 1907), military captives had the right to receive letters, money orders, and parcels while they were being held. These matters were to be handled for them by national Red Cross societies. On the eastern front, the Austrian, German, and Hungarian Red Cross societies relied on neutral channels – meaning the Danish and Swedish Red Cross societies – to send letters and packages to their POWs. Mail to Russian prisoners was handled by the Aid Committee for Prisoners of War, which had an office in Denmark, and by the Russian Red Cross.[20] The situation for civilian prisoners was somewhat murkier since their plight had not been anticipated when the formal agreements governing the treatment of prisoners had been drawn up. So, in October 1914, the International Committee of the Red Cross established a Civilian Prisoners Bureau to handle the correspondence of this group.[21] But, these paper rights meant little in practice.

The number of POWs in German hands almost immediately exceeded the military's capability to house, feed, and care for them. Fearing reprisals against German prisoners in Russia, German officials issued a number of orders that tried to raise the conditions of POW camps so that they met agreed-upon international standards. The Prussian War Ministry, the body that oversaw the treatment of POWs, sent journalists and photographers into the camps to document the conditions. "Soon these images of enemy soldiers and officers," notes historian Oxana Nagornaja, "found their way onto postcards and into illustrated magazines and newspapers, military exhibitions, slide shows, and books."[22]

The Russian government also had not anticipated having to provide more than two million foreign POWs with access to the postal system, and to further complicate matters, the prisoners were dispersed in camps and on work sites across the entire country. Simply put: it proved to be impossible for the existing number of postal censors to read all the mail sent home by prisoners on Russian soil or the items sent by Russian prisoners from their places of captivity in Europe. The number of items involved was staggering: in one week in May 1915, the Viatka military censorship office alone handled more than fifty thousand letters and, by July 1915, according to the Head of the Press and Telegraph Organization, prisoners of war from a single region were posting seventy thousand letters a day – twenty thousand more than could be read by the censors.[23]

The Russian government responded to the situation by issuing new guidelines, the "Regulations on the Organization and Execution of Military Censorship," on 26 September 1915. They specified that foreign POWs were now only allowed to mail postcards. The standardized postcards were devoid of pictures since apparently military authorities were worried about the designs on some picture postcards (such as those

Для военноплѣнныхъ.
Kriegsgefangenensendung.
ОТКРЫТОЕ ПИСЬМО.   ✚   POSTKARTE.
РОССІЯ.   RUSSLAND.

Военноплѣнному №
Лагерь Военноплѣнныхъ №
Dem Kriegsgefangenen №
Kriegsgefangenenlager №
Kompagnie   Baracke

6.7 Blank postcard for use by prisoners of war, n.d.

of battleships) providing the enemy with information about Russia's military capabilities (see Figures 6.7 and 6.8).

While the designs were nowhere near as restrictive as the Field Service postcard used by the British and Canadian militaries, which forced soldiers to choose from only a limited number of preprinted phrases as they literally constructed their messages, they did still control the information prisoners could convey.[24] The small size of the postcards limited the number of words a message could contain. One prisoner remembered being told he could only state he had been captured and give a short comment about his health.[25] Rules were also established concerning what languages could be used for correspondence. Prisoners were only allowed to write in Russian, French, German, and something referred to as "Slavic" (likely to have been Ukrainian).[26] Given there were Hungarian, Czech, Slovak, Serb, and Croat prisoners in Russian captivity, to say nothing of Jewish soldiers who may have wanted to write in Yiddish, one could see how these restrictions limited the stories that could be told on postcards.

Absender: / Отправитель

Correspondance des prisonniers de guerre

АВСТРО - ВЕНГРІЯ

Antwort — Réponse — Для отвѣта

CARTE POSTALE

Adresse: / Адресъ

NO CHARGE FOR POSTAGE — PRISONER OF WAR MAIL — NEW YORK N.Y.

Portofrei   Verlag der Österr. Ges. vom „Roten Kreuze"   Nachdruck verboten
Безплатно   Изданіе Австр. Общ. Краснаго Креста.   Перепечатка воспрещается

6.8 Prisoner-of-war postcard. While the date is illegible, the addressee lived in New York City, so the sender has crossed out "Austria-Hungary" in the top corner and written in "America," instead.

We see the same desire for standardization in the picture postcards created by charitable groups. They show how philanthropic organizations actively constructed an image of the captive male – one that provided no personal information about specific prisoners, but instead treated them as examples of an anonymous type. The Red Cross was responsible for one large transnational series of postcards showing the conditions of POWs. According to postal history collector Prince Dimitry Kandaouroff, the series contained general views of POW camps as well as of certain aspects of camp life such as the prisoners' work and recreational activities. Even camp cemeteries were included. Seventeen of the 306 Red Cross postcards related to POWs in Russia, but they did not differ from the other 289, meaning the impact of captivity was assumed to override other identities prisoners may have had or wanted to claim for themselves, including national affiliation.[27] Similar postcards were issued by Russian philanthropic organizations like the St. Eugenia Society to raise money for POWs.[28] These stark documentary-style photographs

6.9 Prisoners of war. No manufacturer or date listed.

capture scenes of men milling about in open spaces marked off by barbed wire (see Figure 6.9). Their very inactivity lends them an air of passivity. Rather than heroism, defeat, separation, isolation, and even personal tragedy were conveyed by such picture postcards.

Despite these attempts to impose structures on the life stories of prisoners, the grasp of the Russian government and charitable groups was not total. Cracks in the official discourse came from a number of sources. For instance, high-ranking foreign visitors brought cameras to the front and faced few restrictions about what they photographed. Robert McCormick, the son of a former U.S. ambassador to Russia, visited the eastern front in the first year of the war with the blessing of Russia's commander-in-chief, Grand Duke Nikolai Nikolaevich. McCormick describes photographing both POWs and Polish refugees who had been given work repairing roads.[29] Other foreigners volunteered to fight in the Russian Army and, again, took cameras with them. One of them, Malcolm Grow, served as a lieutenant-colonel in the Imperial Russian Army Medical Corps. Grow's book about his experiences contains twenty-seven of his own photographs, including one showing German officers captured by his regiment.[30] These two examples are deliberately singled out because the books they generated appeared in print while the war was still going on. Their photographs were outside the bounds of official control, and they did not reflect state-sponsored patriotic narratives of the war. They illustrate the kinds of materials that became available as the conflict progressed. Nor were these images unique, for Russian soldiers, too, were able to use their private cameras to document the war. In the years leading up to the conflict, more than twenty-five thousand foreign-made cameras were imported into Russia each year, and it is safe to assume many of them accompanied men to the front.[31] It is also worth noting that the illustrations of POWs and refugees used in this chapter were photographs printed on postcard stock; hence, they could be considered either as photographs or postcards.

In this, postcards reflected the sympathy that some Russian soldiers and civilians felt towards the prisoners of war they encountered and offered a chance to document the lives of people seen as helpless. Sympathy could emerge because captivity neutralized the threat posed by former combatants. As a Russian nurse, Tatiana Alexinsky, put it in 1916, "And the simple natural kindness with which our soldiers treated their 'enemy' prisoners! I remember our men saying: 'When a man is disarmed he is not an enemy!'"[32] She was not alone in expressing such sentiments. On 11 August 1916, Princess Catherine Sayn-Wittgenstein wrote the following in her diary, "À vrai dire, des Austrichiens prisonniers travaillent aux champs mais ils ne sont pas plus des ennemis; ils ne sont, comme l'écrit Papa, 'pas venus pour détruire Bronitsa [her family's country estate], mais pour aider.' Sans eux, il serait impossible cette année de rentrer la récolte."[33]

As we shall see, via photographs and picture postcards, former enemies engaged in behaviours, and sometimes forged relationships, that would have deeply concerned their governments. In many war memoirs, expressions of compassion and humane treatment were illustrated by stories involving mail. For example, when A.G. Martin, a British-born German soldier, was being held in Lazaret No. 109 in Petrograd, awaiting his exchange for a Russian POW, he was officially prohibited from having books and writing materials. However, he remembered, "when the gendarme on duty happened to be amiably disposed he might appear with a packet of postcards and a bundle of pencils, intimating that we could each write one card home."[34] Small acts of kindness like these indicate not everyone viewed prisoners with suspicion and hostility.

Friendships, of a sort, could also develop between men fighting on opposing sides. Paul Iogolevitch's account of his wartime service shows how he became friendly with some German soldiers. Iogolevitch, who because he managed to join a group of Dragoons at the age of twelve was one of the youngest members of the Russian Army, captured a number of prisoners during his encounters with the enemy. As one of them was preparing to be sent to a POW camp, he gave Iogolevitch a photo postcard of himself and the address of his relatives in Germany. He begged the young man to write to them, which Iogolevitch eventually did via Red Cross channels. Iogolevitch remembered the prisoner sufficiently fondly that he kept the postcard and included detailed information about the German in his memoirs.[35]

The formulaic ready-made postcards sent by POWs – in addition to the picture postcards showing prisoners in captivity or those exchanged between prisoners and their captors – reminded people that the senders and subjects were no longer masculinized heroic figures fighting for their countries at the front. As such, these postcards offered a startling contrast with the patriotic discourse that stretched across all officially produced popular visual media. Posters, *lubki*, and patriotic postcards showed men imbued with fighting spirit, especially in scenes of hand-to-hand combat. In these dynamic illustrations, soldiers fought on and on, even when they were wounded. Stephen Norris concludes that the contradiction between the images – where Russian soldiers were always heroic – and the defeats suffered by the real Russian soldiers on the battlefield contributed to the political crises in Russia that followed the Crimean, Russo-Japanese, and First World wars.[36] His point can be taken even further since the defeats were not the end of the story, for defeated soldiers often became POWs – POWs who, via the postcards they sent and were depicted on constantly, undermined the perceptions of the war that their government was trying to create. As we can see from the stories above, real prisoners and those they encountered behaved in unpredictable, individualized ways that defied efforts at standardization.

Picture Postcards and Creating "Refugeedom"

"As for their being refugees – refugees are, I suppose, much the same the world over. Homeless – perhaps hopeless – helpless. Pathetic bundles of pathetic belongings."[37] While Scotland Liddell's words offer little in the way of commiseration, they do point to the way refugees were frequently seen in the First World War. Marginalized and desperate figures, refugees were a visible reminder that the war was not going well for Russia. By August 1915, the Russian Army had been pushed more than three hundred miles into the heartland of its own country. As a result, millions of civilians fled from the advancing enemy armies or were summarily ordered to leave their homes by Russian Army commanders. Estimates of the total number of Russian refugees run as high as six million or roughly 5 per cent of the total population.[38]

This flood of refugees provoked tremendous consternation since it proved impossible to control. Apart from unpredictable movement, the refugees posed a serious health risk since they frequently fell ill with such highly infectious diseases as cholera, typhus, and dysentery. They also created massive economic dislocation. The movement of such large numbers certainly generated a sense of catastrophe and threatened existing social structures. The refugees appeared like a primordial force beyond the control of the political authorities. Hence, some attempt was made to neutralize the image of refugees by standardizing the narrative of their plight and by connecting them to patriotic relief efforts.

Only a couple of months into the war, for instance, the Tatiana Committee for the Relief of War Victims (Komitet Ee Imperatorskogo Vysochestva Velikoi Kniazhny Tatiany Nikolaevny) was founded. Local branches followed with at least one in Tver' selling postcards with pictures of their patron, the tsar's daughter Tatiana, to raise money.[39] But, the Tatiana Committee could not handle such a vast problem on its own, and eventually, there was no way to contain the stories of refugees solely within the confines of official patriotism.

This was so because photographs of refugees appeared widely in Russian illustrated periodicals and newspapers. The images printed there were reflected, and in some cases literally reprinted, on picture postcards. They told of a humanitarian crisis that erased pre-war categories of identity since the markers of class and legal estate – property, clothing, occupation, and income – disappeared once people fled from the fighting. Moreover, the anonymity of those pictured obliterated their individual stories. No captions were printed on the postcards identifying the subjects, their locations, or the reasons behind their situations (see Figure 6.10).

Caroline Brothers' work on the representation of refugees from the Spanish Civil War is useful here; she argues that the "notion of refugee as passive victim was expressed in open-ended, or incomplete narratives."[40] Certainly, that is the case vis-à-vis Russian postcards of refugees. They are never shown reaching their final destinations, gaining employment and/or stability in the process. Moreover, like the postcards of POWs discussed earlier, most surviving examples appear to have been photographs printed on postcard stock. Hence, no manufacturers are listed on the back and, frustratingly, none of the postcards I have seen have been written on.[41] They remain somewhat of a puzzle for historians since it is hard to fathom why the postcards were created in the first place and in what capacities they may have been used apart from fundraising.

Nor was their open-endedness their only troublesome feature. Postcards whose photographs included male refugees such as Figure 6.11 were problematic for a number of additional reasons. Simply by not being at the front fighting with the Russian Army, male refugees were behaving in a way that was not consistent with the government-sponsored patriotic narrative. Far from putting the needs of an imperilled country first, these men appeared to have prioritized the survival of their families and what was left of their possessions. By acting in this way, they were effectively outside of government control, and their behaviour suggested that state propaganda could not effectively motivate men to fight.

At the same time, the powerlessness of large numbers of people was implied by other images, like in Figure 6.12. This postcard shows life in a Latvian refugee camp in 1915. By focusing on the crowd, rather than on an individual or particular family, the image makes reference to the

6.10 Russian refugees. No manufacturer or date listed.

6.11 Russian refugees. No manufacturer or date listed.

size of the refugee problem in Russia. The camera angle used is significant since it underscores the vulnerability of these people. By taking the
picture from above, the photographer conveys a sense of distance, as if
the refugees were being put on display like specimens, and implies that
they have little control over their situation.[42]

In other images, we see efforts to hold family units together despite
the crisis that has affected them and to create makeshift new homes
(see Figures 6.13 and 6.14). Perhaps in an attempt to replicate life
under normal conditions, the refugees in both instances posed as if
they were having a family portrait taken in a studio.[43] The way the images are framed, with their subjects centred and looking at the camera,
clearly reflected the aesthetics of conventional photographic portraiture. The very poverty and temporary nature of these shelters, however,
reinforced the impression of their victimhood instead. Such postcards
are, to quote Gatrell, "an exhibition of refugee life."[44] It was through
these kinds of photographs that the stories of individual refugees
merged in the minds of the government and general public so that all

6.12 Latvian refugee camp. No manufacturer or date listed.

refugees came to share a common narrative. It was through this process that the category of "refugeedom" was created.

Families, Photographs, and Memory

In the First World War, images were not always controlled by philan-thropic organizations or the Russian government. From the mid-nineteenth century, soldiers of all ranks had been having cartes-de-visite portraits and larger cabinet photographs made to give to friends and relatives. Taken in formal studios, the photographs typically showed the head and upper torso of the subjects against a background devoid of details. Similar photographs continued to be made throughout the First World War, and they paved the way for the eventual use of photo post-cards by soldiers and their families. In times of peace, the postcards were often used to send holiday greetings to friends and relatives while a sol-dier was stationed away from home, as in Figure 6.15, where the writer used such a card to send an Easter greeting in 1913. In times of war,

6.13 Russian refugees. No manufacturer or date listed.

these postcards took on added significance for the subjects and the re-cipients. Now, with photographs taken both in studios and in posed situ-ations outdoors, the images show uniformed soldiers, sometimes alone but also often in groups, capturing their individuality for posterity (see Figure 6.16). Given the limited means of most soldiers, who could not afford fancier paper, and the accepted use of postcard stock for printing photographs, it should not be surprising that this picture is actually a postcard, as are the next two.

Family members frequently insisted on having these portraits taken. J. Oskine's brother Vassili came to see him just before his regiment left for the front. Oskine recorded in his diary that his brother brought him all the money he could spare – 5 roubles – and the pair promptly spent half of it being photographed together. "À vrai dire je ne voulais pas de-penser cet argent," wrote Oskine, "mais mon frère a insisté: il voulait avoir au moins un portrait de moi, car sait-on si je retournerai."[45]

Other postcards show soldiers with their wives, again, mostly likely just prior to their departure for the front (see Figures 6.17 and 6.18). Like

6.14 Russian refugees. No manufacturer or date listed.

religious icons, these photo postcards were displayed in people's homes, providing a constant reminder of the family member at the front.

Soldiers treasured them, too. It was not uncommon for wounded men to show family photographs (no doubt some of which were printed on postcard stock) to the women nursing them back to health, or for family portraits to be found in the pockets of Russians soldiers who had been killed at the front. When Scotland Liddell emptied the pockets of men killed by a gas attack near Staro-Radziwillow, he found one soldier "had a faded photograph of a woman, wrapped in a piece of coloured cloth. Some had pocketbooks with letters in them and photographs of their folks and of themselves. These latter were of fine, brave, clean-looking men, moustaches very well waxed and faces looking very proudly from out of the glossy card."[46]

Historian Catherine Moriarty notes the power of photographs at this time when she discusses Ivor Gurney's 1917 poem "Photographs." "Gurney refers to the distance which the images traversed between home and front, seeing them as a link between places and people, the past and

6.15 Postcard of a Russian soldier. Postally used in 1913.

the present, peace and war," she writes. "Amid the official communications and the censoring of letters the photograph assumed authenticity; incorruptible evidence of dearly loved faces."[47] Hence, the prevalence with which we find photographs and postcards mentioned among the belongings of the dead. Memoir after memoir lists their discovery on the bodies of soldiers killed in action. In some instances, the finding of a postcard sparked altruistic responses, as in the case of Mary Britnieva when she and some friends came across the bodies of five Russian soldiers. On one of the bodies, they found a postcard sent to the officer by his wife in Moscow. The next day, the group buried the bodies, putting the officer in a separate grave which they marked with a cross. But, their efforts on behalf of the fallen man did not stop there. As Britnieva records, "That same day, one of our nurses who had an aunt in Moscow, sent her the postcard and begged her to try and find the unfortunate writer and tell her that her husband had been discovered and that he was now buried near Wirballen." The aunt was able to track down the widow in question, who was extremely grateful for the information. "Some months later, when we

6.16 Group of Russian soldiers. No manufacturer or date listed.

6.17 Russian soldier and a woman, presumably his wife. No manufacturer or date listed.

6.18 Russian soldier and a woman, presumably his wife. No manufacturer or date listed.

had been transferred to the Polish front," wrote Britnieva, "we got a touching letter from the unfortunate woman in which she told us that thanks to us she had been able to find her husband's body and brought it back to Moscow, where it was now buried in the family vault."[48]

Photographic postcards empowered soldiers and their families since they allowed for the creation of their own histories – narratives commemorating something different, and more personal, than officially produced images. Unlike other forms of remembrance, such as monuments to the war dead, which take away the individuality of those depicted, photo postcards, and photographs in general, to quote Moriarty, "have the power to remind us of the humanity of the dead, their ordinariness and their differences."[49] Such desires spurred thousands of Russian families to send portraits of their lost fathers, brothers, and husbands to illustrated periodicals, which then memorialized the dead in specially designed collages.[50]

In the Russian context, these images took on additional significance once the Bolsheviks came to power. The Bolsheviks rejected the First World War as what they termed an "imperialist war," and chose to publicly celebrate only the revolution and civil war. In terms of official memory, the First World War was largely overlooked. First World War memorials, at either the local or national level, were not constructed. Returning soldiers were not encouraged to write their memoirs, and relatively few literary works dealing with the war, let alone official military histories like those produced elsewhere in Europe, were published.[51] Moreover, there was a deliberate attempt by the Soviet authorities to break linkages with the past. For instance, by restructuring military units, the Red Army purposely destroyed regimental continuity and the identities given to soldiers prior to the revolution. As Peter Gatrell notes, "The kind of camaraderie evident in the veteran's organisations of the French, British and Germans lacked any equivalent in Russia's generation of 1914, except among small numbers of émigré officers."[52] This official silence negated ways that the First World War dead could be mourned. Unlike in Britain, for example, where the creation and public unveiling of local memorials meant that "loss became a collective experience," in the Soviet context, there was no public sanctification.[53] Under the circumstances, one of the few ways to remember the dead was to do so privately. Keeping photo postcards became part of the process whereby a veteran could remember his friends and wartime experiences, and relatives could honour the memory of a dead family member. They could carve out a private niche, separate from the official memory being imposed by the state.

Keeping such images was not without its dangers, however. Once Russia descended into civil war following the Bolshevik seizure of power, photographs could be problematic, for things like uniforms and other pieces of clothing were a way to fix someone's class identity. Class identity then served to mark the individual as friend or foe. In *Memoirs of the Russian Revolution*, Aleksandr Lukomskii provides an example of the power of a single photograph. Lukomskii, who served as chief of staff to both General Brusilov and General Kornilov and as assistant minister of war in 1916, was captured by the Bolsheviks in southern Russia. As he sat in a court waiting room contemplating his fate, Lukomskii watched a soldier wipe up a pool of blood. The soldier explained that, on the previous day, five people had been given death sentences by the court, and when one of them refused to move, his Bolshevik captors bayoneted him before using their rifle butts to finish him off. The soldier added that a photograph was found in the lining of the prisoner's fur cap. Its placement there suggested not only that the photograph was precious, but that its owner wished to conceal it. The reason was obvious in the eyes of the Bolshevik guards since the picture showed the man in a colonel's uniform with his wife and children. A colonel was automatically assumed to be hostile to the revolution, and this man was obviously taking pains to conceal his class identity. The soldier talking to Lukomskii concluded, "They were, therefore, quite right to kill him."[54]

Conclusion

In the words of an advertising writer at Eastman Kodak, "every man can write the outline of his own history, and that ... outline will be a hundredfold more interesting if it is illustrated."[55] Russia's withdrawal from the First World War and descent into revolution and civil war did not immediately alter the way in which people used picture postcards. Attempts to personalize these conflicts and to insert individual stories into the grand narrative of history persisted, allowing ordinary men and women to fight different wars than the ones constructed in state-sponsored narratives. Examining picture postcards reveals the breadth of visual materials available and consumed during the First World War in Russia. From the brightly coloured postcards that promoted the purchase of war bonds to images mocking the enemy or emphasizing the solidarity of the Russian population, the role of picture postcards in creating patriotic discourse has already been recognized by historians. Less attention has been devoted to other attempts to standardize the experience of the war. Drawing on the work of Paul Fussell, the first half of this chapter described efforts to impose a kind of uniformity on prisoners of war and refugees, thereby standardizing their stories. That these labours failed only makes the picture more interesting, for as we have seen in the second half of the chapter, which describes how soldiers and their families actually used photographs and picture postcards, it implies the war years offered a richer tapestry of experiences than several generations of scholarship have suggested. As the First World War years come under new scrutiny from scholars such as Peter Gatrell and Joshua Sanborn, picture postcards can tell us much about how the Russian population really fought and lived through all kinds of "different wars." The turmoil did not, however, end once the guns on the eastern front fell silent. If anything, the situation became more complicated once Russia descended into revolution and civil war. As we shall see in the next chapter, postcards have much to say about those subjects as well.

Chapter Seven

Picture Postcards
and the Russian Revolution, 1905–1922

Nikolai Nabokov was an indifferent student. This nephew of Duma member Vladimir Nabokov and future chief cultural assistant to the American Military Government in Berlin in his own right passed only one subject the first year he attended a formal educational institution. His parents resorted to the traditional remedy of the Russian elites – the hiring of special tutors to coach the boy during his holidays – but they may have gotten more than they bargained for during the last year before the February Revolution. Judging by his uniform, the tutor was a sergeant of the Petrograd *oborona*, a group that supplemented the city garrison. He also turned out to be a Bolshevik. "From him I heard outlandish names," wrote Nabokov in his memoirs, "and he showed me photographs of Marx, Engels, Plekhanov, Martov, and his special hero, Ulyanov-Lenin."[1] Apparently, the young man was far more interested in revolutionary ideas than the Latin and mathematics he was hired to impart.

This final chapter uses picture postcards of figures like those mentioned by Nabokov to examine revolutionary culture during the last turbulent years of Imperial Russia. I outline how revolutionary groups came to employ picture postcards for correspondence, fundraising, and propaganda purposes. Later, a specific examination of the picture postcards generated by revolutionary groups from 1905 to 1922 reveals the visual language of self-representation that groups in the middle and on the left end of the political spectrum, each of whom will be discussed below, used to win followers and grasp at political power.[2] Russia's revolutionaries also explicitly targeted audiences abroad with these materials. Donations from foreign sympathizers offered a crucial source of support to revolutionary organizations, and it was believed that favourable coverage in European media would put pressure on the tsarist government to change. Finally, as revolution twice swept through Russia in 1917 and the country descended into civil war, picture postcards became a kind of photojournalism that chronicled and constructed the event for the masses.

Postcards and Revolutionaries before 1917

Before the October Revolution, all postcards created by revolutionary groups were self-published and could not legally be sent through the mail.[3] In an effort to hide their identities, the makers of such materials did not print dates, their names, or usually any other kind of information on the reverse side of their postcards.[4] Consequently, the precise dating of materials is often a challenge. Because of reforms to the written language introduced by the Provisional Government – reforms that removed a letter from the Russian alphabet and modernized the Cyrillic orthography – as well as some other clues provided by internal evidence, it is possible to say if a postcard is pre- or post-revolutionary, but sometimes that is all that is revealed. It is also impossible to say how many postcards were produced by the various revolutionary groups in Russia. Private collections of illegal postcards were dangerous to keep, and public collections did not include them. Almost a hundred years later, these items are scarce and the market for them among collectors is fierce.

In spite of the frustrations they pose for historians, postcards had an important role in the revolutionary movement. Revolutionaries were familiar with postcards for a number of reasons. For instance, prisoners in Siberia could only legally communicate with their families by writing postcards submitted to the police for censorship before being mailed to their final destination. In return, scenic picture postcards were often sent to prisoners by friends and relatives in the hopes they would brighten up the walls of prison cells.[5] The right to send and receive mail was apparently so important to prisoners' well-being that it became a way for prison authorities to control their charges and enforce discipline. A law of 23 May 1901 listed deprivation of mail as one of the severe punishments that could be inflicted upon a prisoner, right after being given fifty strokes with a birch rod.[6] Postcards of leading socialists or revolutionary figures, usually imported from abroad or drawn by hand, presented Russian radicals with a canon of revolutionary icons. Elena Stasova records in her memoirs that the Bolsheviks used the sale of such portraits to partly fund their activities.[7] The postcards were never written on, but were kept, instead, as treasured, though illegal, items. Nadezhda

Krupskaia noted that Lenin, while in Siberian exile, had postcards of Emile Zola, Herzen, Pisarev, and Chernyshevsky in his album.[8] Nor was Lenin's collection unique. Roman Malinovsky, Lenin's close comrade-in-arms, Duma deputy, and police spy, used a 1914 trip to Western Europe not only to update Russian émigrés on Duma affairs but to acquire new picture postcards for his collection.[9] And, finally, as we saw in chapter 5, Orlando Figes and Boris Kolonitskii's work has quite convincingly argued that pornographic postcards mocking the royal family damaged the tsar's public image and undermined popular support for the monarchy.[10] While we have no concrete evidence linking these postcards with specific revolutionary organizations, it seems evident they would only be produced by opponents of the regime.

The 1905 Revolution brought revolutionary postcards more into the open. Changes in censorship in the wake of the year's upheavals affected all forms of printed matter. The system for inspecting printing plants and bookstores broke down, and the printers themselves became more radicalized, frequently refusing to print materials they did not approve of.[11] V.D. Bonch-Bruevich, who was in charge of Bolshevik publishing at this time, later noted that fifty-nine different printing plants were willing to print material for the revolutionaries.[12] Both the Bolsheviks and the Socialist Revolutionaries used the opportunity to establish legal bookstores that openly sold socialist literature. The Bolshevik Vpered publishing venture established a storefront on Karavannaia Street in St. Petersburg.[13] In addition to its array of pamphlets and books, the store sold picture postcards. Its first postcards were reproductions of works of art depicting revolutionary scenes. Another group was composed of portraits of Russian émigrés such as Aleksandr Herzen, Mikhail Bakunin, and Nikolai Ogarev. By the time Vpered was shut down, in July 1907, it had covered roughly 120 different subjects in postcard form.[14] The cards continued to circulate illegally for months after the publishing venture and its store were closed. The emergence of other manufacturers, such as A.S. Levinson who created a series of satirical postcards in Odessa, ensured that this type of material spread across the country.[15] John Foster Fraser's account of his trip to Russia at this time, for example, notes that revolutionary images were being sold openly in Samara.[16]

Along with the varieties of hand-drawn postcards still being made, these revolutionary postcards provided the public with artistic representations of events such as the French Revolution or the Paris Commune as well as with portraits of key figures such as Marx, Engels, and Lieutenant Schmidt (a martyr of the 1905 Revolution). Song lyrics, particularly for

"The Marseillaise," proved to be another popular topic, as they would be again in 1917.[17] These postcards demonstrate a new form of publicity that came to be used as the public sphere expanded during the 1905 Revolution. Caspar Ferenczi argues that in 1905–06 "through the establishment of a parliament, the authorization of political parties, and the easing of censorship laws, public opinion gained a significance that it had not hitherto possessed."[18] In this new contested arena, revolutionaries challenged the legitimacy of the regime by presenting a different historical narrative – one that deliberately did not celebrate the achievements of the tsarist regime and one that was peopled by revolutionary heroes. Figure 7.1, for example, is a montage of images spelling out "May 1" in Russian. It frames the revolutionary holiday as a celebration of efforts to overthrow the regime. The eclectic array of images places Christ's crucifixion alongside pictures of Karl Marx, Georgii Plekhanov (the father of Russian Marxism), and Ivan Kaliaev (who was responsible for assassinating Grand Duke Sergei Aleksandrovich in February 1905).

A second postcard pointed to the Decembrists as the start of the revolutionary tradition by including Pavel Pestel and Kondratii Ryleev in a montage with Lieutenant Schmidt and Egor Sazonov (who killed government minister Viacheslav Plehve in 1904). Its caption read, "Glory to the fighters for the people's cause, / Glory to the heroes of our native land, / Glory to those who gave both soul and body / For eternal freedom and holy truth!"[19] A montage with similar photographs can be found in Figure 7.2, which contains small portraits of a wide array of Russians who actively resisted autocracy in the nineteenth century. Despite its poor quality, the postcard includes images of such disparate people as Pavel Pestel, Sofiia Perovskaia (who was hanged for her part in the 1881 assassination of Alexander II), and Egor Sazonov. It links them together under the heading "Fighters for Freedom." The content stretches the history of the revolutionary movement back almost a century, and visually, the postcard resembles the family tree iconography used in the portraits of the royal family discussed two chapters ago. Moreover, by providing a pantheon of heroic portraits, the image can be interpreted as a sign of the strength of the revolutionary movement.

Postcards did not confine themselves to the past. Instead, they provided political commentary as events were happening. The attention paid to Lieutenant Schmidt, who became a revolutionary martyr, provides an example. In 1905, Pyotr Schmidt, who had earlier been disciplined for making a speech defending the liberties promised by the

7.1 Montage celebrating May 1 holiday. No manufacturer or date listed.

October Manifesto, led a mutiny aboard a cruiser in Sevastopol. After a battle at Severnaia Bay, the mutiny was repressed and Schmidt was eventually executed, in 1906. His likeness appeared on a number of postcards. Figure 7.3 connects Schmidt's sacrifice to the broader European revolutionary tradition by using sheet music for "The Marseillaise" as a frame for his portrait. The caption describes Schmidt as a "true Russian hero" (*istinnyi Russkii geroi*).

Other postcards of Schmidt used the same portrait, but without the background details. To Tobie Mathew, one of the world's foremost collectors of Russian revolutionary postcards, this second group of images had religious overtones. "This appropriation of [religious] language can be seen to some extent in the picture of Schmidt, in which his head and shoulders stand out against a plain background, consciously mimicking the traditional composition," he writes. Schmidt's "deeds are undoubtedly being equated with those of the saints, further reinforcing his sacrifice in a form that would be immediately understandable to the Russian people."[20]

7.2 "Fighters for Freedom" montage. No manufacturer or date listed.

7.3 Lieutenant Schmidt with "The Marseillaise" as background. No manufacturer or date listed.

7.4 Cossacks charging the crowd on Bloody Sunday. No manufacturer or date listed. Mailed from St. Petersburg to Brooklyn, New York, in 1910.

Other postcards singled out key events in 1905 like the Bloody Sunday massacre that happened on 9 January. The images were deliberately provocative because they highlighted state violence inflicted upon helpless civilians. In Figures 7.4 and 7.5, the scenes include women and children in melodramatic poses to compound the effect. In the first instance, the postcard also provides a clue to the type of person who bought and used these kinds of postcards, for he refers to his correspondent as "Dear Comrade Fritz" (*Darogoi tovarishch Fritz*).

The events of Bloody Sunday, as well as other moments of violence that year, also provoked a response abroad where some rather fanciful and lurid postcards quickly appeared. In France, a Monsieur Laville published a series of six postcards, including one showing Father Gapon, who led the demonstration on Bloody Sunday, and a crowd of peasants surrounding a blood-stained guillotine.[21] Another postcard (see Figure 7.6) commented on the assassination of Grand Duke Sergei Aleksandrovich. The text says, "From the country of crimes," implying that such events were widespread in Russia. In a rather sinister fashion, the postcard refers

7.5 Bloody Sunday massacre. No manufacturer or date listed.

to the grand duke's proximity to the throne by calling him "Uncle Serge" rather than by his official titles. But, by far the most striking element was the postcard's use of colour, for bright red blood is shown spurting from the grand duke's severed body parts.

In Britain, the images were less violent but postcard manufacturers still rushed to provide consumers with items that commented on events in Russia. The postcard in Figure 7.7, part of a series entitled "The Revolutionary Outbreak in St. Petersburg," was mailed at the end of February 1905, which gives some sense of how quickly postcards like these appeared on the European market.

The interest of foreign manufacturers did not diminish after the revolution ended, and their wares added an important dimension to debates about Russian politics. Not only were these postcards available to Russian tourists as they travelled the continent in ever increasing numbers, but by the turn of the century, sizeable Russian émigré communities existed in the larger European cities, and they could be appealed to by revolutionaries for financial and moral support. The émigré community in

7.6 The assassination of Grand Duke Sergei Aleksandrovich. L'arc en ciel, n.d.

Paris alone doubled in size between 1911 and 1931. It eventually encompassed more than eighty thousand people.[22] Events in Russia garnered new-found attention in the West, and Russian groups began to actively court public opinion in other countries as well. As we will see, revolutionary parties sent representatives on speaking tours and made sure sympathetic articles and books appeared telling their stories. Picture postcards offered another form of publicity. Some revolutionaries evidently already understood the power of photography to shape the perception of events. Henry Nevinson, who passed the winter of 1905–06 in Russia as a special correspondent for the *Daily Chronicle*, describes being caught by demonstrators as he tried to photograph barricades erected in the streets of Moscow. Eventually able to convince the crowd that he was not a spy, he still had to turn over his roll of film. He argues that "by their action their finest barricades lost a chance of immortality."[23] But, it can also be posited that this seizure allowed the revolutionaries, rather than outsiders like Nevinson, to control what images circulated of the events both at home and abroad.

7.7 Father Gapon. Manufactured by Lankester & Co., Tunbridge Wells. Postally used in 1905.

The final decade of Imperial Russia saw Europeans watching the Russian political scene with great interest. Postcard manufacturers responded to assumed Western sympathies by producing postcards that openly supported the new Duma in its contests of power with the tsar. Figure 7.8, which depicts Nicholas II clubbing the Duma into submission, may contain a reference to the Fundamental Laws promulgated on 6 May 1906, in other words, on the eve of the first meeting of the Duma. The text on the club says "ukase" ("Imperial decree" in Russian) and gives the date 7/06. The laws severely restricted the activities of the Duma in Russian political life. They enabled the tsar to keep complete control of foreign policy, the military, and the executive branch. He also retained his autocratic title and the right to determine succession to the throne. To many people, both in Russia and the wider European community, the Fundamental Laws were a betrayal of the promises the regime had made in the October Manifesto. A later example, made by a French firm, demonstrates that interest in the Duma continued throughout the decade. The postcard informs the public about the arrest of members of the

7.8 Nicholas II clubbing the Duma. No manufacturer or date listed. Artist Molynk.

Bolshevik faction in the Duma in January 1915.[24] To gain support and sympathy for the men who are named in the image, the postcard's makers drew prison bars over a pre-existing photograph of them, reinforcing the idea that they were suffering behind bars for their beliefs.

Chronicling 1917: Postcards as Photojournalism

A new wave of postcards captured, chronicled, and publicized events in 1917, Russia's year of revolutions. Documentary-style postcards played an active part in what Frederick Corney described as the "battle to 'frame public understanding of events.'"[25] In 1917, documentary postcards staked a claim for the masses in the political life of the country. The postcards captured moments of popular protest – demonstrations, marches, and mass meetings – marking them for posterity as key incidents or sites in the revolution. Some of the postcards, such as Figure 7.9, also included dates in their captions, thereby claiming the event was worthy of remembrance and establishing a chronology of the revolution.

7.9 Political demonstration in Petrograd on 18 June 1917. No manufacturer or date listed.

For the people depicted – workers, soldiers, and even women – this was the first time that power was visibly assigned to them in visual materials. The size of the crowds involved suggested an elemental force surging into traditional places and buildings of power. This force usually appeared leaderless, as no famous revolutionaries or politicians were depicted on these picture postcards. Individual faces were often difficult to distinguish, and no names were included in the captions. Frequently issued in numbered series, these postcards became what Peter Burke terms "narrative strips."[26] Thus, they presented images in a given order so as to tell a story and, like the postcard in Figure 7.9, establish a fixed chronological narrative of events.

One locus of power assigned by the images was the Petrograd Soviet of Soldiers' and Workers' Deputies, housed in the Tauride Palace. Publicity was thereby given to the body that was the main rival for power of the Provisional Government in 1917, that met in the same building as the Provisional Government, and that served as a beacon for opposition to the new regime. For instance, Figure 7.10 captures a meeting of the Petrograd Soviet. Its setting is reminiscent of postcards depicting sessions of the state Duma. However, whereas the Duma meetings appeared orderly and staid, with members seated and the aisles clear, the postcard of the Petrograd Soviet thrums with activity and energy. Members of the crowd have crammed into every available space. And several people were moving when the photograph was snapped so their blurred figures contribute to the dynamic created by this postcard. As was the case on the documentary postcards showing mass demonstrations and marches, the crowd at the meeting of the Petrograd Soviet also appears as a force sweeping its way into power.

Another kind of postcard commemorated the celebration of May 1, 1917, as a revolutionary holiday. May Day demonstrations were legalized by the Provisional Government, but it is unclear which group organized the events held in Petrograd in 1917. While the Provisional Government probably made a contribution, it did not use the occasion to claim legitimacy by having its supporters occupy the central spaces of power on that day. None of the documentary postcards show staged moments. Instead, they featured anonymous crowds milling on Palace Square (see Figure 7.11). The masses, again, appear seemingly without leaders, thus reinforcing Eric Hobsbawm's observation that May Day involved workers parading as a class to demonstrate their strength.[27] The point was reinforced by the banners carried by members of the crowd, as (with the

Засѣданіе Совѣта Рабочихъ и Солдатскихъ Депутатовъ въ Государственной Думѣ.   9

7.10 Meeting of the Soviet of Workers' and Soldiers' Deputies in the state Duma (in the Tauride Palace). Published by Shteinberg, n.d.

exception of one reading, "Land and Freedom," a slogan connected to the Socialist Revolutionaries) they endorsed neither the leadership of the Provisional Government nor any specific political party.[28] In all of these postcards, the people, rather than political leaders, are the dominant force in the revolution.

Finally, a group of postcards associated with the *Izvestiia Petrogradskogo Soveta* newspaper should be mentioned as they, too, helped to chronicle the key events of the revolution. Richard Bartmann's collection shows one such card announcing the tsar's abdication.[29] As an organ of the Petrograd Soviet, the newspaper provided information to the masses and often gave voice to views opposing the new government. To reach their audience quickly, the newspaper's producers also turned to postcards. They had sympathetic printers reproduce the front page of the newspaper in postcard form, and the postcards were then sold at kiosks and railway stations.

7.11 Demonstration celebrating the May 1 holiday, Palace Square in St. Petersburg, 1917. Published by Izdanie S. Sobchinskii, St. Petersburg, n.d.

Kerensky and the Provisional Government

The revolutionary narratives laid out in documentary postcards from 1917 did not go unchallenged by the Provisional Government, and the focus of this section will be on how the Provisional Government used picture postcards as part of efforts to bolster its own legitimacy. The Provisional Government lacked a consistent cultural policy and the political stability needed to develop one.[30] The various coalitions that made up the Provisional Government during its lifespan involved men of such disparate ideological views and party affiliations that it made agreement on political, let alone cultural, matters impossible. Its visual legacy is slim. In terms of picture postcards, there was one series featuring individual portraits of ministers of the Provisional Government that must have been printed very early in 1917 (see Figure 7.12), but additional offerings were not created as the government changed its composition.

7.12 Minister of Trade and Industry A.I. Konovalov. No manufacturer or date listed. Drawing by S. Kushchenko.

Instead, postcard makers soon moved to capitalize on Alexander Kerensky's charisma and reputation as a revolutionary figure.[31]

Kerensky, a lawyer well known for his ties to the Socialist Revolutionaries as well as for his legal defence of radicals, first emerged on the political scene in October 1912 when he was elected to the Duma. Since Duma deputies had immunity from prosecution, they could voice political opinions that others in Russia were not free to give. Kerensky quickly became a leading national representative of populism and the Socialist Revolutionary party. Kerensky's public stature was such that, with the overthrow of the monarchy, he was included in the new Provisional Government as minister of justice. His profile continued to rise over the next several months: a new governing coalition was announced in early May, shifting Kerensky's portfolio from Justice to the Ministry of War and Marine; and, on 7 July, he reached the apex of his power when he was appointed prime minister while continuing to serve as minister of war.

Throughout the year, Kerensky, in the words of his biographer Richard Abraham, worked "to enhance the prestige of the Provisional Government by the only means at hand, his own charisma."[32] An early postcard with his likeness was issued by the publishers of a mass-circulation St. Petersburg newspaper, *Gazeta kopeika*, when he became minister of justice. A simple portrait, it shows Kerensky looking seriously at the viewer and is reminiscent of similar photographs made of tsarist ministers.[33] The image reminds one of Peter Burke's analyses of portrait paintings, where he quotes the work of Erving Goffman. Burke writes, "Thus the portrait is not so much a painted equivalent of a 'candid camera' as a record of what the sociologist Erving Goffman has described as 'the presentation of self,' a process in which the artist and sitter generally colluded."[34] The firebrand known for his passionate speeches in the Duma is nowhere in evidence, having been replaced with the stern expression of a statesman. This image seems to have circulated widely and in a number of formats: two photographs in Laurie Stoff's study of Russian women soldiers in the First World War demonstrate how it was carried in processions in an iconlike fashion, and how it came to replace tsarist portraits on the walls of government buildings.[35] French diplomat Louis de Robien described Cossacks parading after military victories in July 1917. They carried bunches of flowers and large photographs of Kerensky.[36]

Despite this portrait, Kerensky as minister of justice also continued to court the revolutionary end of the political spectrum. He very publicly surrounded himself, at first, with returning revolutionaries like Vera

Figner and Ekaterina Breshko-Breshkovskaia, both of whom acted as official hostesses for some of his breakfast meetings. Kerensky also reworked his image once he became minister of war. He now assumed the uniform of a common soldier for his public appearances and in visual materials created for those who could not see him in person. Figure 7.13 captures this new image.

The caption reads, "The revolution creates a new life, a source of light and joy," and the overall impression of the postcard implies that Kerensky is the embodiment of the revolution, linking him with promises of a better future. Later, when his policies as prime minister strained his relationship with his fellow Socialist Revolutionaries, Kerensky's public persona underwent a third shift. He came to associate himself more with the trappings of the deposed monarchy, for instance, by living in the Winter Palace and using a train that had once belonged to the tsar.[37] In the eyes of Meriel Buchanan, the daughter of the English ambassador, Kerensky's behaviour began to irritate the general public by the late summer of 1917. She remarked, "Kerensky's popularity was increasingly on the wane. His arrogance had set people against him; all sorts of stories as to his mode of life in the Winter Palace were afloat in the town."[38] Perhaps an even more telling incident was recorded in the diary of history professor Iurii Got'e, on 19 September 1917: "Today I saw a marvelous depiction of Mr. Kerenskii in an emperor's crown – on a postcard, with the crown added by hand."[39] The Socialist Revolutionaries responded to this change in Kerensky's behaviour by dropping any reference to him from their visual propaganda.

The Socialist Revolutionaries

The Socialist Revolutionary party was not at a loss for heroic figures to celebrate. As perhaps the most visible revolutionary group for more than a decade, the party had an established canon to fall back on once Kerensky had been abandoned as a symbol. For years, Socialist Revolutionary terrorist acts kept the party constantly in the public eye, and its members worked to create an aura of martyrdom around their arrested comrades, particularly those who were women. In this, the Socialist Revolutionaries were building upon earlier Russian cultural constructions of women.[40] Throughout the nineteenth century, novels placed in the foreground heroines who were morally superior and intellectually equal to the men around them.[41] In the 1870s, when women played a very visible role as defendants in the trials of the Populists, they

7.13 Alexander Kerensky as minister of war. No manufacturer or date listed.

garnered much sympathy from educated society. The sacrifices of women were held up as a legitimizing force for the revolutionary movement as a whole. Moreover, the hardships endured by revolutionary women harkened back to an even older tradition in Russian culture – that of the ascetic hero. After experiencing a transcendent moment, an ascetic hero sheds the material trappings of a comfortable life in order to focus on the pursuit of a shining vision of the future. Asceticism re-entered Russian literature in the nineteenth century with the creation of Rakhmetov in Chernyshevsky's *What Is to Be Done?*[42] Rakhmetov and other characters from the novel quickly came to be seen by radical youths as models for emulation. Their legacy is demonstrated by the myth making that surrounded the careers of Maria Spiridonova and Ekaterina Breshko-Breshkovksaia, both of whom would be the focus of sustained publicity campaigns by branches of the Socialist Revolutionary party in the first two decades of the twentieth century.

Born in 1884, the daughter of a minor (non-hereditary) noble from Tambov, Maria Spiridonova burst onto the public scene in Russia when she assassinated a police official in 1906. Her case attracted widespread attention in the press after a letter she wrote in prison was smuggled out and published in a liberal newspaper. In it, Spiridonova described how she was beaten during her arrest, subjected to further violence during questioning, and hinted she had been sexually assaulted as she was being transported to prison. The letter – excerpts from which were later printed on picture postcards as in Figure 7.14 – gave rise to what one historian has termed "the Spiridonova legend," whereby certain details of her personal life were deliberately suppressed and, instead, Spiridonova came to embody an image of physical beauty, moral purity, and courageous dignity in the face of extreme physical abuse.[43] Her actual crime (she shot G.N. Luzhenovskii five times) was largely forgotten in the subsequent outpouring of opinions concerning her treatment at the hands of the authorities. The publicity was so intense her death sentence ultimately had to be commuted to penal servitude for life.

The February Revolution brought Spiridonova's release from a women's prison in Nerchinsk. She quickly emerged as one of the most visible Socialist Revolutionary publicists even though she did not become active in actual policy decision-making. For instance, Nina Berberova remembers that, following the February Revolution, she and her classmates "abolished the prayer before the beginning of lessons, and hung portraits of Herzen, Plekhanov and Spiridonova on the classroom wall."[44] Another witness to the revolution, Albert Rhys Williams, recalls how

Выдержки изъ письма Спиридоновой.

. . . . Я вошла въ вагонъ и на разстоянiи 12—13 шаговъ, съ площадки вагона, сдѣлала выстрѣлъ въ Луженовскаго. . . . . Руками я закрывала лицо; прикладами руки снимались съ него. Потомъ казачiй офицеръ, высоко поднявъ меня за закрученную на руку косу, сильнымъ взмахомъ бросилъ на платформу. . . . Потомъ за ногу потащили внизъ по лѣстницѣ. Голова билась о ступеньки, за косу внесена на извозчика. . . . . Ударомъ ноги Ждановъ перебрасывалъ меня въ уголъ камеры, гдѣ ждалъ меня казачiй офицеръ, наступалъ мнѣ на спину и опять перебрасывалъ Жданову, который становился на шею. . . Раздѣтую, страшно ругаясь, они били нагайками (Ждановъ) и говорили: „Ну, барышня (ругань), скажи зажигательную рѣчь!" Одинъ глазъ ничего не видѣлъ и правая часть лица была страшно разбита. Они нажимали на нее и лукаво спрашивали: „Больно, дорогая? Ну, скажи, кто твои товарищи?" . . . . выдергивали по одному волосу изъ головы и спрашивали, гдѣ другіе революцiонеры. Тушили горящую папиросу о тѣло и говорили: „кричи же, сволочь!"
Показанiя слѣдующiя: 1) Да, хотѣла убить Луженовскаго по предварительному соглашенiю и т. д. 2) По постановленiю тамбовскаго комитета партiи соцiалистовъ-революцiонеровъ за преступное засѣканiе и безмѣрное истязанiе крестьянъ во время аграрныхъ и политическихъ безпорядковъ и послѣ нихъ въ тѣхъ уѣздахъ гдѣ былъ Луженовскiй, за разбойничьи похожденiя Луженовскаго въ Борисоглѣбскѣ въ качествѣ начальника охраны, за организацiю черной сотни въ Тамбовѣ и какъ отвѣтъ на введенiе военнаго положенiя и чрезвычайной и усиленной охраны въ Тамбовѣ и другихъ уѣздахъ. Тамбовскимъ комитетомъ партiи соцiалистовъ-революцiонеровъ былъ вынесенъ приговоръ Луженовскому: въ полномъ согласiи съ этимъ приговоромъ и въ полномъ сознанiи своего поступка, я взялась за исполненiе этого приговора.
Слѣдствiе кончено, до сихъ поръ сильно больна, часто брежу. Если убьютъ, умру спокойно и съ хорошимъ чувствомъ въ душѣ.
Спиридонова.

7.14 Postcard with excerpts from Spiridonova's famous letter. No manufacturer or date listed.

Spiridonova captured the imagination of left-leaning foreigners: "We all admired Spiridonova, who had worked with Lenin and the other Bolsheviks at the All-Russian Congress of Peasants and was largely instrumental in swinging a majority to the Soviets for the coalition government. [John] Reed thought her the most striking and powerful woman in Petrograd."[45] In terms of her actual activities, in May 1917, Spiridonova travelled to Moscow as a delegate to the party's third national congress. By July, she was making speeches critical of the Provisional Government to mass meetings, and joining comrades on the extreme left wing of the party in advocating a second socialist revolution. After the October Revolution, she supported the Bolshevik-Left Socialist Revolutionary coalition government until the harshness of Bolshevik-forced grain requisitioning in the countryside and the economic concessions granted to Germany in the Treaty of Brest-Litovsk forced her to reconsider. In July 1918, she was arrested in connection with her participation in the failed Left Socialist Revolutionary uprising and the assassination of Count

Mirbach, the new German ambassador to Russia. Thereafter, her life followed a pattern of release from prison, continued agitation against the regime, and re-arrest. She was finally executed with a group of political prisoners in 1945.[46]

Spiridonova was the image of the Left Socialist Revolutionaries in 1917 and 1918. Years earlier, she had already established herself in the public eye. In the wake of the assassination of Luzhenkovskii, Spiridonova was visited in prison by Kellogg Durland, an American correspondent whose writings were published in *Harper's Weekly* and *Collier's Weekly*. Durland was accompanied by Nahum Luboshitz, a photographer. A couple of his pictures were published in *Rech'*, a newspaper associated with the Constitutional Democratic party before being reprinted as postcards. Durland noted that the postcards were briefly available for sale at a Moscow bookstore. Eventually, however, they were seized by the police, and the shop was forced to close.[47] A second periodical, the more conservative organ *Rus'*, sent reporter V.N. Vladimirov to Tambov to investigate the affair. The story generated enough interest that Vladimirov's articles were quickly gathered into a book. It contained six photographs, some of which Spiridonova posed for during her conversation with the reporter.[48] These pictures, too, found their way onto picture postcards. Moreover, Spiridonova was an effective public speaker, able to draw and sway crowds during the stops made by the train taking her to prison in Nerchinsk. Now she re-emerged on the main political stage and old photographs of her were quickly repackaged into new postcards. News of her amnesty was publicized, for instance, by the postcard shown in Figure 7.15, which includes one of the photographs taken by Luboshitz as well as three pictures from Vladimirov's book.

After her release, Spiridonova became a regular speaker at mass political rallies. Her reputation was further enhanced by the attention she received on the twelfth anniversary of Luzhenovskii's assassination. That day, the main Left Socialist Revolutionary newspaper devoted its two front pages to tributes to her and, when she stood to speak at the Congress of Soviets, she was greeted by an ovation from the delegates. Another postcard further exemplifies how her life story was turned into that of an ascetic heroine of the revolutionary movement.[49] The caption, printed below a rather earnest-looking portrait, remarks that following her arrest, Spiridonova was beaten "half-to-death" by policemen and that she remained in prison until only recently. The implication is clear: for her beliefs, Spiridonova was willing to suffer great physical torment and material deprivations. However, postcards did not go on to show her

7.15 Postcard announcing Spiridonova's release from prison after the February Revolution. No manufacturer or date listed.

participating in events after she had been amnestied. Physically, she may have returned to the revolutionary struggle, but visually, she remained frozen in time, victimized either in prison or exile.[50] The power of Spiridonova's image was such that the Bolsheviks could not permit her to remain at large after the failed Left Socialist Revolutionary uprising of July 1918. Once she recast herself as a martyr-heroine who was now leading the fight against the Soviet government, she became a dangerous threat to the new regime, hence the harshness with which she was treated throughout the remainder of her life.

As Spiridonova came to embody the public face of the Left Socialist Revolutionaries, the party mainstream countered by promoting the image of another revolutionary legend, that of Ekaterina Breshko-Breshkovskaia. Born in 1844, Breshkovskaia had already had a long and celebrated career as a revolutionary by the time Nicholas II was overthrown. As a participant in the "to the people" movement, Breshkovskaia was arrested for the first time in 1874 and, four years later, she became the first Russian women sentenced to hard labour in the Kara mines for political reasons. She was released in 1892, but was forced to spend the next few years as a "free exile" in Siberia. When her term of exile finally ended, in September 1896, Breshkovskaia immediately returned to agitating in the countryside. She joined the Socialist Revolutionary party at its founding, in 1901, and set to work recruiting others and building support for the party among the peasantry. Since she did not agitate under an assumed name, Breshkovskaia's activities drew constant attention from the tsarist authorities. Forced to flee across the border to Rumania in 1903, she then became a leading revolutionary spokesperson and fundraiser abroad.

In December 1904, Breshkovskaia began a speaking tour of the United States. The tour's arrangements were handled by the American branch of the Society of Friends of Russian Freedom and included engagements in a number of American cities.[51] On her tours, she honed her public persona. In addition to public lectures, Breshkovskaia met with wealthy Americans at private parties and teas. She became known by her nickname "Grandmother of the Russian Revolution," and by being deliberately vague about her support for terror, the sixty-year-old Breshkovskaia appeared to be a harmless, but morally inspiring, elderly woman. She met with much sympathy, not least because her tours coincided with an image crisis abroad for the tsarist regime. The 1903 Kishinev pogrom received very negative press in the West, and the regime also blundered its way through the Russo-Japanese War. By the end of her tour, in March 1905, Breshkovskaia had raised more than $10,000 – a not inconsiderable amount for the day – which she turned over to an anarchist who bought a shipload of arms that was eventually smuggled to the Finnish coast later in 1905.[52] She made a lasting name for herself and established valuable contacts abroad that she would continue to tap for financial support in years to come. Her reputation was such that a number of petitions were presented to Russian authorities when she was arrested in December 1907.[53] Subsequently exiled in perpetuity to Siberia, she then formed one of her most important relationships.

Breshkovskaia met Alexander Kerensky when he travelled to eastern Siberia to investigate the Lena Goldfields massacre of 1912, and the two struck up a lasting friendship. When, in March 1917, Breshkovskaia was freed from exile and quickly returned to European Russia, Kerensky organized her official welcome in Petrograd. According to historians Good and Jones, "Kerensky believed Babushka's unique stature among the peasants made her the ideal representative to send to the countryside to explain the Provisional Government's land and war policies."[54] Consequently, she was soon provided with a railway car and toured several provinces, making frequent speeches in favour of Kerensky and generally supporting the Provisional Government. Not content with mere speech making, Breshkovskaia also established a publishing house that by mid-summer had printed over four million brochures.[55] As her party became factionalized, she also drew on a million-dollar donation from an American admirer to fund other ventures that publicized Right Socialist Revolutionary viewpoints.

While historians have paid some attention to Breshkovskaia's propagandizing efforts during the revolution, they have not discussed the visual materials that celebrated her role in revolutionary movements and that publicized her image to the peasantry. Breshkovskaia herself had long realized the power of photography. During her arrest in 1874, tsarist officials asked to take her photograph; Breshkovskaia responded by closing her eyes and pulling a face. As she writes in *Hidden Springs of the Russian Revolution*, "In the course of my long life, I was to undergo this same procedure several times, and I always, during the first months of my imprisonment, refused to be photographed. This gave my friends time to hear of my arrest and to think things out before there was an opportunity for searches and inquiries."[56] Apart from concern for co-conspirators, it was also important to control the dissemination of images of revolutionaries so that they could have the correct impression on the masses. In Breshkovskaia's case, her history of arrest, imprisonment, and exile seems to have resonated sympathetically with the intended audience, even if some of its members were repulsed by Breshkovskaia's actual physical appearance. A passage from future Nobel laureate Ivan Bunin's diary records a conversation that he overheard in the summer of 1917. A group of peasants were discussing Breshkovskaia, mixing fact and fiction:

> The owner of the hut says in a measured way: "I've heard about this old lady for quite some time. She's a soothsayer, that's for sure. The word on her is that she's been predicting all these goings-on for the past fifty years. But God help us, she's really beastly looking: fat, angry, with very small, penetrating eyes – I once saw her portrait in a feuilleton. She was chained up in a stockade for forty-two years, but they couldn't hold her back: even in the stockade she managed to get hold of a million rubles!"[57]

Breshkovskaia's image was disseminated in a number of ways, including in a feature film by Aleksandr Drankov's studio in 1917.[58] Her likeness also appeared on a number of picture postcards. Most referred to her as the "Grandmother of the Russian Revolution" in their captions and used photographs that emphasized her advanced age (see Figure 7.16).

As revolutionary symbols, these images of Breshkovskaia drew upon the same traditions that were linked to her rival Spiridonova, the visual personification of the Left Socialist Revolutionaries. Breshkovskaia, too, was a martyr-heroine who had adopted an ascetic lifestyle, only her asceticism was even more extreme than Spiridonova's for she had dramatically renounced family happiness when she turned her infant son over to relatives to be raised. One of the greatest ironies of revolutionary myth making was that Breshkovskaia, depicted as the grandmother of the entire movement and of its members, had forsaken her own biological child. The importance of her work is further underscored in other postcards. For instance, Figure 7.17 is a particularly interesting and personal composition.

The postcard reproduces a sample of her handwriting – the text exhorts the people to elect deputies who will give them land and freedom – and shows her working at a desk. The papers covering the desk as well as the dark background suggest she may have been engaged for some time, and the entire scene is reminiscent of what Peter Burke refers to as the image of the "ruler as bureaucrat."[59] Breshkovskaia's stance co-opts a position of power and the legitimacy of traditional governing elites.

Breshkovskaia was, indeed, elected as a deputy to the Constituent Assembly, but by then power had already slipped from the grasp of any of the Right Socialist Revolutionaries. After the Bolshevik seizure of power, the country's new leaders moved quickly to silence Breshkovskaia. Her publishing ventures were shut down one by one, and she chose to go underground rather than openly oppose the Bolsheviks. She eventually left Russia, stopping briefly in the United States (long enough to testify in front of the U.S. Senate concerning Bolshevism), before finally settling in Czechoslovakia, in the summer of 1919. She died in 1934.

Bolshevik Revolutionary Narrative

No discussion of picture postcards and the Russian Revolution would be complete without addressing Bolshevik efforts in this sphere, particularly since these were the years when the Bolsheviks established their claim to political legitimacy, in part, by spelling out their own revolutionary narrative. Unlike the Socialist Revolutionaries, who immediately

7.16 Breshkovskaia, the "Grandmother of the Russian Revolution." No manufacturer or date listed.

7.17 Breshkovskaia at work. Produced by the publishing firm D. Khromov and B. Bakhrakh (Moscow), n.d.

focused their publicity campaigns around images of key leaders, the earliest Bolshevik postcards harkened back to other aspects of the Russian revolutionary tradition by featuring photographs of 1917 funeral processions like the one in Figure 7.18.

Funerals had long served political purposes in socialist circles. Wilhelm Liebknecht's funeral, in August 1900, was the first such public event. An active member of the International, Liebknecht's demise connected a large demonstration with fundraising opportunities. Picture postcards with his portrait or featuring photographs of the funeral procession were soon on sale.[60] Similarly large public processions were arranged following the funerals of Ignaz Auer, Paul Singer, and Paul and Laura Lafargue. This tradition of the socialist movement fit well with established conventions of the Russian intelligentsia, whose members regularly held large funerals or commemorative events to honour Russian cultural icons. Funerals were also the only legal private demonstrations in the tsarist era.

In 1917, they had an added importance for, as Catherine Merridale notes, they were "an opportunity no politician could ignore, a chance to claim the bodies for the cause and turn their blood into a sacrifice, a

7.18. Funeral of revolutionaries killed in Helsingfors (Helsinki) in 1917. Manufactured by Kustannusliike Vapaus, n.d.

secular communion."[61] It was an effective strategy. The events resonated with revolutionaries of all stripes. Pitrim Sorokin's diary, for example, contains a very positive reaction to a revolutionary funeral:

> Today was held the funeral of the victims who died for the Revolution. What a moving spectacle. Hundreds of thousands of people moving behind thousands of red and black banners with the words: "Glory to Those Who Perished for Liberty." Marvelous music, voices, and bands joining in the funeral hymn. Perfect order and discipline as for hours the endless procession wound through the streets. The faces of the marchers were solemn and uplifted. Such a crowd thrills me. It is so human.[62]

These were the words of a university professor, member of the Socialist Revolutionary party, and eventually, an active opponent of the Bolsheviks throughout the civil war era. However, the funeral is clearly presented by Sorokin as a moment when all revolutionary factions overcame their differences to honour their dead.

Apart from commemorating the sacrifices of revolutionary martyrs, funerals celebrating those killed during the October Revolution, such as the victims of street fighting in Moscow, allowed the country's new leaders to lay claim to, and create, new sacred spaces. The victims mentioned above, for instance, were buried on Red Square. Their graves were situated at the very heart of Soviet power, since they bridged the gap between the Kremlin Wall and Lenin's Mausoleum, once it had been constructed. In Petrograd, fallen revolutionaries were laid to rest with elaborate festivities in the Field of Mars, quite close to the tsarist seat of power, the Winter Palace. By devising these separate cemeteries for their fallen comrades, the Bolshevik leadership was able to denote them as more than just mere mortals.

Other postcards were made that gave living soldiers a place in this new heroic narrative. Figure 7.19 shows two Red Guards in Sverdlovsk in 1918. In what appears to be a staged photograph, the men stare intensely into the camera and are equipped with a variety of weapons. They are presented as determined Bolshevik supporters although neither man is particularly physically imposing. Such an image – which celebrated the common soldier – legitimized Bolshevik claims concerning the depth of their support and the nature of their party's constituency. Eliisa Vaha has written that for the October Revolution to be labelled as a foundation event, it had to be "held up as a landmark in the history of humankind and the event that separated the Soviet people from other nations of the world."[63] Consequently, commemorations of the October Revolution, as well as of the Russian Civil War, became in postcard form components of Soviet popular culture and its unique historical narrative.

It was not until well into 1918, however, that Bolshevik postcards also began to lay claim to the general pantheon of Russian revolutionary heroes or to single out the image of Lenin for special attention. For the first anniversary of the Bolshevik seizure of power, the Central Bureau on the Organization Celebrating the First Anniversary of the October Revolution (Tsentral'noe biuro po organizatsiii prazdnestv pervoi godovshchiny Oktiabr'skoi revoliutsii) created postcards reminiscent of those circulated in 1905. Portraits of Marx, Engels, and Lassalle were all included in this series.[64] The year also saw the emergence of the first postcards bearing Lenin's likeness, thereby identifying him as a key leader to the masses. The postcards provided basic information, in visual form, about the major events in Lenin's life prior to the revolution. They also occasionally used photographs from the Okhrana archives to do so.[65] Such images defined Lenin as an active opponent of the old regime

7.19 "Red Guard Types," Sverdlovsk, 1918. Manufactured by Izd. "Ural'sk oblast-nogo muzeia revoliutsii," n.d.

and cast his life in heroic terms. The postcards also marked the beginnings of the Lenin cult, which would so visibly explode after his death, in 1924.[66]

Émigrés and the Debate Abroad

In part, the Bolsheviks felt pressured to develop visual propaganda because as long as the civil war continued, and especially while foreign intervention troops remained on Russian soil, they faced ongoing threats from a variety of forces. Those groups, in turn, often relied on picture postcards to disseminate their anti-Bolshevik messages. Research by Tobie Mathew has revealed that while the White Volunteer Army merely designed a handful of propaganda postcards, other opponents of the new regime like nationalists looking for their independence, the Allied Expeditionary Force, and the Czechoslovak Legion in Siberia, or non-Bolshevik revolutionary parties continued to produce them in significant numbers. Most anti-Bolshevik postcards were created in peripheral regions of the former empire such as Finland, the Baltic states, and the Far East as well as by the pro-German government briefly established in Ukraine. "These areas," writes Mathew, "had easier access to raw materials and were at certain periods in a far stronger position to print postcards than the White Army in southern Russia."[67] Because people in other countries had a hard time understanding why their forces were fighting the Bolsheviks, particularly after the final armistice ended the First World War, visual materials were needed to explain who the new enemies were.[68] The postcards stereotyped the Bolsheviks as criminals whose leadership would certainly ruin the country and possibly threatened democracies and market economies elsewhere in Europe. The threat of a spreading revolution was a real one. In April 1919, the Bavarian Soviet Republic was proclaimed. It was soon joined by similar entities in Hungary and Slovakia. While none of these Soviet-styled regimes lasted long, they did indicate that Soviet ideas were popular, particularly in places facing political and economic collapse. Hence, postcards of atrocities committed by the Bolsheviks were quickly produced and dispersed as widely as possible as were a few postcards satirizing leaders such as Lenin and Trotsky.

Russian émigrés jumped into the fray. A host of Russians followed the retreating German armies in the winter of 1918–19. They were joined by Cossacks and the remnants of the White armies after these were defeated in 1920–21. Finally, once the contours of Soviet life became increasingly clear, many liberals and members of defeated socialist parties moved westward to escape persecution. With these disparate groups came ongoing political debate. Both monarchists and socialists alike continued to struggle against the new Soviet government, targeting both Russian and non-Russian audiences for support. At this point, most Russian émigrés viewed their exile as temporary. Marc Raeff, whose *Russia Abroad: A Cultural History of the Russian Emigration, 1919–1939* provides one of the best portraits of this era, explains that the refugees believed they were following a pattern established by earlier political émigrés.[69] It was assumed that moving abroad would give them a better chance to keep fighting, since they would have access to printers. Residence in Germany had an added benefit in those early years: a common border with Russia that would facilitate the smuggling of illegal literature. In the words of historian Robert Williams, "With the end of the Russian Civil War and the apparent triumph of the Bolsheviks, the written words became a substitute for political activity and at the same time a means of putting the case for or against the Soviet regime before the emigration."[70] Indeed, publishing ventures sprang up wherever sizeable Russian communities formed, with the most important centres being Berlin, Paris, Prague, and Harbin. Smaller outposts were established in Belgrade, Riga, and Sofia. They, too, had vibrant literary scenes.

Historians such as Raeff and Williams, as well as Paul Robinson in his study of White soldiers in exile and Elizabeth White in her account of the Socialist Revolutionaries in Czechoslovakia, have emphasized the degree to which Russian émigrés isolated themselves from their host societies.[71] Venturing beyond the literary works and political newspapers of the era, however, suggests isolation may not have been as total as we have been led to believe. Picture postcards, especially ones produced from 1918 to 1922, tell a different story. They show a continuing effort to create a cultural dialogue that would engage non-Russians in Russian affairs. As such, the postcards harken back to 1904–05, when Breshkovskaia and others toured the United States to create a positive impression of Russian "freedom fighters" and to drum up financial assistance for the revolutionary movement, or to the post-1907 period when Nicholas II's consistent efforts to thwart the proper functioning of the Duma received much publicity in European newspapers and postcards. Now opponents of the Bolshevik regime used picture postcards to undermine the new state by highlighting the brutality of its leaders to foreign audiences. For instance, Figure 7.20 is a postcard of Ia.I.

Triapitsyn, apparently convalescing in a hospital bed.[72] Whereas the Russian caption simply reads, "Commander of the Red Army in the city of Nikolaevsk on the Amur," the English-language caption has been greatly embellished in an effort to undermine any sympathy the viewer might have had for the man. It says, "J.I. Triapitzin, under whose command Nikolaevsk on Amur has been burned down and citizens have been murdered by the Red Army."

The violent nature of the new Bolshevik regime is also underscored on a postcard (see Figure 7.21) showing some of the thirty-four Socialist Revolutionaries who were put on trial in Moscow from 8 June to 7 August 1922. Within Soviet Russia, the trial was surrounded by a vehement campaign justifying the destruction of the Socialist Revolutionary party.[73] A special agitation committee was even established in order to provide the press with materials on a daily basis. Protests against the trial were mounted abroad by émigré members of the party as well as by foreign socialists. The Socialist Revolutionaries based in Berlin, for example, reached out to German socialists and even Iulii Martov's Mensheviks. As early as April 1922, they lobbied members of a conference of European socialists to create a "united front" against the new Soviet government.[74] This postcard is an interesting, and previously unnoted, part of the effort. It played on Western sympathies in a number of ways. By using French – as opposed to Russian – for the text, the postcard had a wider audience and appeal. Furthermore, the defendants shown in the image are not pictured as bomb-throwing terrorists or sinister individuals, but as a well-dressed, calm but serious group of people. The defendants can be identified by the list of names on one side of the composition, so they become individuals, not just anonymous members of a revolutionary group. Their plight is further emphasized by the remaining words on the postcard. The text says that from the moment they fell into Bolshevik hands, the arrested Socialist Revolutionaries were convinced they would be executed and they will not ask for mercy.

Twelve defendants were, indeed, given death sentences. However, in January 1924, it was announced by the Soviet authorities that all of the sentences were hereby reduced and no one would be executed. Those who protested the trial abroad took credit for this modest victory. Vladimir Zenzinov, who sat on the board of the Paris-based Union of Russian Writers and Journalists, for example, claimed, "In my opinion, the campaign that we unleashed in Europe at the time saved the lives of our comrades."[75]

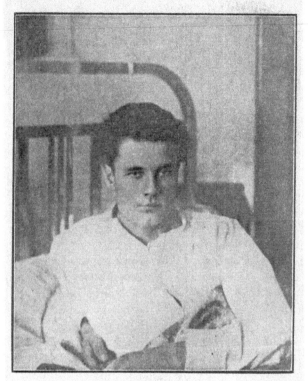

Я. И. ТРЯПИЦЫНЪ,
командовавшій красной арміей въ гор. Николаевскѣ на Амурѣ.

J. I. TRIAPITZIN,
under whose command Nikolaevsk on Amur has been burned
down and citizens have been murdered by the Red Army.

7.20 Triapitzin. No manufacturer or date listed.

Procès des Socialistes-Révolutionnaires à Moscou.

En haut:
1. M. Wedeniapin.
2. N. Artemiev.
3. N. Jdanov
         (avocat).
4. M. Lvoff.
5. A. Wauters
         (avocat).
6. E. Timofeev.
7. C. Rosenfeld
         (avocat).
8. P. Zlobin.

En bas:
1. D. Donskoi.
2. E. Ratner.
3. E. Vandervelde
         (avocat).
4. A. Gotz.

„Dès le moment même où nous sommes tombés entre vos mains il n'y avait aucun doute pour nous que vous nous condamnerez à mort Il nous est parfaitement indifférent, si vous allez nous amnistier ou non Mais une demande de grâce ne partira jamais de ces bancs."

7.21 The trial of the Socialist Revolutionaries in Moscow. No manufacturer or date listed.

Conclusion

By the mid-1920s, the Soviet regime had consolidated its grip on power, silenced most of its political opponents, and standardized the narrative that was told about the revolution. Images that complicated the picture by offering alternative versions, or that mentioned the role of now discredited political opponents, were abandoned. This chapter has recaptured some of that lost imagery. Examining the picture postcards created by various opposition groups from 1905 to 1922 deepens our understanding of how revolutionary groups depicted themselves as they sought to win adherents and, ultimately, political power. The postcards demonstrate how Russia's revolutionaries created a new pantheon of heroes, and put forward rival candidates for that status. They further show how the events of 1917 came to be chronicled and interpreted in visual form.

Picture Postcards
across the Revolutionary Divide

On 14 October 1941, Soviet art historian and critic Nikolai Punin received a postcard relaying some important news from his former wife, the famous poet Anna Akhmatova. The postcard informed Punin that another cultural icon known to both of them, the poet Marina Tsvetaeva, had committed suicide.[1] That Akhmatova chose to convey her news via a postcard was not particularly surprising for the Punin family had sent important communications that way for decades, most notably during Punin's first and last arrests in 1921 and 1951, respectively. Like pre-revolutionary political prisoners, the jailed Punin was often restricted to postcards for his correspondence with friends and relatives.[2]

The use of postcards by political prisoners is just one of a number of continuities between the pre- and post-revolutionary eras. The pages that follow will briefly describe some of the others. To begin with, like the Romanovs before them, Soviet leaders turned to popular media to bolster support in times of political instability. Picture postcards were an integral part of the early cult of Lenin, when portraits of him served as a legitimizing force for the regime. By the late 1920s, however, postcards of Lenin had served their purpose and been superseded by others bearing the likeness of a new generation of political leaders, including Stalin. Nor were Politburo members the country's only celebrities. As the 1930s progressed, a plethora of new heroes and heroines emerged in popular culture. As they had when celebrity culture was a new phenomenon, postcards again played an important role in constructing the images of famous pilots, shock workers, and cultural luminaries. They also, via photographs of athletes, continued to eroticize the bodies of women, although it must be admitted, in a less blatant fashion than pre-revolutionary erotic postcards had done. Finally, postcards actively publicized the reconstruction of the Soviet landscape. Like their tsarist predecessors, Soviet postcards contained maps and symbols of state that claimed control over contested regions, and they catalogued the massive infrastructure projects the new regime was undertaking to modernize the country.

Postcards, Political Legitimacy, and the Cult of Lenin

In 1918, Fania Kaplan's attempted assassination of Lenin changed the way that the country's leader was presented in the media. That event, to quote Soviet historian Dmitri Volkogonov, "suddenly brought home to the Party leadership just how much Lenin meant to them."[3] The realization was reflected in a concentrated upsurge of materials about Lenin in the press and led to his being praised extravagantly for the first time. Lenin's deep dislike of this kind of publicity was emphatically ignored.[4] Postcards joined in by having special series link Lenin to the established pantheon of great Marxist theoreticians and by publicizing his past revolutionary activities for the first time. A number of manufacturers – including the Moscow-based book-publishing firm Kommunist as well as the Petrograd firm Ukrainian Commune (Ukrainskaia kommuna) – copied portraits of Lenin by M.S. Nappelbaum and P.S. Otsup for their postcards.[5] The pictures, which were taken in Lenin's office in the Smolny Institute in St. Petersburg and the Kremlin in Moscow, respectively, provided iconic images that became the mainstays of the cult in years to come. By showing Lenin reading newspapers or working at his desk, the photographs tapped into a familiar trope: the "ruler as bureaucrat" pose we have already encountered in connection with postcards of leading Socialist Revolutionaries.

In 1922, Lenin suffered his first stroke and his health remained precarious from that point until his death, in January 1924. Photographs and visual materials like postcards were used to deceive the public about the seriousness of the situation so that political stability could be maintained while the remaining leaders determined what to do in light of Lenin's incapacity. While they jockeyed for position behind the scenes, the public was led to believe Lenin was still at his desk handling the day-to-day governance of the country.

When Lenin died, picture postcards assumed a new purpose. They became part of the official mourning process. Commemorative postcards, including some special albums, were rushed into production. Centralized control over their creation was facilitated by two decrees

E.1 Funeral procession in Lenin's honour. Photograph taken on 27 January 1924 in Leningrad's Square of Fallen Revolutionaries. No manufacturer or date listed.

issued by the Central Executive Committee in the first half of the year. One ordered all photographers with Lenin materials to turn them over to the Lenin Institute, while the other made it a criminal offence to make or sell portraits of Lenin without the permission of the Commission for the Immortalization of the Memory of V.I. Ul'ianov (Lenin). These orders ensured the growing cult of Lenin would be directed to serve the political purposes of his heirs. Old Bolsheviks Grigorii Zinoviev and Lev Kamenev were particularly keen to base their bids for power on their long-standing relationships with Lenin, so they fostered the development of his cult.[6]

Picture postcards proved useful when it came to documenting Lenin's funeral (see Figure E.1). As we have seen, seriality had long been a feature of postcard production. Now numbered series of postcards showed all the stages of Lenin's funeral as well as the mass response to it. They

E.2 The Lenin Mausoleum. Izdanie Moskovskogo kommunal'nogo khoziaistva, 1925.

legitimized the regime at this moment of crisis by portraying the event as one that sparked an outpouring of grief across the nation and united the population to face the challenges ahead.

Later postcards recorded the construction of Lenin's Tomb. The process lasted until 1930 when the red-and-black granite mausoleum was finally completed. However, even the earlier wooden monuments had served a purpose: they anchored Lenin's body (the most sacred relic of the cult), as well as his weight as a political symbol, to the Kremlin in Moscow.

In many of the postcards, like the one in Figure E.2 from 1925, parts of the Kremlin itself are clearly visible in the background, and such images were repeated time and again. For example, *Izdanie Moskovskogo kummunal'nogo khoziaistva* reprinted the exact same image the following year. The postcards, which frequently showed long queues of people waiting to see the preserved body, implied an imagined community – one where the population was in perpetual mourning and devoted to the Soviet state – existed. The left edge of the postcard in Figure E.3

E.3 A view of the Lenin Mausoleum. Soiuzfoto-Fotokhudoznik, 1938.

shows one of these queues in 1938. The unknown foreigner who jotted down impressions of his or her visit to the mausoleum on the back of the postcard noted that the line was half a mile long and five deep that day.

Within two years of his death, the nadir of the Lenin cult had been reached. As the political climate changed – notably, Zinoviev and Kamenev suffered a series of defeats at the 12th and 13th Party Congresses – the cult of Lenin came to be downgraded and eventually superseded. Fewer postcards with his portraits were issued as Lenin's image as a source of political legitimacy was needed less and less. By the time the First Five-Year Plan was announced, the country had a new generation of political leaders to celebrate. Postcards of Stalin, as in Figure E.4, as well as ones of other Soviet leaders now came to the fore.

The legacy of this outpouring of postcards had to be a mixed one, probably proving no more effective in generating mass loyalty than the similar barrage launched by the Romanovs in the fin-de-siècle era. Not everyone collected postcards with the gusto of the most well-known

E.4 Portrait of Stalin. Izdanie Muzeia Revoliutsii Soiuza SSR, 1930.

Soviet collector, Nikolai Tagrin, who over the course of his fifty-year career amassed more than forty thousand postcards that he could connect
in some way or other to Lenin.[7] Other memoirists and diarists left scathing comments about portraits of Lenin, often drawing on the racialized
discourse of the nineteenth century to express their hatred of the
Bolsheviks and especially Lenin. Professor Pitrim Sorokin remarked that
Lenin's face "reminds me of those congenital criminals in the albums of
Lombroso," while writer Ivan Bunin declared, "even in ancient times
there was a universal hatred for people with red hair and high cheek-
bones."[8] In his diary entry, Bunin went on to outline the physical characteristics of the "born criminal" before asking the rhetorical question,
"How can one not recall this when one thinks of Lenin and thousands
like him?" More innocent criticism of the Lenin cult's visual aspects is
perhaps best expressed by Mary Britnieva's son during his mid-1920s
visit to the USSR. Pointing to one of the many Lenin portraits he had
seen, the boy asked, "Why do they have that ugly face stuck everywhere,
mummy?" His embarrassed, and somewhat fearful, mother quickly
hushed him and led him away.[9] Despite the wide-ranging responses they
generated, millions of picture postcards with portraits of Soviet leaders
continued to be printed until the regime itself collapsed.

Celebrity Culture – Soviet Style

Soviet political leaders were not the only ones to receive this kind of
publicity. Celebrity culture returned in full force in the 1930s as a generation of film stars, aviators, arctic explorers, and Stakhanovites came to
the fore. The heroic pantheon seemingly offered something for everyone since it embraced both men and women engaged in all kinds of
activities.

Female celebrities, who will be the focus of this short discussion,
emerged at a time when women in Soviet propaganda changed from being symbols of backwardness to blazing beacons of modernity. Their very
public devotion to Stalin, as well as to the current political system and its
embodiment in the Soviet nation, meant female celebrities also served
to legitimize the regime. As Elena Shulman writes concerning the
Khetagurovites (women who responded to a 1937 call in *Komsomol'skaia
Pravda* to go and develop the Soviet Far East), "These women exemplified and facilitated the rise of a new model of womanhood based on an
explicit link to Soviet civilization-building on the peripheries. Such
women appeared as active subjects in official culture precisely in the
second half of the 1930s."[10] Nor were Khetagurovites the only women to

have their images manipulated this way; the exploits of female pilots, too, underpinned Soviet attempts at nation building. In the mid-1930s, public interest in aviation reached a fever pitch, and Soviet media regularly trumpeted the records set by women in flying, gliding, and parachute jumping (see Figure E.5). Soon the figure of the female pilot became a strong staple of Soviet propaganda.

The fanfare reached a crescendo in 1938 when the all-female crew of the *Rodina* established a new long-distance flight record by flying from Moscow to the Far East. Despite the fact the women crash-landed before reaching their final objective, their adventure was publicized via daily newspaper coverage, books in both Russian and English, and a documentary film. Their likenesses were reproduced on a political poster, a series of postage stamps, and a picture postcard.[11] The goal behind this publicity was to convince twenty thousand women to join aviation circles. That was the target set by Osoaviakhim, the Soviet Union's paramilitary organization.[12] Many women did flock to aviation over the course of the decade: between a quarter and a third of the pilots trained by Soviet air clubs in the 1930s were women.[13]

For women who were not attracted to such extreme pursuits, other role models were developed. The life stories of the most outstanding female Stakhanovites were publicized, and similar narratives were woven into Soviet feature films. Like the publicity that surrounded and typecast Vera Kholodnaia in the pre-revolutionary era, the best-known Soviet actresses, too, had picture personalities created for them. Liubov' Orlova is a good example, although the same could be said for Valentina Serova, Marina Ladynina, or Vera Maretskaia. First noticed for her role in the 1934 feature *Happy Guys* (*Veselye rebiata*), platinum blonde Orlova starred in a series of films directed by her husband Grigorii Aleksandrov, including *Circus* (*Tsirk*, 1936), *Volga-Volga* (1938), and *The Radiant Path* (*Svetlyi put'*, 1940). She was said to be Stalin's favourite actress.[14] In the first decade of her career, Orlova usually played slightly naïve but well-intentioned heroines. Full of comedic misunderstandings, her films also featured chaste Soviet romances as well as heroes who worked hard, and frequently excelled, at their jobs. A touch of glamour crept into *Circus*, where Orlova played the lavishly dressed circus performer Marion Dixon, and into *The Radiant Path*, after her Stakhanovite character was rewarded for her work with luxury material goods. Hence, while Orlova's characters could be imagined as ordinary Soviet women, their lives also contained attractive fairy-tale elements. In other words, Orlova's picture personality fulfilled a similar function to that of Vera Kholodnaia by presenting women with an idealized world of consumption. Figure E.6, a montage

E.5 *Young Girl – Pilot* (*Devushka-Pilot*) sculpture included in the All-Union Art Exhibition "Industry of Socialism." Iskusstvo, 1940.

E.6 Liubov' Orlova. Izdanie Biuro propagandy sovetskogo kinoiskusstva, n.d.

E.7 Physical culture parade on Red Square in 1932. No manufacturer or date listed.

showing Liubov' Orlova in some of her most famous roles, reminds us that the construction of picture personalities extended beyond the screen, even in the Soviet era.

Soviet Bodies on Display

On May Day in 1931, Red Square played host to its first, and definitely not its last, sports display. The annual physical culture day parade ballooned in size as the decade progressed. From forty thousand participants in 1931, the parade grew to 120,000 people in 1934 and 1935, before settling back to forty thousand per year from 1937 to 1940.[15] Some sense of the spectacle can be garnered from the postcard that is Figure E.7, where tiny and tightly packed groups of athletes gather in front of the Lenin Mausoleum and the Kremlin walls. What this aerial photograph hides, however, is the extent to which these parades were

E.8 Uzbek delegation to the 1937 All-Union Physical Culture Parade in Moscow. Soiuzfoto, n.d.

opportunities to put Soviet bodies on view and how eroticized interpretations could be generated from at least some of the displays.

It is worth remembering at this point that while the Soviet regime fixated on corporeality in the 1930s, thereby linking private bodies to state ideology, it did so in a way that was meant to be as chaste as possible.[16] Party authorities frowned upon the viewing of pornographic images throughout the Soviet era. As historian Julianne Fürst explains, "As an expression of personal pleasure and an activity devolved from the control of youth authorities, it was as subversive as outright opposition."[17] Indeed, nudes ceased to be produced in official Soviet culture, with the sole exception of a few paintings and sculptures of nude athletes. Otherwise, the kinds of images discussed in chapter 4 were meant to disappear.[18] Under these circumstances, scholars like Mikhail Zolotonosov have suggested that statues of nude athletes took over the role previously played by pornographic postcards.[19]

Всесоюзный физкультурный парад 1937г в Москве. гимнастические упражнения физкультурниц Узбекской ССР на Красной площади   фото С.Лоскутова 255996

E.9 Uzbek delegation to the 1937 All-Union Physical Culture Parade in Moscow. Soiuzfoto, n.d.

It is also possible that postcards continued to provide some erotic stimulation even if the bodies they showed were no longer completely nude. The postcards that are Figures E.8 and E.9 illustrate this. Both show Uzbek women participating in the 1937 All-Union Physical Culture Parade in Moscow. This was the first time groups from all of the non-Russian republics were part of the parade, and it was organized as a symbol of national unity. To quote *Pravda*'s coverage of the event, "the physical culture parade did not just show the successes and achievements of sportsmen, but also [it] was a political demonstration of the unity and cohesion of the peoples of the Soviet Union."[20] The participation of young Muslim women – who appeared without veils and with parts of their upper bodies bare – was meant to signify their adoption of Soviet values on the way to becoming exemplary New Soviet Women. However, the images on the postcards are erotically charged in several ways. First, as some viewers of the parade as well as purchasers of the postcards must surely have been aware, this was a time when violent assaults continued against Muslim women who sought to reject traditional mores.[21] These attacks were often described in the central press and, certainly, in Soviet periodicals for women. Perhaps the knowledge that one could openly see what Muslim men were so desperate to keep hidden added a frisson of titillation to viewing these images. But, even viewers who were not particularly well versed in Central Asian developments could certainly look at these postcards, as well as others showing sportswomen from other parts of the USSR, and see tight clothing framing the women's bodies. Here, clothing did not conceal but rather underscored sexuality. In the second postcard, in particular, this is the case, for the women's tank tops are stretched across their chests, hugging and highlighting their breasts. While not so blatant as some prerevolutionary erotic postcards, these examples demonstrate that women's bodies continued to be objectified and commodified long after the revolution that had supposedly emancipated them.

Soviet Visions Transform Space into Territory

In 1935, German Communist Wolfgang Leonhard visited Moscow with his parents. The trio, who had only an old map from 1924, bought a newer version to guide them as they explored the city. That map included changes to be implemented according to the official plan for the reconstruction of Moscow, even though not all of the projects were due to be completed until 1945. Imagine their confusion. "We used to take both town plans with us on our walks," Leonhard writes, "one showing what Moscow had looked like ten years before, the other showing what it would look like in ten years hence."[22] Like their tsarist predecessors, it is clear from this example that Soviet leaders understood the power of maps and popular media to influence people's ideas of spatial geography.

The same year that Leonhard and his parents were stumbling around Moscow, the NKVD (Narodnyi komissariat vnutrennykh del) took over Soviet cartography. Putting the secret police in charge of maps and mapmaking indicates how important the subject was to the Soviet leadership. Once again, maps and other symbols of state were used to conceptualize and consolidate the borders (as well as the imagined community) of the nation. It became a common trope to include such items on postcards commemorating arctic expeditions and record-breaking long-distance flights. In terms of the first, it is worth remembering that in the late 1920s, official international boundaries had yet to be fixed in the arctic.

E.10. "Heroes of the Soviet Union – Conquerors of the North Pole." No manufacturer or date listed.

Hence, postcards were part of a multipronged effort to assert Soviet territorial claims in that region. On the postcard in Figure E.10, whose caption reads, "Heroes of the Soviet Union – Conquerors of the North Pole," ownership is symbolized by the heavy line tracing the route from Moscow to the pole and by the flags planted there.

The same design features appear in the postcard in Figure E.11, which was included in a commemorative set called *Shining Victories of Soviet Aviation* (*Blestiashchaia pobeda sovetskoi aviatsii*) in celebration of the July 1937 transpolar flight of Mikhail Gromov, Andrei Iumashev, and Sergei Danilin.[23] Feats such as these – in addition to the propaganda materials they spawned – reminded other nations of Soviet claims in the north and projected an image of technological prowess and modernity.

Nor were they unique. The first two decades of Soviet power were rife with construction projects connecting industrial development to control

E.11 Postcard celebrating a transpolar flight. Iskusstvo, 1937.

E.12 A dam under construction at Volkhovstroi. V.M.S. RKKA, n.d.

of the landscape. From the smallest power plant to the most ambitious railway, these projects were, to quote Emma Widdis, "acts of surveying – the transformation of space (the unknown) into territory (the known and mapped)."[24] As the sample of images included here reveals, in every case, picture postcards were issued to document the changes being wrought. Figure E.12 shows a dam being built at Volkhovstroi. Completed in 1927 under the supervision of G.O. Graftio, the Volkhov hydroelectric station provided power to Leningrad and was a component of Lenin's plan to electrify the country.[25]

A second postcard (see Figure E.13) shows a train carrying slag from a blast furnace. It records the development of Magnitostroi, a new coal and metallurgical works constructed with great fanfare in the Urals in the 1930s.[26] The economic importance of the region was emphasized in the information printed on the back of the postcard: it stated that

E.13 Magnitostroi. Izd. Ural'skogo oblastnogo komiteta VLKSM, n.d.

Magnitostroi would generate 2.5 million tons of cast iron per year.

Finally, Figure E.14 provides information about the Stalin White Sea to Baltic Sea Canal (Belomorsko–Baltiiskiiy Kanal imeni Stalina, or Belomor Canal). A signature project of the First Five-Year Plan, the now-infamous canal was built by forced labourers in only twenty months and officially opened in August 1933.[27]

As was the case in the pre-revolutionary era, postcards such as these noted with great pride the investment in impressive infrastructure, particularly in underdeveloped areas. Such projects were hallmarks of modernity and expressed a Soviet form of economic nationalism. These continuities, like those noted earlier, show that Soviet visual culture relied heavily on tropes developed before the revolution. Picture postcards, as one of the cheapest and easiest forms of propaganda to produce, were positively vital to the regime as it sought to build a new society,

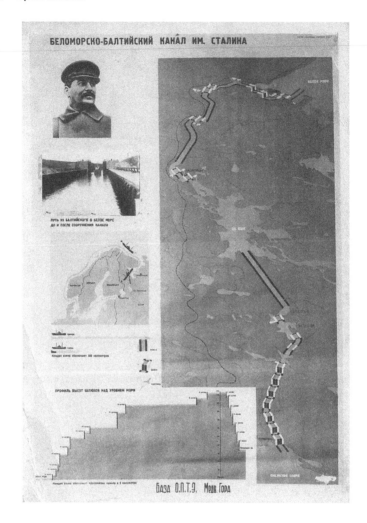

E.14 The Belomor Canal. No manufacturer or date listed.

one that was to be inhabited by the New Soviet Man and Woman. To do justice to that subject, a more in-depth study of picture postcards in the Soviet era needs its own volume. Perhaps, this study of pre-revolutionary postcards will inspire someone to take up that task.

Notes

Introduction

1 Tim Jon Semmerling, *Israeli and Palestinian Postcards: Presentations of National Self* (Austin: University of Texas Press, 2004).

2 Claudia Verhoeven, *The Odd Man Karakozov: Imperial Russia, Modernity and the Birth of Terrorism* (Ithaca: Cornell University Press, 2009), 9.

3 Eric J. Evans and Jeffrey Richards, *A Social History of Britain in Postcards, 1870–1930* (London: Longman, 1980); Hubertus F. Jahn, *Patriotic Culture in Russia during World War I* (Ithaca: Cornell University Press, 1995); Semmerling, *Israeli and Palestinian Postcards*; and the articles in *Delivering Views: Distant Cultures in Early Postcards*, eds. C.M. Geary and V.L. Webb (Washington, DC: Smithsonian Institution Press, 1998) are all good examples.

4 See Richard Carline, *Pictures in the Post*, 2nd ed. (London: Gordon Fraser, 1971); M. Chapkina, *Khudozhestvennaia otkrytka* (Moscow: Galart, 1993); A. Melitonian et al., *Privet iz Moskvy* (Moscow: Magma, 2004); and Frank Staff, *The Picture Postcard and Its Origins* (London: Praeger, 1966).

5 Louise McReynolds, *Russia at Play* (Ithaca: Cornell University Press, 2002); Richard de Cordova, "The Emergence of the Star System in America: An Examination of the Institutional and Ideological Function of the Star, 1907–1922" (Ph.D. diss., University of California at Los Angeles, 1986); and Paul McDonald, *The Star System: Hollywood's Production of Popular Identities* (London: Wallflower, 2000).

6 Christine Ruane, "Clothes Shopping in Imperial Russia: The Development of a Consumer Culture," *Journal of Social History* 28, no. 4 (1995): 765–82.

7 Richard Wortman, *Scenarios of Power: Myth and Ceremony in Russian Monarchy*, vol. II (Princeton: Princeton University Press, 2000); Richard Wortman,

"Publicizing the Imperial Image in 1913," in *Self and Story in Russian History*, eds. L. Engelstein and S. Sandler (Ithaca: Cornell University Press, 2000), 94–119; and Helen Baker, "Monarchy Discredited? Reactions to the Khodynka Coronation Catastrophe of 1896," *Revolutionary Russia* 16, no. 1 (2003): 1–46.

8 Orlando Figes and Boris Kolonitskii, *Interpreting the Russian Revolution: The Language and Symbols of 1917* (New Haven: Yale University Press, 1999).

9 See Richard Williams, *The Contentious Crown: Public Discussion of the British Monarchy in the Reign of Queen Victoria* (Aldershot: Ashgate, 1997); Alexis Schwarzenbach, "Royal Photographs: Emotions for the People," *Contemporary European History* 13, no. 3 (2004): 267–86; and David Cannadine, "The Context, Performance and Meaning of Ritual: The British Monarchy and the 'Invention of Tradition,' c. 1820–1977," in *The Invention of Tradition*, eds. E. Hobsbawm and T. Ranger (Cambridge: Cambridge University Press, 1983), 101–64.

10 Janet Watson, *Fighting Different Wars: Experience, Memory, and the First World War in Britain* (Cambridge: Cambridge University Press, 2004).

11 Mikhail Zolotonosov, *Gliptokpratos: Issledovanie nemnogo diskursa* (St. Petersburg: Inapress, 1999), 19.

1. The Market for Picture Postcards

1 Ilya Ehrenburg, *People and Life, 1891–1921* (New York: Alfred A. Knopf, 1962), 35, 43, and 77.

2 For information on the Russian postal system before the nineteenth century, see M.N. Vitashevskaia, *Starinnaia russkaia pochta* (Moscow: Sviaz' izdat', 1969).

3 O.N. Bukharov, *Marki iz starogo al'boma* (Moscow: Radio i sviaz', 1981), 13.

4 Examples can be seen in ibid., 19.

5 Ibid., 22.

6 Ibid., 27.

7 K.V. Bazilevich, *The Russian Posts in the XIX Century*. Trans. by D. Skipton (Rossica Translation no. 2, 1987), 2.

8 Ibid., 121.

9 Ibid.

10 For a detailed analysis of the problems hampering Russian railway development, see Steven G. Marks, *Road to Power: The Trans-Siberian Railroad and the Colonization of Asian Russia, 1850–1917* (Ithaca: Cornell University Press, 1991).

11 Bazilevich notes that steamships bearing mail were used on the Kama, Oka, Dnepr, Neman, and Sheksna rivers, as well as across lakes Ladoga, Onega, and Chudskoe. Bazilevich, *Russian Posts*, 124.

12 Ibid., 141.

13 N.I. Vladinets, *Filatelisticheskaia geografiia* (Moscow: Radio i sviaz', 1982), 19.

14 Bazilevich, *Russian Posts*, 145.

15 Ibid., 156.

16 There is some evidence that the number of provinces where the first Soviet stamps circulated varied widely from year to year. Mazur gives the following figures: in 1918, the stamps were available in 18 gubernii; in 1919, in 40 gubernii; and in 1920, in 31 gubernii. See P. Mazur, "O pochtovom obrashchenii revoliutsionnykh marok vypuska 1918 goda," *Filateliia SSSR*, no. 12 (1972): 34.

17 N. Safonov and V. Karlinskii, *Pis'mo otpravliaetsia v put': Rasskazy o zarozhdenii i razvitii otechestvennoi pochty* (Moscow: Izdatel'stvo sviaz', 1965), 37.

18 Bukharov, *Marki*, 104.

19 Safonov and Karlinskii, *Pis'mo otpravliaetsia v put'*, 50.

20 On the history of the envelope, see Michael Kernan, "Pushing the Envelope," *Smithsonian Magazine*, http://www.smithsonianmag.si.edu/smithsonian/issues97/oct97/mall_oct97.html. Accessed 18 June 2002.

21 Newsprint costs in the United States, e.g., fell from 25 cents per pound in the 1860s to 2 cents per pound in 1897. Susan Strasser, *Waste and Want: A Social History of Trash* (New York: Owl Books, 1999), 91.

22 Beautiful reproductions of these items can be seen in Frank Staff, *The Picture Postcard and Its Origins* (New York: Praeger, 1966).

23 The best book on the subject is William C. Darrah, *Cartes de Visite in Nineteenth-Century Photography* (Gettysburg: privately published, 1981), although Robin and Carol Wichard, *Victorian Cartes-de-Visite* (Risborough: Shire Press, 1999) also provides a solid introduction to the subject. Darrah's collection of 62,608 cartes is housed in the Special Collections Department of the Paterno Library at Pennsylvania State University, University Park, Pennsylvania.

24 Darrah, *Cartes de Visite*, 4.

25 For information about these photographers, see S. Morozov, "Early Photography in Eastern Europe: Russia," *History of Photography* 1, no. 4 (1977): 327–47.

26 The presses of Neue Photographische Gesellschaft, e.g., used continuous rolls of bromide card which were 34 inches wide and printed 50 cards per yard. See W. Turner Berry, "The Picture Postcard Craze," *Graphic Arts Focal Point* (June 1957): 5.

27 Information about the development of the postcard industry can be found in Richard Carline, *Pictures in the Post*, 2nd ed. (London: Gordon Fraser, 1971); Eric J. Evans and Jeffrey Richards, *A Social History of Britain in Postcards, 1870–1930* (London: Longman, 1980); Staff, *Picture Postcard*;

and Howard Woody, "International Postcards: Their History, Production, and Distribution (Circa 1895 to 1915)," in *Delivering Views: Distant Cultures in Early Postcards*, eds. C.M. Geary and V.L. Webb (Washington, DC: Smithsonian Institution Press, 1998), 13–45.

28 In Britain, e.g., at the height of the craze, there were 278 different firms making postcards. See Evans and Richards, *Social History*, 4. In turn-of-the-century France, the postcard industry employed about 30,000 people. See Naomi Schor, "Collecting Paris," in *The Cultures of Collecting*, eds. J. Elsner and R. Cardinal (London: Reaktion Books, 1994), 263.

29 N. Tagrin, *Mir v otkrytke* (Moscow: Izobrazitel'noe iskusstvo, 1978), 33.

30 For additional examples of foldout postcards, see A. Melitonian et al., *Privet iz Moskvy*(Moscow: Magma, 2004), 54–5.

31 On novelty postcards in general, see Staff, *Picture Postcard*, 67–8.

32 One Easter card in my collection was not used until 1951, in other words, decades after it was made.

33 M. Chapkina, *Khudozhestvennaia otkrytka* (Moscow: Galart, 1993), 177.

34 For a good short history of the Society, see G.A. Polikarpova and L.A. Protsai, "Iz istorii izdatel'stva Obshchiny sviatoi Evgenii," in *Izdaniia Obshchiny sviatoi Evgenii* (St. Petersburg: Palace Editions and Graficart, 2008).

35 Tagrin, *Mir v otkrytke*, 50.

36 I.A. Zolotinkina, "Otkrytye pis'ma Obshchiny sviatoi Evgenii i russkaia grafika nachala XX veka," in *Izdaniia Obshchiny sviatoi Evgenii* (St. Petersburg: Palace Editions and Graficart, 2008), 24.

37 A photograph of one of these kiosks can be seen in Polikarpova and Protsai, "Iz istorii izdatel'stva," 11.

38 The competitions are described in Komitet populiarizatsii khudozhestvennykh izdanii, *Za tridtsat' let, 1896–1926* (Leningrad: Author, 1928), 18–21.

39 Quoted in Zolotinkina, "Otkrytye pis'ma Obshchiny," 31.

40 On this phenomenon see Joseph Bradley, "Voluntary Associations, Civic Culture, and Obshchestvennost' in Moscow," in *Between Tsar and People*, eds. E.W. Clowes, S.D. Kassow, and J.L. West (Princeton: Princeton University Press, 1991), 131–48.

41 See Richard Bartmann, *Picture Postcard Encyclopaedia of Russia* (Erlangen: privately published, 1992), entry on "Special Welfare Organisations in Russia."

42 For other examples of Soviet relief postcards, see Iakov Belitskii and Georgii Glezer, *Rasskazy ob otkrytkakh* (Moscow: Radio i sviaz', 1986), 41–2.

43 Nora Lourie Percival, *Weather of the Heart: A Child's Journey Out of Revolutionary Russia* (Boone, NC: High Country Publishers, 2001), 163. Percival's uncle worked for the ARA depot in Samara.

44 A survey of the images reproduced in Anne Goulzadian, *L'empire du dernier Tsar* (Paris: Editions Astrid, 1982), as well as the postcards in my own collec-

tion, revealed at least six booksellers who had postcards printed. One card does not say where the shop was located, but the others were in Tomsk, St. Petersburg, Kremenchug, Tiflis, and Smolensk.

45 D.A. Zasosov and V.I. Pyzin, *Iz zhizni Peterburga 1890–1910x godov* (Leningrad: Lenizdat, 1991), 99.

46 H.V. Keeling, *Bolshevism: Mr. Keeling's Five Years in Russia* (London: Hodder and Stoughton, 1919), 69.

47 Evans and Richards, *Social History*, 3.

48 N. Teleshov, *A Writer Remembers* (London: Hutchinson, 1946), 19.

49 *Sergey Prokofiev Diaries, 1907–1914: Prodigious Youth*, trans. and ed. A. Phillips (Ithaca: Cornell University Press, 2006). The entry for 19 June 1911, e.g., refers to a postcard notifying Prokofiev when two of his works will be performed in Moscow (219).

50 Naomi Schor discusses the association of gender and postcards. "Collecting Paris," 262.

51 On the company's innovative marketing techniques, see chapter 7 of Ruth Brandon, *Singer and the Sewing Machine: A Capitalist Romance* (New York: Kodansha International, 1977).

52 A poster of the same image can be seen, e.g., in A.E. Snopkov et al., *Zhenshchiny v russkom plakate* (Moscow: Kontakt-kul'tura, 2001), 13.

53 Tagrin, *Mir v otkrytke*, 58.

54 Izogiz was renamed the "Iskusstvo" publishing house in 1938 and continued to issue postcards.

55 Examples can be seen in I. Bugaevich, "Otkrytka v arsenale pedagoga," *Sovetskii kollektsioner*, no. 5 (1967): 91–8.

56 For examples, see G.V. Shalimoff and G.B. Shaw (eds.), *Catalogue of Propaganda-Advertising Postal Cards of the USSR, 1927–1934* (Norfolk, VA: United Postal Stationery Society, 2002).

57 Iiakov Belitskii and Georgii Glezer, *Otkrytka prodolzhaet rasskaz* (Moscow: Radio i sviaz', 1982), 101.

58 Edmund Swinglehurst, *Cook's Tours: The Story of Popular Travel* (Poole: Blandford Press, 1982), 71.

59 A collected volume of articles on the history of tourism in Eastern Europe has been edited by Anne Gorsuch and Diane Koenker; however, the publication of that book has not led to an outpouring of new scholarship on tourism. See Anne Gorsuch and Diane Koenker (eds.), *Turizm: The Russian and East European Tourist under Capitalism and Socialism* (Ithaca: Cornell University Press, 2006).

60 The office was closed a year later when its two main employees left in the wake of the revolutions. Their escapes are described in Alden Hatch, *American Express: A Century of Service* (Garden City, NY: Doubleday, 1950), 136–7.

61 See International Sleeping Car and European Express Trains Ry., *Guide for the Use of Travellers to the Far-East by the Trans-Siberian Ry.* (London: Author, 1910); Karl Baedeker, *Baedeker's Russia 1914*, reprint ed. (London: George Allen and Unwin, with David and Charles, 1971); and Stephen Graham, *A Vagabond in the Caucasus* (London: John Lane, 1911).

62 J.H. Wisdom, *The Briton in Russia* (London: Leopold B. Hill, 1915).

63 Ibid., 29–31; Baedeker, *Baedeker's Russia*, xxviii.

64 G.P. Dolzhenko, *Istoriia turizma v dorevoliutsionnoi Rossii i SSSR* (Rostov: Izdatel'stvo Rostovskogo universiteta, 1988), 42.

65 Ibid., 75.

66 On Intourist, see Samantha Kravitz, "The Business of Selling the Soviet Union: Intourist and the Wooing of American Travelers, 1929–1939" (MA thesis, Concordia University, 2006).

67 Turner Berry, "Picture Postcard Craze," 3.

68 Esther Milne, *Letters, Postcards, Email: Technologies of Presence* (New York: Routledge, 2010), 110.

69 Steven Dotterer and Galen Cranz, "The Picture Postcard: Its Development and Role in American Urbanization," *Journal of American Culture* 5, no. 1 (1982): 45.

70 *Prokofiev Diaries, 1907–1914*, 221–2, 257, 272, 303, 306, 307, 310, and 358. These references are just a small sample of the instances where Prokofiev sent postcards to his friends.

71 Ibid., 430.

72 McReynolds was writing about tourist publications but her words are equally applicable to postcards. Louise McReynolds, *Russia at Play* (Ithaca: Cornell University Press, 2003), 155.

73 Ruth Kedzie Wood, *Honeymooning in Russia* (New York: Dodd, Mead, 1911), 24.

74 Marks, *Road to Power*, 199.

75 Ruth Kedzie Wood, *The Tourist's Russia* (New York: Dodd, Mead, 1912), 42.

76 Chapkina, *Khudozhestvennaia otkrytka*, 15.

77 Owen Tweedy, *Russia at Random* (London: Jarrolds, 1931), 32. Tweedy had a three-day shore excursion to St. Petersburg and Moscow as part of a cruise he took in the 1930s.

78 Ibid., 15.

79 See Shalimoff and Shaw, *Catalogue*, 35, 37, 39, and 129.

80 Indeed, some scholars argue that seriality is a defining feature of postcard collecting. See Schor, "Collecting Paris," 255–6.

81 Evans and Richards, *Social History*, 4.

82 Carline, *Pictures in the Post*, 65.

83 Examples can be seen in Bartmann, *Picture Postcard Encyclopaedia*, entry on "Postcard Trade Ties between Russia and Western Europe."

84 V.V. Shleev and E.B. Fainshtein, *Khudozhestvennye otkrytki i ikh sobiranie* (Moscow: Gosudarstvennoe izdatel'stvo izobrazitel'nogo iskusstva, 1960), 29.
85 Our knowledge is further hampered by the fact that through subsequent decades collections, including recently Bartmann's own, have been broken apart and sold off card by card. Today's collectors do not have to have much contact with one another as Internet auctions have increasingly replaced human interaction in the postcard world.
86 On stamp collecting in the USSR, see Jonathan Grant, "The Socialist Construction of Philately in the Early Soviet Era," *Comparative Studies in Society and History* 37, no. 3 (1995): 476–93; Alison Rowley, "Miniature Propaganda: Self-Definition and Soviet Postage Stamps, 1917–41," *Slavonica* 8, no. 2 (2002): 138; and A.N. Sudakov, "Sovetskaia filateliia," in *Sto let russkoi pochtovoi marki, 1858–1958* (Moscow: Sviaz'izdat', 1958).
87 *Zhurnal "Sredi kollektsionerov" (1921–1924) ukazatel' soderzhaniia* (Leningrad: DOK RSFSR, 1986).
88 For information on Soviet postcard collecting in general after the Second World War, see Shleev and Fainshtein, *Khudozhestvennye otkrytki*, 29–31. Today, Tagrin's collection is housed at the State Museum of the History of St. Petersburg (*Gosudarstvennyi muzei istorii Sankt-Peterburga*).
89 Staff, *Picture Postcard*, 47.
90 Bazilevich. *The Russian Posts*, 96.
91 M. Eager, *Six Years at the Russian Court* (London: Hurst and Blackett, 1906), 242–3.
92 Carline, *Pictures in the Post*, 68.
93 David Skipton and Peter Michalove, *Postal Censorship in Imperial Russia*, vol. I (Urbana: John H. Otten, 1989), 96.
94 On the changes in censorship in the wake of the 1905 revolution, see A.F. Berezhnyi, *Tsarskaia tsenzura i bor'ba bol'shevikov za svobody pechati (1895–1914)* (Leningrad: Izdatel'stvo Leningradskogo universiteta, 1967); Caspar Ferenczi, "Freedom of the Press under the Old Regime, 1905–1914," in *Civil Rights in Imperial Russia*, eds. O. Crisp and L. Edmondson (Oxford: Clarendon Press, 1989), 191–214; and Charles A. Ruud, *Fighting Words: Imperial Censorship and the Russian Press, 1804–1906* (Toronto: University of Toronto Press, 1982).
95 Skipton and Michalove, *Postal Censorship*, 103.
96 Quoted in Evans and Richards, *Social History*, 4.

2. The Landscapes of Russian Imperialism

1 Peter Osborne, *Traveling Light: Photography, Travel and Visual Culture* (Manchester: Manchester University Press, 2000), 79.

2 Christopher Ely, *This Meager Nature: Landscape and National Identity in Imperial Russia* (DeKalb: Northern Illinois University Press, 2002), 5.

3 Benedict Anderson, *Imagined Communities*, rev. ed. (London: Verso, 2006), 86.

4 Ibid., 36.

5 Michael Biggs, "Putting the State on the Map: Cartography, Territory, and European State Formation," *Comparative Studies in Society and History* 41 (1999): 374.

6 Valerie Kivelson, *Cartographies of Tsardom: The Land and Its Meanings in Seventeenth-Century Russia* (Ithaca: Cornell University Press, 2006), 29.

7 Ibid., 30.

8 J.B. Harley, "Maps, Knowledge, and Power," in *The Iconography of Landscape*, eds. D. Cosgrove and S. Daniels (Cambridge: Cambridge University Press, 1988), 294.

9 On the history of this symbol and its use by the region of Moscow, see A. Melitonian et al., *Privet iz Moskvy* (Moscow: Magma, 2004), 71.

10 Ibid., 73.

11 The importance of the funds, which allowed for the wider spread of education in Russia, was clearly recognized by the purchaser who wrote some lines from Pushkin on the blank area of the postcard. The lines can be roughly translated as follows: "Do I see a people freed / And slavery fallen by the passion of the Tsar / And under a free fatherland enlightened / Finally has the longed-for star risen." I am grateful to Sergey Lobachev for helping me decipher the writing on this postcard.

12 June Hargrove, "Shaping the National Image: The Cult of Statues to Great Men in the Third Republic," in *Nationalism in the Visual Arts*, ed. R. Etlin (Washington, DC: National Gallery of Art, 1991), 49.

13 My thinking here has been influenced by a brief comment about memorials in Gail Turley Houston's book, *Royalties: The Queen and Victorian Writers* (Charlottesville: University Press of Virginia, 1999). She writes, "For that matter, any artwork memorializing another in the name of the queen would always manifest her authority, for the subject of commemoration would not have been honored in the first place had Victoria not authorized the testimonial" (49).

14 Tatiana Alexinsky, *With the Russian Wounded* (London: T. Fisher Unwin, 1916), 169.

15 Princess Julia Cantacuzene, *Revolutionary Days*, ed. T. Emmons (Chicago: R.R. Donnelley & Sons, 1999), 270.

16 Kornilov, along with Vice-Admiral Nakhimov, spearheaded the defence of the city during the Crimean War. He was killed in battle in October 1854.

17 Serhii Plokhy, "The City of Glory: Sevastopol in Russian Historical Mythology," *Journal of Contemporary History* 35, no. 3 (2000), 377.

18 Scholarly work on nighttime landscapes is rare apart from several works by

John Jakle. See his *City Lights: Illuminating the American Night* (Baltimore: Johns Hopkins University Press, 2001), and *Postcards of the Night: Views of American Cities* (Santa Fe: Museum of New Mexico Press, 2003).

19 The moment is described in Christopher Warwick, *Ella: Princess, Saint and Martyr* (Chichester: Wiley, 2006), 187.

20 Richard Harding Davis, *A Year from a Reporter's Note-book* (New York: Harper and Brothers, 1897), 21–2.

21 A.S. Suvorin, *Dnevnik A.S. Suvorina*, ed. M. Krichevskii (Moscow: Izdatel'stvo L.D. Freikel', 1923), 101.

22 James von Geldern notes the importance of staging revolutionary demonstrations in city centres, but his analysis is equally applicable to tsarist celebrations. See his *Bolshevik Festivals, 1917–1920* (Berkeley: University of California Press, 1993), 45.

23 Jakle, *Postcards of the Night*, 14.

24 Ibid., 17.

25 Andrea Schönle, *The Ruler in the Garden: Politics and Landscape Design in Imperial Russia* (Bern: Peter Lang, 2007), 39.

26 Lindsey Hughes, "Monuments and Identity," in *National Identity in Russian Culture*, eds. S. Franklin and E. Widdis (Cambridge: Cambridge University Press, 2004), 174.

27 Schönle, *Ruler in the Garden*, 75.

28 Dea Birkett, *Spinsters Abroad: Victorian Lady Explorers* (New York: Barnes and Noble Books, 1989), 96.

29 See Lucile H. Brockway, *Science and Colonial Expansion: The Role of the British Royal Botanic Garden* (New York: Academic Press, 1979).

30 Priscilla Roosevelt's research shows how the process of using plants to indicate power was replicated on the Russian country estate. She writes, "In defiance of Russia's short growing season and inhospitable clime, aristocrats also lavished attention on more utilitarian hothouses and forcing beds, proud of being able to produce throughout the year an abundance of fresh flowers for every room and fruits for their table." See her *Life on the Russian Country Estate* (New Haven: Yale University Press, 1995), 78.

31 Gary D. Sampson, "Unmasking the Colonial Picturesque: Samuel Bourne's Photographs of Barrackpore Park," in *Colonial Photography: Imag(in)ing Race and Place*, eds. E.M. Hight and G.D. Sampson (London: Routledge, 2002), 84.

32 Scherer, Nabholzh & Co. printed the tsarist double-headed eagle next to the company's name on their landscape postcards.

33 Thomas M. Barrett, "Lines of Uncertainty: The Frontiers of the North Caucasus," *Slavic Review* 54, no. 3 (1995): 581.

34 Susan Layton, "The Creation of an Imaginative Caucasian Geography," *Slavic Review* 45, no. 3 (1986): 484.

35 Mary Louise Pratt, *Imperial Eyes: Travel Writing and Transculturation* (London: Routledge, 1992), 201.

36 The various views of Siberia are described in Mark Bassin, "Inventing Siberia: Visions of the Russian East in the Early Nineteenth Century," *American Historical Review* 96, no. 3 (1991): 763–94.

37 Ibid., 766.

38 Quoted in Steven Marks, *Road to Power: The Trans-Siberian Railroad and the Colonization of Asian Russia, 1850–1917* (Ithaca: Cornell University Press, 1991), 143.

39 The figure includes both legal and illegal settlers. See ibid., 155.

40 Harley, "Maps, Knowledge, and Power," 292.

41 *Sergei Prokofiev Diaries, 1907–1914: Prodigious Youth*, trans. and ed. A. Phillips (Ithaca: Cornell University Press, 2006), 221.

42 Joan M. Schwartz, "*The Geography Lesson*: Photographs and the Construction of Imaginative Geographies," *Journal of Historical Geography* 22, no. 1 (1996): 33.

43 *Sergey Prokofiev Diaries, 1915–1923: Behind the Mask*, trans. and ed. A. Phillips (Ithaca: Cornell University Press, 2008), 19.

44 Most surviving Russian landscape postcards have never been mailed or written on. The ones in this chapter that have been used feature – with one exception – messages written in Russian or German. They were purchased from sellers who live in the Baltic region today.

45 Christopher Ely, "The Origins of Russian Scenery: Volga River Tourism and Russian Landscape Aesthetics," *Slavic Review* 62, no. 4 (2003): 670.

46 Ibid., 675.

47 Paul Grabbe, *Windows on the River Neva* (New York: Pomerica Press, 1977), 149.

48 John Jakle and Keith Sculle, "The American Hotel in Postcard Advertising: An Image Gallery," *Material Culture* 37, no. 2 (2005), 1–25.

3. Gender and Celebrity Culture

1 Nina Berberova, *The Italics Are Mine*, trans. P. Radley (New York: Alfred A. Knopf, 1992), 22.

2 Laurence Senelick, "Eroticism in Early Theatrical Photography," *Theatre History Studies* 11 (1991): 2.

3 As I discuss in detail in the next chapter, pornographic postcards were sold openly in major Russian cities and could also be purchased through the mail. See Laura Engelstein, *The Keys to Happiness: Sex and the Search for Modernity in Fin-de-Siècle Russia* (Ithaca: Cornell University Press, 1992), 361. On pornographic images in general, see Senelick, "Eroticism"; Maria-Elena Buszek, "Representing 'Awarishness': Burlesque, Feminist

Transgression, and the 19th-Century Pin-up," *Drama Review* 43, no. 4 (1999): 141–62; and Elizabeth Anne McCauley, *A.A.E. Disderi and the Carte de Visite Portrait Photograph* (New Haven: Yale University Press, 1985).

4 On the position of actresses in general, see Christopher Kent, "Image and Reality: The Actress and Society," in *A Widening Sphere: Changing Roles of Victorian Women*, ed. M. Vicinus (Bloomington: Indiana University Press, 1977); and Sandra Richards, *The Rise of the English Actress* (New York: St. Martin's Press, 1993). Stella Arbenina's memoir provides an interesting case study of an aristocratic woman in Russia who wanted to become an actress (and eventually did after the revolution). See her, *Through Terror to Freedom* (London: Hutchinson, 1929).

5 Richards, *Rise of the English Actress*, 90.

6 V.R. Leikina-Svirskaia, *Russkaia intelligentsiia v 1900–1917 godakh* (Moscow: Mysl', 1981), 193.

7 Ibid., 203.

8 On the difficulties women faced in obtaining professional qualifications, see Mary Schaeffer Conroy, "Women Pharmacists in Russia before World War I: Women's Emancipation, Feminism, Professionalization, Nationalism and Class Conflict," in *Women and Society in Russia and the Soviet Union*, ed. L. Edmondson (Cambridge: Cambridge University Press, 1992), 48–76; and Christine Johanson, *Women's Struggle for Higher Education in Russia* (Montreal: McGill-Queen's University Press, 1987).

9 Catherine Schuler, *Women in Russian Theatre: The Actress in the Silver Age* (London: Routledge, 1996), 19.

10 Catherine Schuler, "Actresses, Audience and Fashion in the Silver Age: A Crisis of Costume," in *Women and Russian Culture*, ed. R. Marsh (New York: Berghahn, 1998), 111.

11 See Linda Edmondson, *Feminism in Russia, 1900–1917* (Stanford: Stanford University Press, 1984), and her, "Women's Rights, Civil Rights and the Debate over Citizenship in the 1905 Revolution," in *Women and Society in Russia and the Soviet Union*, ed. L. Edmondson (Cambridge: Cambridge University Press, 1992), 77–100.

12 Senelick, "Eroticism," 11.

13 Samuel Marshak, *At Life's Beginning: Some Pages of Reminiscence* (New York: E.P. Dutton, 1964), 160.

14 Louise McReynolds, *Russia at Play* (Ithaca: Cornell University Press, 2003), 114.

15 The evening is described in Sergei Prokofiev's diary for 1913. See *Sergey Prokofiev Diaries, 1907–1914: Prodigious Youth*, trans. and ed. A. Phillips (London: Faber and Faber, 2006).

16 Anna Pavlovna Vygodskaia, *The Story of a Life: Memoirs of a Young Jewish Woman in the Russian Empire* (DeKalb: Northern Illinois University Press, 2012), 88.

17 The firm Bamforth & Co. in Britain, e.g., was noted for its song and hymn postcards. See A.W. Coysh, *The Dictionary of Picture Postcards in Britain, 1894–1939* (Woodbridge: Antique Collectors' Club, 1984), 27 and 32.

18 McReynolds, *Russia at Play*, 272.

19 Denise Youngblood, *The Magic Mirror: Moviemaking in Russia, 1908–1918* (Madison: University of Wisconsin Press, 1999), 9 and 11.

20 S. Ginzburg, *Kinematografiia dorevoliutsionnoi Rossii* (Moscow: Izdatel'stvo iskusstvo, 1963), 158.

21 McReynolds, *Russia at Play*, 268.

22 Ginzburg, *Kinematografiia*, 11.

23 Prince A. Lobanov-Rostovsky, *The Grinding Mill: Reminiscences of War and Revolution in Russia, 1913–1920* (New York: Macmillan, 1935), 226.

24 The British occupied Baku from 25 July to 14 September 1918. They had been invited to do so by the non-Bolshevik majority in the city soviet. Anna Andzhievskaia, "A Mother's Story," in *In the Shadow of Revolution*, eds. S. Fitzpatrick and Yu. Slezkine (Princeton: Princeton University Press, 2000), 80–1.

25 McReynolds, *Russia at Play*, 269.

26 A sample of these posters, including several publicizing movies starring Vera Kholodnaia, can be seen in A.E. Snopkov, P.A. Snopkov, and A.F. Shkliaruk, *Russkii kinoplakat* (Moscow: Kontakt-kul'tura, 2002).

27 See Q. David Bowers, "Souvenir Postcards and the Development of the Star System, 1912–1914," *Film History* 3, no. 1 (1989): 1–10.

28 Veronica Kelly, "Beauty and the Market: Actress Postcards and Their Senders in Early Twentieth-Century Australia," *New Theater Quarterly* 20, no. 2 (2004): 100.

29 Quoted in Jay Leyda, *Kino: A History of the Russian and Soviet Film* (Princeton: Princeton University Press, 1973), 53. The film's title was changed to *The Defence of Sevastopol* prior to its release.

30 Biographical information about Kholodnaia is drawn from the collection *Vera Kholodnaia: K 100-letiiu so dnia rozhdeniia*, ed. B.B. Ziukov (Moscow: Iskusstvo, 1995); Elena Prokof'eva, *Koroleva ekrana* (Moscow: Izdatel'skii dom "I.G.S.," 2001); and Aleksandr Varakin, *V luchakh slavy: Zvezdy russkogo kino* (Moscow: Veche, 2006).

31 Quoted in Prokof'eva, *Koroleva ekrana*, 42.

32 *Vera Kholodnaia*, 40.

33 Ginzburg, *Kinematografiia*, 370.

34 Prokof'eva, *Koroleva ekrana*, 85.

35 On the changes wrought by the new Bolshevik regime, see Peter Kenez, *Cinema and Soviet Society, 1917–1953* (Cambridge: Cambridge University Press, 1992).

36 *Vera Kholodnaia*, 39.

37 Leyda, *Kino*, 79.

38 The film has survived and is included in vol. 9 of the British Film Institute collection, *Early Russian Cinema*. At the request of relatives, Kholodnaia was reburied in Moscow in 1931.

39 Konstantin Paustovsky, *Slow Approach of Thunder*, trans. M. Harari and M. Duncan (London: Harvill Press, 1965), 93.

40 Konstantin Paustovsky, *In That Dawn*, trans. M. Harari and M. Duncan (London: Harvill Press, 1967), 139–40.

41 Paustovsky, *In That Dawn*, 205.

42 "Russkii amerikanets," *Teatr i kino* (8 Oct. 1916): 14.

43 See Richard de Cordova, "The Emergence of the Star System in America: An Examination of the Institutional and Ideological Function of the Star, 1907–1922," (PhD diss., University of California at Los Angeles, 1986); and Paul McDonald, *The Star System: Hollywood's Production of Popular Identities* (London: Wallflower Press, 2000).

44 A similar blurring is often repeated in the scholarship on Kholodnaia. In Neia Zorkaia's book on mass art, e.g., photographs of Kholodnaia in movie roles are mixed with studio poses. The caption given below them merely says, "Vera Kholodnaia in roles and in life." It does not identify which photographs belong to each category. See N.M. Zorkaia, *Na rubezhe stoletii: U istokov massovogo iskusstva v Rossii 1900–1910 godov* (Moscow: Izdatel'stvo Nauka, 1976), 287 and 291.

45 McDonald, *Star System*, 27.

46 Quoted in *Vera Kholodnaia*, 21.

47 Yuri Tsivian, *Early Cinema in Russia and Its Cultural Reception* (London: Routledge, 1994), 193. He provides an example of one such review where the author writes, "V. Kholodnaya's acting in the main role was no better than average; perhaps the director was guilty of not taking many close-ups, which are so effective with this actress, and of giving us only very short scenes."

48 Senelick, "Eroticism," 29.

49 Ibid., 7.

50 E. Anthony Swift, *Popular Theater and Society in Tsarist Russia* (Berkeley: University of California Press, 2002), 31; and Steve Smith and Catriona Kelly, "Commercial Culture and Consumerism," in *Constructing Russian Culture in the Age of Revolution, 1881–1940*, eds. C. Kelly and D. Shepherd (Oxford: Oxford University Press, 1998), 107.

51 Michael Hamm, "Introduction," in *The City in Late Imperial Russia*, ed. M. Hamm (Bloomington: Indiana University Press, 1986), 2.

52 On the emergence of department stores, see D.A. Zasosov and V.I. Pyzin, *Iz zhizni Peterburga 1890–1910x godov* (Leningrad: Lenizdat', 1991), 96–100.

53 Christine Ruane, "The Development of a Fashion Press in Late Imperial Russia – *Moda: Zhurnal dlia svetskikh liudei*," in *An Improper Profession: Women, Gender, and Journalism in Late Imperial Russia*, eds. B. Norton and J. Gheith (Durham: Duke University Press, 2001), 75.

54 Christine Ruane, "Clothes Shopping in Imperial Russia: The Development of a Consumer Culture," *Journal of Social History* 28, no. 4 (1995): 767. Ruane also discusses the subject in her book, *The Empire's New Clothes: A History of the Russian Fashion Industry, 1700–1917* (New Haven: Yale University Press, 2009).

55 Lisa Tiersten, *Marianne and the Market: Envisioning Consumer Society in Fin-de-Siècle France* (Berkeley: University of California Press, 2001), 128.

56 Smith and Kelly, "Commercial Culture," 112.

57 Semen Kanatchikov, *A Radical Worker in Tsarist Russia*, trans. and ed. R. Zelnik (Stanford: Stanford University Press, 1986), 71.

58 Barbara A. Engel, *Between the Fields and the City: Women, Work, and Family in Russia, 1861–1914* (Cambridge: Cambridge University Press, 1996), 154.

59 Ruane, *Empire's New Clothes*, 220.

60 Tiersten, *Marianne*, 5.

61 Jane Gaines, "Costume and Narrative: How Dress Tells the Woman's Story," in *Fabrications: Costume and the Female Body*, eds. J. Gaines and C. Herzog (New York: Routledge, 1990), 188.

62 Boris Pil'niak, *The Naked Year*, trans. A.R. Tulloch (Ann Arbor: Ardis, 1975), 42.

63 Swift, *Popular Theater*, 231.

4. Bodies on Display

1 Ilya Ehrenburg, *People and Life, 1891–1921* (New York: Alfred A. Knopf, 1962), 35.

2 Quoted in Laura Engelstein, *The Keys to Happiness: Sex and the Search for Modernity in Fin-de-Siècle Russia* (Ithaca: Cornell University Press, 1992), 386. The latest study of *Sanin* questions whether the label "pornographic" was, indeed, appropriately used in discussions of the novel. See Otto Boele, *Erotic Nihilism in Late Imperial Russia* (Madison: University of Wisconsin Press, 2009).

3 Lynn Hunt, "Introduction," in *The Invention of Pornography: Obscenity and the Origins of Modernity, 1500–1800*, ed. L. Hunt (New York: Zone Books, 1993), 10.
4 Lynn Hunt, "Pornography and the French Revolution," in *The Invention of Pornography: Obscenity and the Origins of Modernity, 1500–1800*, ed. L. Hunt (New York: Zone Books, 1993), 305.
5 These developments are outlined in Paula Findlen, "Humanism, Politics and Pornography in Renaissance Italy," in *The Invention of Pornography: Obscenity and the Origins of Modernity, 1500–1800*, ed. L. Hunt (New York: Zone Books, 1993), 49–108; and Steven Marcus, *The Other Victorians: A Study of Sexuality and Pornography in Mid-Nineteenth-Century England* (New Brunswick, NJ: Transaction Publishers, 2009).
6 Three hundred copies were printed for subscribers only. As the copper plates were destroyed, the modern reprint used offset lithography to reproduce one of the original volumes. See Mihaly Zichy, *The Erotic Drawings of Mihaly Zichy* (New York: Grove Press, 1969).
7 Paul Goldschmidt, "Pornography in Russia," in *Consuming Russia*, ed. Adele Barker (Durham: Duke University Press, 1999), 319; and Edvard Radzinsky, *Alexander II* (New York: Free Press, 2005), 57–9.
8 Olga Matich, *Erotic Utopia: The Decadent Imagination in Russia's Fin-de-Siècle* (Madison: University of Wisconsin Press, 2005), 79–80.
9 Malek Alloula, *The Colonial Harem* (Minneapolis: University of Minnesota Press, 1986).
10 See, e.g., Elizabeth Anne McCauley, *A.A.E. Disderi and the Carte de Visite Portrait Photograph* (New Haven: Yale University Press, 1985), 106; examples of pornographic cartes are reproduced on page 108.
11 Lisa Z. Sigel, "Filth in the Wrong People's Hands: Postcards and the Expansion of Pornography in Britain and the Atlantic World, 1880–1914," *Journal of Social History* 33, no. 4 (2000): 859–85.
12 Laurie Bernstein, *Sonia's Daughters: Prostitutes and Their Regulation in Imperial Russia* (Berkeley: University of California Press, 1995), 3.
13 Allison Pease, *Modernism, Mass Culture, and the Aesthetics of Obscenity* (Cambridge: Cambridge University Press, 2000), 51.
14 Examples are included in Sigel, "Filth," 873–6. Unfortunately, an examination of the *Vigilance Record* showed the publication only turned its attention to Russia and Eastern Europe in conjunction with fears of white slavery, in other words, the trafficking of women tricked into prostitution.
15 Sigel, "Filth," 880–1n8.
16 Katalin Szoverfy Milter and Joseph W. Slade, "Global Traffic in Pornography: The Hungarian Example," in *International Exposures:*

Perspectives on Modern European Pornography, 1800–2000 (New Brunswick, NJ: Rutgers University Press, 2005), 173.

17 Robert Blobaum, "Criminalizing the 'Other': Crime, Ethnicity, and Antisemitism in Early Twentieth-Century Poland," in *Antisemitism and Its Opponents in Modern Poland*, ed. R. Blobaum (Ithaca: Cornell University Press, 2000), 89.

18 See M. Levitt and A. Toporkov (eds.), *Eros i pornografiia v russkoi kul'ture* (Moscow: "Ladomir," 1999).

19 Beth Holmgren, *Rewriting Capitalism: Literature and the Market in Late Tsarist Russia and the Kingdom of Poland* (Pittsburgh: University of Pittsburgh Press, 1998), 5.

20 Thierry Terret, "Sports and Erotica: Erotic Postcards of Sportswomen during France's *Années Folles*," *Journal of Sport History* 29, no. 2 (2002): 276.

21 Sergei Prokofiev, *Sergei Prokofiev Diaries, 1907–1914: Prodigious Youth*, trans. and ed. A. Phillips (Ithaca: Cornell University Press, 2006), 426.

22 Engelstein, *Keys to Happiness*, 360–1, esp. n5.

23 G. B-n, "Bor'ba s pornografiei," *Peterburgsksia gazeta*, 6 Aug. 1906.

24 Ivan Bunin, *Cursed Days: A Diary of Revolution*, trans. T.G. Marullo (London: Phoenix Press, 1998), 114.

25 Sally West, *I Shop in Moscow: Advertising and the Creation of Consumer Culture in Late Tsarist Russia* (DeKalb: Northern Illinois University Press, 2011), 84–5.

26 John Foster Fraser, *Red Russia* (London: Cassell, 1907), 117.

27 Paul Hammon, *French Undressing: Naughty Postcards from 1900 to 1920* (London: Jupiter Books, 1976); Erik Nørgaard, *With Love to You: A History of the Erotic Postcard* (New York: Clarkson N. Potter, 1969); and William Ouellette and Barbara Jones, *Erotic Postcards* (New York: Excalibur Books, 1977).

28 These postcards are catalogued under the title "Russian Erotic Postcards."

29 Esther Milne, *Letters, Postcards, Email: Technologies of Presence* (New York: Routledge, 2010), 95.

30 Nora Lourie Percival, *Weather of the Heart: A Child's Journey Out of Revolutionary Russia* (Boone, NC: High Country Publishers, 2001), 36, 247–9.

31 See, e.g., the entries for 2 March 1913 and 22 May 1914. Prokofiev, *Sergei Prokofiev Diaries, 1907–1914*, 332 and 686.

32 Beverly Seaton's study of the language of flowers shows how meanings varied from reference manual to reference manual, to say nothing of from country to country, as well as how difficult it would have been to coordinate meanings with what flowers were in season. See her, *The Language of Flowers: A History* (Charlottesville: University Press of Virginia, 1995).

33 The French postcard can be seen in Ado Kyrou, *L'âge d'or de la carte postale* (Paris: André Balland, 1966), 128.

34 Valentin Berezhkov, *At Stalin's Side* (New York: Birch Lane Press, 1994), 123–4.

35 This strain can be traced through *lubki* and *chastushki* to at least the 18th century. Usually more suggestive than sexually explicit, both offered a humorous view of relations between the sexes. Scholars using these sources argue that they were not direct predecessors of modern pornography. Rather, in the case of lubki, they became more sanitized in the 19th century, or, in the case of chastushki, remained merely suggestive. See Dianne Ecklund Farrell, "The Bawdy Lubok: Sexual and Scatalogical Content in Eighteenth-Century Russian Popular Prints," and A.V. Kulagina, "Russkaia eroticheskaia chastushki," both in *Eros i pornografiia v russkoi kul'ture*, ed. M. Levitt and A. Toporkov (Moscow: "Ladomir," 1999), 16–41 and 94–120, respectively.

36 I am referring to Figures 21–39 in the volume. They include images from more than one series.

37 Marcus, *Other Victorians*, 59–60.

38 Kathryn Norberg makes this connection with respect to novels whose narrators are prostitutes but her conclusions are just as applicable for other female narrators. See her "The Libertine Whore: Prostitution in French Pornography from Margot to Juliette," in *The Invention of Pornography: Obscenity and the Origins of Modernity, 1500–1800*, ed. L. Hunt (New York: Zone Books, 1993), 230.

39 See Figure 54 in *Eros i pornografiia*.

40 Marcus, *Other Victorians*, 270.

41 Ellen Bayuk Rosenman, *Unauthorized Pleasures: Accounts of Victorian Erotic Experiences* (Ithaca: Cornell University Press, 2003), 65.

42 G.Iu. Sternin, *Khudozhestvennaia zhizn' Rossii: Na rubezhe XIX–XX vekov* (Moscow: Izdatel'stvo "Iskusstvo," 1970), 251–2.

43 The story is retold in Douglas Greenfield, "From the Hothouse to the Harem: Rozanov and Decadence," *Ulbandus* 8 (2004): 71.

44 This defence was not always successful, particularly in Germany, where the courts ruled that nude paintings were acceptable but that postcards reproducing the same works were obscene. Even reproductions of works on display at the Dresden Royal Gallery were destroyed by the police. Gary D. Stark, "Pornography, Society, and the Law in Imperial Germany," *Central European History* 14, no. 3 (1981): 225.

45 M. Chapkina, *Khudozhestvennaia otkrytka* (Moscow: Galart, 1993), 14.

46 G. B-n, "Bor'ba s pornografiei."

47 Nadezhda Teffi, letter to Ivan Bunin dated 19 May 1944. Reproduced in Thomas Gaiton Marullo, *Ivan Bunin: The Twilight of Émigré Russia, 1934–1953* (Chicago: Ivan R. Dee, 2002), 240.

48 Pease, *Modernism*, 124.

49 M.A. Chlenov, *Polovaia perepis' moskovskogo studenchestva i ee obshchestvennoe znachenie* (Moscow, 1909), 49–52, quoted in Engelstein, *Keys to Happiness*, 373.

50 Postcard versions of these paintings are mentioned and reproduced in Ludmilla Jordanova, *Sexual Visions: Images of Gender in Science and Medicine between the Eighteenth and Twentieth Centuries* (Madison: University of Wisconsin Press, 1989); and Elaine Showalter, *Sexual Anarchy: Gender and Culture at the Fin de Siècle* (Harmondsworth: Penguin, 1990).

51 See Karl Toepfer, "Nudity and Modernity in German Dance, 1910–1930," *Journal of the History of Sexuality* 3, no. 1 (1992): 58–108; and Karl Toepfer, *Empire of Ecstasy: Nudity and Movement in German Body Culture, 1910–1935* (Berkeley: University of California Press, 1997).

52 Toepfer, "Nudity and Modernity," 80.

53 John Bowlt, *Moscou et Saint-Péterbourg, 1900–1920* (Paris: Hazan, 2008), 288 and 292. A photograph of a naked Andreev with his young son is reproduced on page 292.

54 Matich, *Erotic Utopia*, 257.

55 Laurence Senelick, "The Erotic Bondage of Serf Theatre," *Russian Review* 50, no. 1 (1991): 30.

56 Katherine Lahti, "On Living Statues and Pandora, *Kamennye baby* and Futurist Aesthetics – The Female Body in *Vladimir Mayakovsky: A Tragedy*," *Russian Review* 58 (1999): 439.

57 Irene Masing-Delic, "Creating the Living Work of Art: The Symbolist Pygmalion and His Antecedents," in *Creating Life: The Aesthetic Utopia of Russian Modernism*, eds. I. Paperno and D.D. Grossman (Stanford: Stanford University Press, 1994), 51–82.

58 Kristi Groberg, "Crucified Women in Russian Fin-de-Siècle Art: Why Demons Cling to the Cross," paper presented at the annual conference of the Canadian Association of Slavists, Concordia University, Montreal, 30 May 2010.

59 Theatre historian Laurence Senelick notes that records exist documenting the existence of 173 private gentry theatres in Russia. See his "The Erotic Bondage of Serf Theatre," 24.

60 Priscilla Roosevelt, *Life on the Russian Country Estate* (New Haven: Yale University Press, 1995), 144. The story is also recounted in the memoirs of one of his descendants. See Felix Youssoupoff, *Lost Splendor* (New York: Helen Marx, 2003), 16.

61 Tracy Davis, "The Actress in Victorian Pornography," in *Victorian Scandals: Representations of Gender and Class*, ed. K.O. Garrigan (Athens: Ohio University Press, 1992), 106.

5. Monarchy and the Mundane

1 Jane Robins, *The Trial of Queen Caroline* (New York: Free Press, 2006), 19.
2 Robin and Carol Wichard, *Victorian Cartes-de-Visite* (Risborough: Shire Publications, 1999), 36.
3 For details, see Simon Heffer, *Power and Place: The Political Consequences of King Edward VII* (London: Phoenix, 1998), 74–5.
4 Jamie H. Cockfield, *White Crow: The Life and Times of the Grand Duke Nicholas Mikhailovich Romanov, 1859–1919* (Westport: Praeger, 2002), 101.
5 It is reproduced in Frances Dimond and Roger Taylor, *Crown and Camera: The Royal Family and Photography, 1842–1910* (London: Viking, 1987), 176.
6 Mark Steinberg and Vladimir Khrustalev, *The Fall of the Romanovs* (New Haven: Yale University Press, 1995), 148 and 221. Syroboiarsky was a wounded soldier befriended by Alexandra when he was a patient at the Tsarskoe Selo infirmary.
7 William C. Darrah, *Cartes de Visite in Nineteenth-Century Photography* (Gettysburg: privately published, 1981), 6.
8 Ibid., 43.
9 Peter Hamilton and Roger Hargreaves, *The Beautiful and the Damned: The Creation of Identity in Nineteenth-Century Photography* (London: National Portrait Gallery, 2001), 45.
10 Gail Turley Houston, *Royalties: The Queen and Victorian Writers* (Charlottesville: University Press of Virginia, 1999), 56. Victoria also filled 84 photograph albums with pictures of family and friends. Her collection amounted to roughly 100,000 photographs.
11 See Richard Williams, *The Contentious Crown: Public Discussion of the British Monarchy in the Reign of Queen Victoria* (Aldershot: Ashgate, 1997).
12 Alexis Schwarzenbach, "Royal Photographs: Emotions for the People," *Contemporary European History* 13, no. 3 (2004): 267–86.
13 The postcard is reproduced in Anne Goulzadian, *L'empire du dernier Tsar* (Paris: Editions Astrid, 1982).
14 David Cannadine, "The Context, Performance and Meaning of Ritual: The British Monarchy and the 'Invention of Tradition,' c. 1820–1977," in *The Invention of Tradition*, eds. E. Hobsbawm and T. Ranger (Cambridge: Cambridge University Press, 1983), 106.

15 Elena Hellberg-Hirn, "Imperial Places and Stories," in *Imperial and National Identities in Pre-Revolutionary, Soviet, and Post-Soviet Russia,* eds. C.J. Chulos and J. Remy (Helsinki: SKS, 2002), 26.

16 Nina Berberova, *The Italics Are Mine,* trans. P. Radley (New York: Alfred A. Knopf, 1992), 80.

17 Thomas M. Barrett, "Southern Living (in Captivity): The Caucasus in Russian Popular Culture," *Journal of Popular Culture* 31, no. 4 (1998): 83.

18 Carolyn Harris, "The Succession Prospects of Grand Duchess Olga Nikolaevna (1895–1918)," *Canadian Slavonic Papers* 54, nos. 1–2 (2012): 73.

19 Ibid., 73.

20 Anton I. Denikin, *The Career of a Tsarist Officer: Memoirs, 1872–1916,* trans. M. Patoski (Minneapolis: University of Minnesota Press, 1975), 273.

21 George A. Lensen, "The Attempt on the Life of Nicholas II in Japan," *Russian Review* 20, no. 3 (1961): 251.

22 A.S. Suvorin, *Dnevnik A.S. Suvorina,* ed. M. Krichevskii (Moscow: Izdatel'stvo L.D. Freikel', 1923), 301.

23 On the ritual significance of coronations, see Cannadine, "Context, Performance and Meaning."

24 Samuel Marshak, *At Life's Beginning: Some Pages of Reminiscence* (New York: E.P. Dutton, 1964), 116.

25 Helen Baker, "Monarchy Discredited? Reactions to the Khodynka Coronation Catastrophe of 1896," *Revolutionary Russia* 16, no. 1 (2003): 2.

26 Walter Sablinsky, *The Road to Bloody Sunday* (Princeton: Princeton University Press, 1976), 285.

27 Ibid., 274.

28 Michael Melancon, "The Ninth Circle: The Lena Goldfields Workers and the Massacre of 4 April 1912," *Slavic Review* 53, no. 3 (1994): 793.

29 Here, I disagree with Daniel Field who, with respect to Bloody Sunday, argues that one event in the capital could not possibly have had such a widespread effect. The point is that Bloody Sunday was part of a pattern of mishaps and violence. It was not seen as an isolated event. See his *Rebels in the Name of the Tsar* (Boston: Unwin Hyman, 1989), 20.

30 For more on this subject, see the conclusion in Michael Melancon, *The Lena Goldfields Massacre and the Crisis of the Late Tsarist State* (College Station: Texas A & M University Press, 2006).

31 Asa Briggs, *Victorian Things* (Chicago: University of Chicago Press, 1988), 143 and 145.

32 For a list of occasions marked by the production of postcards, see A.W. Coysh, *The Dictionary of Picture Postcards in Britain, 1894–1939* (Woodbridge: Antique Collectors' Club, 1984), 228.

33 The postcard can be seen in Edmund Swinglehurst, *Cook's Tours: The Story of Popular Travel* (Poole: Blandford Press, 1982), 106.

34 The postcards are discussed in John Grand-Carteret, *Le musée pittoresque du voyage du Tsar* (Paris: Librairie Charpentier et Fasquelle, 1896), 183–8.

35 Roderick McLean, *Royalty and Diplomacy in Europe, 1890–1914* (Cambridge: Cambridge University Press, 2001), 186.

36 Richard Wortman's work mentions coins, postage stamps, and newsreels, as well as commemorative volumes but not postcards. See his "Publicizing the Imperial Image in 1913," in *Self and Story in Russian History*, eds. L. Engelstein and S. Sandler (Ithaca: Cornell University Press, 2000), 94–119.

37 Princess Catherine Sayn-Wittgenstein, *La fin de ma Russie: Journal 1914–1919* (Montricher, Switzerland: Les editions noir sur blanc, 1990), 133. The passage reads: "I honoured little Aleksei with my strongest and devoted love ... I bought all his portraits and to that end I emptied all the stores in Petrograd and Moscow. In Petrograd my big album of postcards of all the members of the Imperial family still exists."

38 For an excellent analysis of this icon, see Isolde Thyrêt, *Between God and Tsar: Religious Symbolism and the Royal Women of Muscovite Russia* (DeKalb: Northern Illinois University Press, 2001), 70–3. A reproduction of the icon is included on page 71.

39 Bishop Herbert Bury, *Russian Life Today* (London: A.R. Mowbray, 1915), 55; and Hubertus Jahn, "For Tsar and Fatherland: Russian Popular Culture and the First World War," in *Cultures in Flux*, eds. S.P. Frank and M.D. Steinberg (Princeton: Princeton University Press, 1994), 136.

40 Anonymous, *The Russian Diary of an Englishman: Petrograd, 1915–1917* (New York: Robert M. McBride and Co., 1919), 51.

41 The St. Nicholas Day celebrations described by Nevinson fell on 19 December 1905. See Henry W. Nevinson, *The Dawn in Russia*, reprint ed. (New York: Arno Press and New York Times, 1971), 127.

42 Richard Wortman, *Scenarios of Power: Myth and Ceremony in Russian Monarchy*, vol. II (Princeton: Princeton University Press, 2000), 422.

43 Peter Baker, "The Social and Ideological Role of the Monarchy in Late Victorian Britain" (MA thesis, University of Lancaster, 1978), 16.

44 See article by Bishop Nikon, "Vera Khristova ne terpit dvoedushiia," *Tserkovnym vedomostiam*, 9 Feb. (1913): 283.

45 Wortman, "Publicizing the Imperial Image," 98.

46 Prince Dimitry Kandaouroff, *Collecting Postal History* (New York: Larousse, 1974), 180.

47 Simon Schama, "The Domestication of Majesty: Royal Family Portraiture, 1500–1850," in *Art and History: Images and Their Meaning*, eds. R. Rotberg and T. Rabb (Cambridge: Cambridge University Press, 1988), 157.

48 Wortman, *Scenarios of Power*, 336.
49 Renate Prochno, "Nationalism in British Eighteenth-Century Painting: Sir Joshua Reynolds and Benjamin West," in *Nationalism in the Visual Arts*, ed. R. Etlin (Washington, DC: National Gallery of Art, 1991), 29.
50 An example can be seen in Orlando Figes and Boris Kolonitskii, *Interpreting the Russian Revolution: The Language and Symbols of 1917* (New Haven: Yale University Press, 1999). A more detailed analysis of Alexandra's image occurs in Boris Kolonitskii, *"Tragicheskaia erotica": Obrazy imperatorskoi sem'i v gody pervoi mirovoi voiny* (Moscow: Novoe Literaturnoe Obozrenie, 2010). That study shows that most pornographic images of the royal couple and Rasputin were put out in pamphlet, rather than postcard, form.
51 She is quoted in Paul Miliukov, *Political Memoirs, 1905–1917* (Ann Arbor: University of Michigan Press, 1967), 235.
52 Marie-Monique Huss, "Pronatalism and the Popular Ideology of the Child in Wartime France: The Evidence of the Picture Postcard," in *The Upheaval of War*, eds. R. Wall and J. Winter (Cambridge: Cambridge University Press, 1988), 334.
53 Figes and Kolonitskii, *Interpreting the Russian Revolution*, 14.
54 Brian Coe and Paul Gates, *The Snapshot Photograph: The Rise of Popular Photography, 1888–1939* (London: Ash and Grant, 1977), 29.
55 Dimond and Taylor, *Crown and Camera*, 77.
56 David Cannadine, *History in Our Time* (New Haven: Yale University Press, 1998), 27.
57 Adele Lindenmeyr, *Poverty Is Not a Vice: Charity, Society, and the State in Imperial Russia* (Princeton: Princeton University Press, 1996), 75.
58 On her charitable work, see Iuliia Kudrina, *Imperatritsa Mariia Fedorovna (1847–1928 gg)* (Moscow: Olma-Press, 2001), 27–30.
59 See Joseph Bradley, "Voluntary Associations, Civic Culture, and Obshchestvennost' in Moscow," in *Between Tsar and People*, eds. E.W. Clowes, S.D. Kassow, and J.L. West (Princeton: Princeton University Press, 1991), 131–48.
60 N. Tagrin, *Mir v otkrytke* (Moscow: Izobrazitel'noe iskusstvo, 1978), 50. For additional information about the Society, which survived into the early Soviet period, see Komitet populiarizatsii khudozhestvennykh izdaniii, *Za tridtsat' let, 1896–1926* (Leningrad: Komitet populiarizatsii khudozhestvennykh izdaniii, 1928).
61 A number of them are described in the entry "Special Welfare Organisations in Russia," in Richard Bartmann, *Picture Postcard Encyclopaedia of Russia* (Erlangen: privately published, 1992).

62 Alexandra came from a family noted for its charitable activities. On the charitable work of her mother and her sister Elizabeth (Ella), see Christopher Warwick, *Ella: Princess, Saint and Martyr* (Chichester: Wiley, 2006). Her own charitable undertakings were not well publicized. They are mentioned extensively in Sophie Buxhoeveden, *The Life and Tragedy of Alexandra Feodorovna* (London: Longmans, Green, 1928); and Anna Viroubova, *Memories of the Russian Court* (New York: Macmillan, 1923).

63 Frank Prochaska, *Royal Bounty: The Making of a Welfare Monarchy* (New Haven: Yale University Press, 1995), 68.

64 Carolly Erickson, *Alexandra: The Last Tsarina* (New York: St. Martin's Griffin, 2001), 224.

65 Kolonitskii, *"Tragicheskaia erotica,"* 274–6.

66 Olga Barkovets, "The Emperor's Camera Obscura," in *Nicholas and Alexandra: At Home with the Last Tsar and His Family – Treasures from the Alexander Palace*, ed. M.P. Swezey (Washington, DC: American-Russian Cultural Cooperation Foundation, 2004), 47.

67 On the healing power of monarchs, see Marc Bloch, *The Royal Touch: Sacred Monarchy and Scrofula in England and France*, trans. J.E. Anderson (London: Routledge and Kegan Paul, 1973).

68 Countess Kleinmichel, *Memories of a Shipwrecked World* (New York: Brentano's, 1923), 216.

69 Figes and Kolonitskii, *Interpreting the Russian Revolution*, 24.

70 Kleinmichel, *Memories*, 217.

71 George Thomas Marye, *Nearing the End in Imperial Russia* (London: Selwyn and Blount, 1929), 211.

6. Beyond Patriotic Discourse

1 Janet Watson, *Fighting Different Wars: Experience, Memory, and the First World War in Britain* (Cambridge: Cambridge University Press, 2004).

2 The point about patriotism and class conflict is made in Hugh Cunningham, "The Language of Patriotism, 1750–1914," *History Workshop Journal* 12 (Autumn 1981): 23.

3 Peter Gatrell, *Russia's First World War* (Harlow: Pearson, 2005), 70.

4 Aaron Cohen, *Imagining the Unimaginable: World War, Modern Art, and the Politics of Public Culture in Russia, 1914–1917* (Lincoln: University of Nebraska Press, 2008); Hubertus F. Jahn, *Patriotic Culture in Russia during World War I* (Ithaca: Cornell University Press, 1995); Stephen Norris, *A War of Images: Russian Popular Prints, Wartime Culture, and National Identity, 1812–1945* (DeKalb: Northern Illinois University Press, 2006); and Richard Stites,

"Days and Nights in Wartime Russia: Cultural Life, 1914–1917," in *European Culture in the Great War: The Arts, Entertainment, and Propaganda, 1914–1918*, eds. A. Roshwald and R. Stites (Cambridge: Cambridge University Press, 1999), 8–31. For a Russian perspective that briefly acknowledges images of suffering and defeat but still fits them into a larger patriotic narrative, see the introductory essay in Nina Baburina, *Russkii plakat pervoi mirovoi voiny* (Moscow: Iskusstvo i kul'tura, 1992).

5 On "photo postcards," see Rosamund B. Vaule, *As We Were: American Photographic Postcards, 1905–1930* (Boston: David R. Godine, 2004), 22–3. As Vaule later notes, "Kodak introduced photo stock specifically for postcards in 1902, and from 1903 until 1941, produced various models of the 3A camera that used postcard size film" (53). These supplies were available in Russia around the time of the First World War. The stock said "Otkrytoe pis'mo" on the back and had a line dividing the space for any message from that left for an address.

6 S. Morozov, "Early Photography in Eastern Europe: Russia," *History of Photography* 1, no. 4 (1977): 331 and 340.

7 Louise McReynolds, *The News under Russia's Old Regime* (Princeton: Princeton University Press, 1991), 136. Additional information can be found in Christopher Stolarski, "Another Way of Telling the News: The Rise of Photojournalism in Russia, 1900–1914," *Kritika: Explorations in Russian and Eurasian History* 12, no. 3 (2011): 561–90.

8 Peter Burke, *Eyewitnessing: The Uses of Images as Historical Evidence* (Ithaca: Cornell University Press, 2001), 147.

9 Jorge Lewinski, *The Camera at War* (London: W.H. Allen, 1978), 68.

10 Ester Milne, *Letters, Postcards, Email: Technologies of Presence* (New York: Routledge, 2010), 53 and 121.

11 William Darrah's work shows that stereographs were made of both the Boer and Russo-Japanese wars. See his *The World of Stereographs* (Gettysburg: privately published, 1977). By the start of the Boer War, the picture postcard had overtaken both cartes-de-visite and stereographs in terms of the number of images sold each year.

12 Ian McDonald, *The Boer War in Postcards* (London: Wren's Park Publishing, 2000).

13 Examples of French postcards commenting on the Russo-Japanese War can be seen in Bruno de Perthuis, "Les cartes postales gravées et lithographiées sur la guerre russo-japonaise (1904–1905)," *Gazette des Beaux-Arts* (Sept. 1984): 86–98.

14 However, I have never seen any postcard from this war that matches some that were mailed during the U.S. conflict with Mexico. In those postcards, American soldiers posed alongside the bodies of their enemies. Paul Vanderwood notes how on postcards "the sailors and Marines stand

like safari hunters over their dead quarry, Mexicans who had resisted the invasion." See his "The Picture Postcard as Historical Evidence: Veracruz, 1914," *Americas* 45, no. 2 (1993): 207.

15 Examples can be seen in Anne Goulzadian, *L'empire du dernier Tsar* (Paris: Editions Astrid, 1982).

16 Yulia Mikhailova, "Images of Enemy and Self: 'Popular Prints' of the Russo-Japanese War," *Acta Slavic Iaponica* 16 (1998): 36.

17 Evgenii Sergeev, "Russkie voennoplennye v Germanii i Avstro-Vengrii v gody pervoi mirovoi voiny," *Novaia i noveishaia istoriia*, no. 4 (1996), 66.

18 Ibid., 71.

19 Quoted in Elsa Brändström, *Among Prisoners of War in Russia and Siberia* (London: Hutchinson, 1929), 26.

20 Gerald H. Davis, "National Red Cross Societies and Prisoners of War in Russia, 1914–1918," *Journal of Contemporary History* 28, no. 1 (1993): 43.

21 The Civilian Prisoners Bureau received items forwarded to it by national Red Cross societies and handled an estimated 30,000 letters and postcards per day for the duration of the war. Matthew Stibbe, "The Internment of Civilians by Belligerent States during the First World War and the Response of the International Committee of the Red Cross," *Journal of Contemporary History* 41, no. 1 (2006): 10.

22 Oxana Nagornaja, "United by Barbed Wire: Russian POWs in Germany, National Stereotypes, and International Relations, 1914–22," *Kritika* 10, no. 3 (2009): 478. Some of the postcards are reproduced in her article.

23 Peter Holquist, "What's so Revolutionary about the Russian Revolution? State Practices and the New-Style Politics, 1914–21," in *Russian Modernity*, eds. D. Hoffmann and Y. Kotsonis (New York: St. Martin's Press, 2000), 93; and John T. Smith, "Russian Military Censorship during the First World War," *Revolutionary Russia* 14, no. 1 (2001): 87. The Russians were not the only ones inundated with mail. The British Army needed more than 4,000 postal employees to handle almost two million pieces of mail per day. See Tonie Holt and Valmai Holt, *Till the Boys Come Home: The Picture Postcards of the First World War* (London: Macdonald and Jane's, 1977), 9.

24 For a discussion of the British Field Service postcard see Paul Fussell, *The Great War and Modern Memory* (New York: Oxford University Press, 1975), 184–6. Fussell's analysis greatly influenced my own thinking about post-cards and the efforts to standardize the wartime experiences of certain groups.

25 A.G. Martin, *Mother Country Fatherland: The Story of a British-Born German Soldier* (London: Macmillan, 1936), 200.

26 Peter A. Michalove and David H. Skipton, *Postal Censorship in Imperial Russia*, vol. II (Urbana, IL: John H. Otten, 1989), 263.

27 Prince Dimitry Kandaouroff, *Collecting Postal History* (New York: Larousse, 1974), 130 and 133.

28 M. Chapkina, *Khudozhestvennaia otkrytka* (Moscow: Galart, 1993), 15.

29 Robert McCormick, *With the Russian Army* (New York: Macmillan, 1915), 78. The photographs appear opposite page 162.

30 Malcolm Grow, *Surgeon Grow: An American in the Russian Fighting* (New York: Frederick A. Stokes, 1918). The photograph appears between pages 56 and 57.

31 Valerii Stigneev, *Vek fotografii, 1894–1994: Ocherki istorii otechestvennoi fotografii* (Moscow: URSS, 2005), 14–15.

32 Tatiana Alexinsky, *With the Russian Wounded* (London: T. Fisher Unwin, 1916), 75.

33 Princess Catherine Sayn-Wittgenstein, *La fin de ma Russie: Journal 1914–1919* (Montricher, Switzerland: Les éditions noir sur blanc, 1990), 67. The passage reads this way in English: "Truth be told, Austrian prisoners are working in the fields but they are no longer enemies. They have not, as Paper writes, 'come to destroy Bronitsa, but to help.' Without them, it would be impossible to bring in the harvest this year."

34 Martin, *Mother Country Fatherland*, 285–6.

35 Iogolevitch carefully relayed that the prisoner was Gottlieb Rittweg from the Fifth Bavarian Cavalry Division, Sixth Volunteer Regiment, Fifth Squadron. Paul Iogolevitch, *The Youngest Russian Corporal* (New York: Harper and Brothers, 1919), 231.

36 Norris, *War of Images*, 189.

37 R. Scotland Liddell, *On the Russian Front* (London: Simpkin, Marshall, Hamilton, Kent, 1916), 169.

38 Peter Gatrell, *A Whole Empire Walking: Refugees in Russia during World War I* (Bloomington: Indiana University Press, 1999), 3.

39 Ibid., 61.

40 Caroline Brothers, *War and Photography: A Cultural History* (London: Routledge, 1997), 142.

41 In the case of Figure 6.12, where the photograph has been reprinted, we can provide some information. According to the Latvian Historical Museum, it shows a Latvian refugee camp in the forest in 1915. See Gatrell, *A Whole Empire Walking*, 103.

42 Brothers, *War and Photography*, 141 and 143–4.

43 I am grateful to my colleague Mary Vipond for suggesting this interpretation to me.

44 Gatrell, *A Whole Empire Walking*, 75.

45 J. Oskine, *Le carnet d'un soldat russe* (Paris: Albin Michel, 1931), 30. The passage reads this way in English: "Truth be told I did not want to spend this

money but my brother insisted. He wanted at least a portrait of me since we do not know if I will be returning."

46 Liddell, *On the Russian Front*, 56.

47 Catherine Moriarty, "'Though in a Picture Only': Portrait Photography and the Commemoration of the First World War," in *Evidence, History and the Great War*, ed. G. Braybon (New York: Berghahn, 2003), 37.

48 Mary Britnieva, *One Woman's Story* (London: Arthur Baker, 1934), 22–3.

49 Moriarty, "'Though in a Picture Only,'" 40.

50 Christopher Stolarski, "Picturing War, Representing Empire: Russian Photojournalism during the First World War," paper presented at the Canadian Association of Slavists Annual Conference, Carleton University, Ottawa, May 2009. I am grateful to him for sending me a copy of the paper after the presentation.

51 Karen Petrone, *The Great War in Russian Memory* (Bloomington: Indiana University Press, 2011).

52 Gatrell, *Russia's First World War*, 258.

53 Catherine Moriarty, "Private Grief and Public Remembrance: British First World War Memorials," in *War and Memory in the Twentieth Century*, eds. M. Evans and K. Lunn (Oxford: Berg, 1997), 126.

54 Aleksandr Sergeevich Lukomskii, *Memoirs of the Russian Revolution* (Westport: Hyperion, 1975), 162–3.

55 Quoted in Susan Strasser, *Satisfaction Guaranteed: The Making of the American Mass Market* (New York: Pantheon, 1989), 102.

7. Picture Postcards and the Russian Revolution

1 Nicholas Nabokov, *Bagazh: Memoirs of a Russian Cosmopolitan* (New York: Atheneum, 1975), 84.

2 Interestingly, right-wing groups do not seem to have issued postcards. Two reasons for this omission can be suggested. The first has to do with the perceived audience for postcards, which was generally assumed to be middle and lower-middle class – therefore, not necessarily one that right-wing groups wanted to reach. I am grateful to Ron Bobroff for suggesting this line of thinking to me. The second reason may be that right-wing groups did not want to associate themselves with something they saw as mundane. As I mentioned earlier, there was conservative resistance to the postage stamps bearing the tsar's likeness that were issued in 1913. It seems highly likely that postcards could garner similar hostility.

3 Instead, they were often distributed like leaflets. See M. Chapkina, *Khudozhestvennaia otkrytka* (Moscow: Galart, 1993), 14.

4 For instance, only one artist who produced satirical postcards during the
   1905 Revolution, Mikhail Mikhailovich Chemodanov, has been identified
   by historians and collectors to date. A doctor with ties to the Bolshevik
   party, he was arrested in December 1906 and charged along with five
   accomplices who were responsible for distributing his postcards. He died
   before he could be brought to trial. See E. Fainshtein, "Russkie revoliutsionnye otkrytki (1905–1907)," *Sovetskii kollekstioner* (1967): 86–90.
5 David Skipton and Peter Michalove, *Postal Censorship in Imperial Russia*, vol. I
   (Urbana, IL: John H. Otten, 1989), 211.
6 Ibid., 211.
7 Elena Stasova, *Vospominaniia* (Moscow: Mysl', 1969), 49.
8 V.V. Shleev and E.B. Fainshtein, *Khudozhestvennye otkrytki i ikh sobiranie*
   (Moscow: Gosudarstvennoe izdatel'stvo izobrazitel'nogo iskusstva, 1960), 6.
9 R.C. Elwood, *Roman Malinovsky: A Life without a Cause* (Newtonville, MA:
   Oriental Research Partners, 1977), 32.
10 Orlando Figes and Boris Kolonitskii, *Interpreting the Russian Revolution: The
   Language and Symbols of 1917* (New Haven: Yale University Press, 1999),
   10–17.
11 See Charles Ruud, *Fighting Words: Imperial Censorship and the Russian Press,
   1804–1906* (Toronto: University of Toronto Press, 1982), 220–1.
12 V.D. Bonch-Bruevich, *Bol'shevistskie izdatel'skie dela v 1905–1907 gg.*
   (Moscow: OGIZ, 1933), 87.
13 Bonch-Bruevich, who ran *Vpered*, gives the address as Karavannaia Street,
   Building 9, Apartment 19. See p. 29; he mentions the postcards on p. 32.
14 Iakov M. Belitskii and Georgii N. Glezer, *Rasskazy ob otkrytkakh* (Moscow:
   Radio i sviaz', 1986), 96. Examples of the *Vpered* postcards can also be seen
   in this work.
15 An example of his work can be found in Fainshtein, "Russkie," 85.
16 John Foster Fraser, *Red Russia* (London: Cassell, 1907), 193. Reprints of
   four satirical postcards from 1905 are included in his book. They are opposite pages 46 and 163.
17 For instance, in St. Petersburg, the Vyborgskii raion committee of the
   RSDRP published a postcard with the lyrics to "The International" in 1917.
   See Belitskii and Glezer, *Rasskazy ob otkrytkakh*, 69. At the end of 1918, the
   lyrics were also printed on the back of calendar postcards made for the Red
   Army. See Chapkina, *Khudozhestvennaia otkrytka*, 175.
18 Caspar Ferenczi, "Freedom of the Press under the Old Regime, 1905–
   1914," in *Civil Rights in Imperial Russia*, eds. O. Crisp and L. Edmondson
   (Oxford: Clarendon Press, 1989), 191.
19 N.L. Brodskii, "Dekabristy v russkoi khudozhestvennoi literature," *Katorga i
   ssylka* 21 (1925): 217.

20 Tobie Mathew, "The Hundred Year War: Russian Political Postcards 1905–2005," www.passportmagazine.ru/article/367.

21 Richard Carline, *Pictures in the Post,* 2nd ed. (London: Gordon Fraser, 1971), 113.

22 Lesley Chamberlain, *Lenin's Private War: The Voyage of the Philosophy Steamer and the Exile of the Intelligentsia* (New York: St. Martin's Press, 2006), 231.

23 Henry W. Nevinson, *The Dawn in Russia,* reprint ed. (New York: Arno Press and New York Times, 1971), 170–1.

24 The deputies were eventually deprived of all civil rights and condemned to perpetual exile in Siberia. Richard Abraham, *Alexander Kerensky: The First Love of the Revolution* (New York: Columbia University Press, 1987), 84. The postcard is reproduced in Alison Rowley, "Popular Culture and Visual Narratives of Revolution: Russian Postcards, 1905–1922," *Revolutionary Russia* 21, no. 1 (2008): 8.

25 Frederick Corney, "Narratives of October and the Issue of Legitimacy," in *Russian Modernity,* eds. D. Hoffmann and Y. Kotsonis (New York: St. Martin's Press, 2000), 188.

26 Peter Burke, *Eyewitnessing: The Uses of Images as Historical Evidence* (Ithaca: Cornell University Press, 2001), 152.

27 Eric Hobsbawm, "Mass-Producing Traditions: Europe, 1870–1914," in *The Invention of Tradition,* eds. E. Hobsbawm and T. Ranger (Cambridge: Cambridge University Press, 1983), 285.

28 The postcard showing an SR banner is reproduced in Charles E. Beury, *Russia after the Revolution* (Philadelphia: George W. Jacobs, 1918), 87.

29 Richard Bartmann, *Picture Postcard Encyclopaedia of Russia* (Erlangen: privately published by author, 1992). See the entry on "Izvestiia Petrogradskago [sic] Soveta."

30 See Daniel T. Orlovsky, "The Provisional Government and Its Cultural Work," in *Bolshevik Culture,* eds. A. Gleason, P. Kenez, and R. Stites (Bloomington: Indiana University Press, 1985), 53.

31 Badges and medals bearing Kerensky's likeness were also produced. See Figes and Kolonitskii, *Interpreting the Russian Revolution,* 86.

32 Abraham, *Alexander Kerensky,* 145.

33 The postcard can be seen in Rowley, "Popular Culture," 14.

34 Burke, *Eyewitnessing,* 26.

35 Laurie Stoff, *They Fought for the Motherland* (Lawrence: University Press of Kansas, 2006), 105 and 115.

36 Louis de Robien, *The Diary of a Diplomat in Russia, 1917–1918* (New York: Praeger, 1970), 79.

37 I have not found any postcards of Kerensky that date from the final couple of months that he was in office. It is likely that some were created but they

may not have survived or may remain in the hands of private collectors.

38 Meriel Buchanan, *Petrograd: The City of Trouble, 1914–1918* (London: W. Collins Sons, 1918), 183–4.

39 Iurii Got'e, *Time of Troubles: The Diary of Iurii Vladimirovich Got'e*, trans. and ed. T. Emmons (Princeton: Princeton University Press, 1988), 60.

40 Interestingly, although the actions of Socialist Revolutionary women were heavily publicized, the party itself remained an organization dominated by men. Women accounted for only about 15 per cent of its members. Sally A. Boniece, "Mariia Spiridonova, 1884–1918: Feminine Martyrdom and Revolutionary Mythmaking" (PhD dissertation, Indiana University, 1995), 90.

41 See Barbara Heldt, *Terrible Perfection: Women and Russian Literature* (Bloomington: Indiana University Press, 1987).

42 See Marcia Morris, *Saints and Revolutionaries: The Ascetic Hero in Russian Literature* (Albany: State University of New York Press, 1993).

43 Boniece, "Mariia Spiridonova," 25.

44 Nina Berberova, *The Italics Are Mine*, trans. P. Radley (New York: Alfred A. Knopf, 1992), 82.

45 Albert Rhys Williams, *Journey into Revolution: Petrograd, 1917–1918* (Chicago: Quadrangle, 1969), 192.

46 Details of Spiridonova's life after 1917 can be found in Boniece, "Mariia Spiridonova"; Alexander Rabinowitch, "Maria Spiridonova's 'Last Testament,'" *Russian Review* 54, no. 3 (1995): 424–46; and V.M. Lavrov, *Mariia Spiridonova: Terroristka i zhertva terrora* (Moscow: Arkheograficheskii tsentr, 1996).

47 Kellogg Durland, *The Red Reign: The True Story of an Adventurous Year in Russia* (New York: Century Co., 1907), 387.

48 V.N. Vladimirov, *Mariia Spiridonova s portretem i risunkami* (Moscow: Vserossiiskago Soiuz ravnopraviia zhenshchin, 1906). The date on the book is mistakenly printed as 1905.

49 It can be seen in Rowley, "Popular Culture," 18.

50 I am grateful to Lars Lih for suggesting this idea to me.

51 The Society was founded in 1890 and published a newspaper, *Free Russia*, in addition to organizing these kinds of tours. Sergei Kravchinskii was another well-known revolutionary who engaged in this kind of publicity under the Society's auspices. See Jane E. Good, "America and the Russian Revolutionary Movement, 1888–1905," *Russian Review* 41, no. 3 (1982): 275–6.

52 Jane E. Good and David R. Jones, *Babushka: The Life of Russian Revolutionary Ekaterina K. Breshko-Breshkovskaia (1844–1934)* (Newtonville, MA: Oriental Research Partners, 1991), 88.

53 Ibid., 90.

54 Ibid., 111.

55 Ibid., 117.

56 Ekaterina Breshko-Breshkovskaia, *Hidden Springs of the Russian Revolution* (Stanford: Stanford University Press, 1931), 67.

57 Ivan Bunin, *Cursed Days: A Diary of Revolution*, trans. T. Marullo (London: Phoenix, 1998), 162.

58 The film is entitled *Babushka russkoi revoliutsii*. See Denise Youngblood, *The Magic Mirror: Moviemaking in Russia, 1908–1918* (Madison: University of Wisconsin Press, 1999), 119, for a discussion of it.

59 Burke argues that this image began with a painting of Napoleon in his study by Jacques-Louis David. He writes that the painting "presented a relatively new aspect of power, the ruler as bureaucrat, tied to his desk even in the small hours of the morning (a candle has been lit and the clock shows nearly quarter past four)." Burke, *Eyewitnessing*, 69.

60 Kevin J. Callahan, *Demonstration Culture: European Socialism and the Second International, 1889–1914* (Leicester: Troubador, 2010), 164.

61 Catherine Merridale, *Night of Stone: Death and Memory in Twentieth-Century Russia* (New York: Viking, 2000), 93.

62 Pitrim A. Sorokin, *Leaves from a Russian Diary – and Thirty Years After* (Boston: Beacon Press, 1950), 32–3. For an interesting contrast, see Bunin's scathing description of a revolutionary funeral. Bunin, *Cursed Days*, 115–16.

63 Eliisa Vaha, "Out of Oppression into Brotherhood: The Meaning of the October Revolution as Part of National Identity in Soviet History Textbooks," in *Imperial and National Identities in Pre-Revolutionary, Soviet, and Post-Soviet Russia*, eds. C.J. Chulos and J. Remy (Helsinki: SKS, 2002), 100.

64 N. Tagrin, *Mir v otkrytke* (Moscow: Izobrazitel'noe iskusstvo, 1978), 58.

65 Iakov Belitskii and Georgii Glezer, *Otkrytka prodolzhaet rasskaz* (Moscow: Radio i Sviaz', 1982), 6.

66 The first actual album of Lenin postcards was issued only after his death. Containing 24 postcards, the album, entitled *Ilich*, had a print run of 15,000 copies. Such modest offerings were dwarfed by the outpouring of materials created in the years to come. On Lenin postcards, see N. Tagrin, "Obraz Lenina v illiustrirovannoi otkrytke," *Sovetskaia knizhnaia torgovlia*, no. 4 (1960): 8–10.

67 Tobie Mathew, "'Wish You Were (Not) Here': Anti-Bolshevik Postcards of the Russian Civil War, 1918–21," *Revolutionary Russia* 23, no. 2 (2010): 185.

68 The difficulty of motivating soldiers in the expeditionary forces is outlined in Benjamin Isitt, *From Victoria to Vladivostok: Canada's Siberian Expedition, 1917–19* (Vancouver: UBC Press, 2010).

69 Marc Raeff, *Russia Abroad: A Cultural History of the Russian Emigration, 1919–1939* (Oxford: Oxford University Press, 1990), 4.

70 Robert C. Williams, *Culture in Exile: Russian Emigrés in Germany, 1881–1941* (Ithaca: Cornell University Press, 1972), 132.

71 See Paul Robinson, *The White Russian Army in Exile, 1920–1941* (Oxford: Oxford University Press, 2002); and Elizabeth White, *The Socialist Alternative to Bolshevik Russia: The Socialist Revolutionary Party, 1921–1939* (London: Routledge, 2011).

72 Unfortunately, it is impossible to determine exactly which group produced the card since no information appears on its reverse side. Mention of Tripitzin's exploits can be found in Emil Lengyel, *Siberia* (New York: Random House, 1943), 261–3.

73 The trial, and the propaganda campaign surrounding it, are described in Marc Jansen, *A Show Trial under Lenin: The Trial of the Socialist Revolutionaries, Moscow, 1922*, trans. J. Sanders (The Hague: Martinus Nijhoff, 1982). Despite devoting close to two chapters to the propaganda campaign, Jansen confines his remarks primarily to print journalism. He does not appear to know of the existence of the postcard shown in Figure 7.20.

74 Williams, *Culture in Exile*, 234.

75 Quoted in Jansen, *Show Trial*, 159.

Epilogue

1 Nikolai Punin, *The Diaries of Nikolai Punin, 1904–1953*, eds. S. Monas and J.G. Krupala (Austin: University of Texas Press, 1999), 188.

2 The texts of some of those postcards are reprinted in *The Diaries of Nikolai Punin*. See ibid., 72–5.

3 Dmitri Volkogonov, *Lenin* (New York: Free Press, 1994), 222.

4 For Lenin's attempts to reign in the burgeoning cult, see Iurii Annenkov, "Vospominaniia o Lenine," *Novyi zhurnal* 25 (1961): 125–50; Nina Tumarkin, *Lenin Lives!: The Lenin Cult in Soviet Russia*, enlarged ed. (Cambridge, MA: Harvard University Press, 1997); and E. Vittenberg, "Lenin protiv kulta Lenina," *Nauka i zhizn'* 4 (1989): 12–14.

5 On the manufacturers, see M. Zabochen', "Otkrytki – propagandisty," *Tvochestvo* 10 (1965): 24; and Iakov Belitskii and Georgii Glezer, *Otkrytka prodolzhaet rasskaz* (Moscow: Radio i sviaz', 1982), 7.

6 See Alexis Pogorelskin, "Kamenev in Early NEP: The Twelfth Party Congress," in *Rude and Barbarous Kingdom Revisited: Essays in Russian History and Culture in Honor of Robert O. Crummey*, eds. C. Dunning, R. Martin, and D. Rowland (Bloomington: Slavica Publishers, 2008).

7 N. Tagrin, *Mir v otkrytke* (Moscow: Izobrazitel'noe iskusstvo, 1978), 89.

8 Pitrim A. Sorokin, *Leaves from a Russian Diary – and Thirty Years After* (Boston: Beacon Press, 1950), 47; and Ivan Bunin, *Cursed Days: A Diary of*

Revolution, trans. T. Marullo (London: Phoenix Press, 1998), 198.

9   Mary Britnieva, *One Woman's Story* (London: Arthur Barker, 1934), 215.

10 Elena Shulman, *Stalinism on the Frontier of Empire: Women and State Formation in the Soviet Far East* (Cambridge: Cambridge University Press, 2008), 23.

11 See Alison Rowley, "Masha Grab Your Gun: 1930s Images of Soviet Women and the Defense of Their Country," *Minerva: Journal of Women and War* 2, no. 1 (2008): 61–2.

12 Z. Kokorina, *Rabotnitsa izuchai voennoe delo* (Moscow: Gosudarstvennoe izdatel'stvo otdel voennoi literatury, 1930), 31.

13 Reina Pennington, *Wings, Women, and War: Soviet Airwomen in World War II* (Lawrence: University of Kansas Press, 2001), 10.

14 Details about her life can be found in the documentary *Liubov' Orlova* (Mosfilm, 1983); and Aleksandr Barakin, *V luchakh slavy: zvezdy russkogo kino* (Moscow: Veche, 2007), 105–38.

15 B.N. Petrov, *Rezhissura massovogo sportivno-khudozhestvennogo teatra* (Leningrad: Leningradskii Gosudarstvennyi institut N.K. Krupskoi, 1986), 6.

16 For a good discussion of corporeality in the Stalin era, see Keith A. Livers, *Constructing the Stalinist Body: Fictional Representations of Corporeality in the Stalinist 1930s* (Lanham: Lexington Books, 2004).

17 Julianne Fürst, *Stalin's Last Generation* (Oxford: Oxford University Press, 2010), 269.

18 One incident included in Vassily Aksyonov's novel, *The Winter's Hero*, suggests they did not. In the scene, which takes place in a nightclub in the late Stalin era, a character named Bogoslovsky produces a pornographic postcard of a couple engaging in sexual intercourse. The group of people at the table play a game where they try to apply headlines from Soviet newspapers to the image on the postcard. Vassily Aksyonov, *The Winter's Hero*, trans. J. Glad (New York: Random House, 1996), 116.

19 Mikhail Zolotonosov, *Gliptokpratos: Issledovanie nemnogo diskursa* (St. Petersburg: Inapress, 1999), 19.

20 The quotation appears in Russian in A.A. Konovich, *Teatralizovannye prazdniki i obriady v SSSR* (Moscow: Vyshaia shkola, 1990), 63.

21 See Shoshana Keller, *To Moscow, Not Mecca: The Soviet Campaign against Islam in Central Asia, 1917–1941* (Westport: Praeger, 2001), 234.

22 Quoted in Orlando Figes, *The Whisperers: Private Life in Stalin's Russia* (New York: Metropolitan Books, 2007), 189.

23 The flight from Moscow to San Jacinto, California, covered a distance of 6,305 miles. It is described in M. Vodopyanov, *Outstanding Flights by Soviet Airmen* (Moscow: Foreign Languages Publishing House, 1939), 24–5; and John McCannon, *Red Arctic: Polar Exploration and the Myth of the North in the Soviet Union, 1932–1939* (New York: Oxford University Press, 1998), 72.

24 Emma Widdis, "To Explore or Conquer?" in *The Landscape of Stalinism: The Art and Ideology of Soviet Space,* eds. E. Dobrenko and E.Naiman (Seattle: University of Washington Press, 2003), 220.

25 For information about Graftio, see Графтио, Генрих Осипович, on http://ru.wikipedia.org; and Volkhovstroi, see Волховская ГЭС, on http://ru.wikipedia.org.

26 See Stephen Kotkin, *Magnetic Mountain: Stalinism as a Civilization* (Berkeley: University of California Press, 1995) for details about Magnitostroi and the city of Magnitogorsk that grew up to house its workers.

27 See Cynthia Ruder, *Making History for Stalin: The Story of the Belomor Canal* (Gainesville: University Press of Florida, 1998).

Bibliography

Abraham, Richard. *Alexander Kerensky: The First Love of the Revolution*. New York: Columbia University Press, 1987.

Aksyonov, Vassily. *The Winter's Hero*. Trans. J. Glad. New York: Random House, 1996.

Alexinsky, Tatiana. *With the Russian Wounded*. London: T. Fisher Unwin, 1916.

Alloula, Malek. *The Colonial Harem*. Minneapolis: University of Minnesota Press, 1986.

Anderson, Benedict. *Imagined Communities*. Rev. ed. London: Verso, 2006.

Andzhievskaia, Anna. "A Mother's Story." In *In the Shadow of Revolution*, eds. S. Fitzpatrick and Yu. Slezkine, 73–81. Princeton: Princeton University Press, 2000.

Annenkov, Iurii. "Vospominaniia o Lenine." *Novyi zhurnal* 25 (1961): 125–50.

Anonymous. *The Russian Diary of an Englishman: Petrograd, 1915–1917*. New York: Robert M. McBride, 1919.

Arbenina, Stella. *Through Terror to Freedom*. London: Hutchinson, 1929.

Baburina, Nina. *Russkii plakat pervoi mirovoi voiny*. Moscow: Iskusstvo i kul'tura, 1992.

Baedeker's Russia 1914. Reprint ed. London and Newton Abbot: George Allen and Unwin with David and Charles, 1971.

Baker, Helen. "Monarchy Discredited? Reactions to the Khodynka Coronation Catastrophe of 1896." *Revolutionary Russia* 16, no. 1 (2003): 1–46. http://dx.doi.org/10.1080/09546540308575763.

Baker, Peter. "The Social and Ideological Role of the Monarchy in Late Victorian Britain." MA thesis, University of Lancaster, 1978.

Barakin, Aleksandr. *V luchakh slavy: Zvezdy russkogo kino*. Moscow: Veche, 2007.

Barkovets, Olga. "The Emperor's Camera Obscura." In *Nicholas and Alexandra: At Home with the Last Tsar and His Family – Treasures from the Alexander Palace,* ed. M.P. Swezey, 39–47. Washington, DC: American-Russian Cultural Cooperation Foundation, 2004.

Barrett, Thomas M. "Lines of Uncertainty: The Frontiers of the North Caucasus." *Slavic Review* 54, no. 3 (1995): 578–601. http://dx.doi.org/10.2307/2501737.

– "Southern Living (in Captivity): The Caucasus in Russian Popular Culture." *Journal of Popular Culture* 31, no. 4 (1998): 75–93. http://dx.doi.org/10.1111/j.0022-3840.1998.3104_75.x.

Bartmann, Richard. *Picture Postcard Encyclopaedia of Russia.* Erlangen: privately published, 1992.

Bassin, Mark. "Inventing Siberia: Visions of the Russian East in the Early Nineteenth Century." *American Historical Review* 96, no. 3 (1991): 763–94. http://dx.doi.org/10.2307/2162430.

Bazilevich, K.V. *The Russian Posts in the XIX Century.* Trans. D. Skipton. Rossica Translation no. 2, 1987.

Belitskii, Iakov M., and Georgii N. Glezer. *Otkrytka prodolzhaet rasskaz.* Moscow: Radio i sviaz', 1982.

– *Rasskazy ob otkrytkakh.* Moscow: Radio i sviaz', 1986.

Berberova, Nina. *The Italics Are Mine.* Trans. P. Radley. New York: Alfred A. Knopf, 1992.

Berezhkov, Valentin. *At Stalin's Side.* New York: Birch Lane Press, 1994.

Berezhnyi, A.F. *Tsarskaia tsenzura i bor'ba bol'shevikov za svobody pechati (1895–1914).* Leningrad: Izdatel'stvo Leningradskogo universiteta, 1967.

Bernstein, Laurie. *Sonia's Daughters: Prostitutes and Their Regulation in Imperial Russia.* Berkeley: University of California Press, 1995.

Berry, W. Turner. "The Picture Postcard Craze." *Graphic Arts Focal Point* (June 1957): 1–5.

Beury, Charles E. *Russia after the Revolution.* Philadelphia: George W. Jacobs, 1918.

Biggs, Michael. "Putting the State on the Map: Cartography, Territory, and European State Formation." *Comparative Studies in Society and History* 41, no. 2 (1999): 374–405. http://dx.doi.org/10.1017/S0010417599002121.

Birkett, Dea. *Spinsters Abroad: Victorian Lady Explorers.* New York: Barnes and Noble Books, 1989.

Blobaum, Robert. "Criminalizing the 'Other': Crime, Ethnicity, and Antisemitism in Early Twentieth-Century Poland." In *Antisemitism and Its Opponents in Modern Poland*, ed. R. Blobaum, 81–103. Ithaca: Cornell University Press, 2000.

Bloch, Marc. *The Royal Touch: Sacred Monarchy and Scrofula in England and France.* Trans. J.E. Anderson. London: Routledge and Kegan Paul, 1973.

Boele, Otto. *Erotic Nihilism in Late Imperial Russia.* Madison: University of Wisconsin Press, 2009.

Bonch-Bruevich, V.D. *Bol'shevistskie izdatel'skie dela v 1905–1907 gg.* Moscow: OGIZ, 1933.

Boniece, Sally A. "Mariia Spiridonova, 1884–1918: Feminine Martyrdom and Revolutionary Mythmaking." PhD dissertation, Indiana University, 1995.

Bowers, Q. "David. "Souvenir Postcards and the Development of the Star System, 1912–1914." *Film History* 3, no. 1 (1989): 1–10.

Bowlt, John. *Moscou et Saint-Péterbourg, 1900–1920.* Paris: Hazan, 2008.

Bradley, Joseph. "Voluntary Associations, Civic Culture, and Obshchestvennost' in Moscow." In *Between Tsar and People*, eds. E.W. Clowes, S.D. Kassow, and J.L. West, 131–48. Princeton: Princeton University Press, 1991.

Brandon, Ruth. *Singer and the Sewing Machine: A Capitalist Romance.* New York: Kodansha International, 1977.

Brändström, Elsa. *Among Prisoners of War in Russia and Siberia.* London: Hutchinson, 1929.

Breshko-Breshkovskaia, Ekaterina. *Hidden Springs of the Russian Revolution.* Stanford: Stanford University Press, 1931.

Briggs, Asa. *Victorian Things.* Chicago: University of Chicago Press, 1988.

Britnieva, Mary. *One Woman's Story.* London: Arthur Baker, 1934.

Brockwary, Lucile H. *Science and Colonial Expansion: The Role of the British Royal Botanic Garden.* New York: Academic Press, 1979.

Brodskii, N.L. "Dekabristy v russkoi khudozhestvennoi literature." *Katorga i ssylka* 21 (1925): 187–226.

Brothers, Caroline. *War and Photography: A Cultural History.* London: Routledge, 1997.

Buchanan, Meriel. *Petrograd: The City of Trouble, 1914–1918.* London: W. Collins Sons, 1918.

Bugaevich, I. "Otkrytka v arsenale pedagoga." *Sovetskii kollektsioner*, no. 5 (1967): 91–8.

Bukharov, O.N. *Marki iz starogo al'boma.* Moscow: Radio i sviaz', 1981.

Bunin, Ivan. *Cursed Days: A Diary of Revolution.* Trans. T. Marullo. London: Phoenix Press, 1998.

Burke, Peter. *Eyewitnessing: The Uses of Images as Historical Evidence.* Ithaca: Cornell University Press, 2001.

Bury, Bishop Herbert. *Russian Life Today.* London: A.R. Mowbray, 1915.

Buszek, Maria-Elena. "Representing 'Awarishness': Burlesque, Feminist Transgression, and the 19th-Century Pin-up." *Drama Review* 43, no. 4 (1999): 141–62. http://dx.doi.org/10.1162/105420499760263606.

Buxhoeveden, Sophie. *The Life and Tragedy of Alexandra Feodorovna.* London: Longmans, Green, 1928.

Callahan, Kevin J. *Demonstration Culture: European Socialism and the Second International, 1889–1914.* Leicester: Troubador, 2010.

Cannadine, David. "The Context, Performance and Meaning of Ritual: The British Monarchy and the 'Invention of Tradition,' c. 1820–1977." In *The Invention of Tradition*, eds. E. Hobsbawm and T. Ranger, 101–64. Cambridge: Cambridge University Press, 1983.

– *History in Our Time*. New Haven: Yale University Press, 1998.

Cantacuzene, Princess Julia. *Revolutionary Days*. Ed. T. Emmons. Chicago: R.R. Donnelley and Sons, 1999.

Carline, Richard. *Pictures in the Post*. 2nd ed. London: Gordon Fraser, 1971.

Chamberlain, Lesley. *Lenin's Private War: The Voyage of the Philosophy Steamer and the Exile of the Intelligentsia*. New York: St. Martin's Press, 2006.

Chapkina, M. *Khudozhestvennaia otkrytka*. Moscow: Galart, 1993.

Clark, Katerina. "Socialist Realism and the Sacralizing of Space." In *The Landscape of Stalinism: The Art and Ideology of Soviet Space*, eds. E. Dobrenko and E. Naiman, 3–18. Seattle: University of Washington Press, 2003.

Cockfield, Jamie H. *White Crow: The Life and Times of the Grand Duke Nicholas Mikhailovich Romanov, 1859–1919*. Westport: Praeger, 2002.

Coe, Brian, and Paul Gates. *The Snapshot Photograph: The Rise of Popular Photography, 1888–1939*. London: Ash and Grant, 1977.

Cohen, Aaron. *Imagining the Unimaginable: World War, Modern Art, and the Politics of Public Culture in Russia, 1914–1917*. Lincoln: University of Nebraska Press, 2008.

Conroy, Mary Schaeffer. "Women Pharmacists in Russia before World War I: Women's Emancipation, Feminism, Professionalization, Nationalism and Class Conflict." In *Women and Society in Russia and the Soviet Union*, ed. L. Edmondson, 48–76. Cambridge: Cambridge University Press, 1992. http://dx.doi.org/10.1017/CBO9780511520877.005

Corney, Frederick. "Narratives of October and the Issue of Legitimacy." In *Russian Modernity*, eds. D. Hoffmann and Y. Kotsonis, 185–203. New York: St. Martin's Press, 2000.

Coysh, A.W. *The Dictionary of Picture Postcards in Britain, 1894–1939*. Woodbridge: Antique Collectors' Club, 1984.

Cunningham, Hugh. "The Language of Patriotism, 1750–1914." *History Workshop Journal* 12, no. 1 (1981): 8–31.

Darrah, William. *The World of Stereographs*. Gettysburg: privately published, 1977.

– *Cartes de Visite in Nineteenth-Century Photography*. Gettysburg: privately published, 1981.

Davis, Gerald H. "National Red Cross Societies and Prisoners of War in Russia, 1914–1918." *Journal of Contemporary History* 28, no. 1 (1993): 31–52. http://dx.doi.org/10.1177/002200949302800103.

Davis, Richard Harding. *A Year From a Reporter's Note-book*. New York: Harper and Brothers, 1897.

Davis, Tracy. "The Actress in Victorian Pornography." In *Victorian Scandals: Representations of Gender and Class*, ed. K.O. Garrigan, 99–103. Athens: Ohio University Press, 1992.

de Cordova, Richard. "The Emergence of the Star System in America: An Examination of the Institutional and Ideological Function of the Star, 1907–1922." PhD dissertation, University of California at Los Angeles, 1986.

de Perthuis, Bruno. "Les cartes postales gravées et lithographiées sur la guerre russo-japonaise (1904–1905)." *Gazette des beaux-arts* (Sept. 1984): 86–98.

de Robien, Louis. *The Diary of a Diplomat in Russia, 1917–1918*. New York: Praeger, 1970.

Denikin, Anton I. *The Career of a Tsarist Officer: Memoirs, 1872–1916*. Trans. M. Patoski. Minneapolis: University of Minnesota Press, 1975.

Dimond, Frances, and Roger Taylor. *Crown and Camera: The Royal Family and Photography, 1842–1910*. London: Viking, 1987.

Dolzhenko, G.P. *Istoriia turizma v dorevoliutsionnoi Rossii i SSSR*. Rostov: Izdatel'stvo Rostovskogo universiteta, 1988.

Dotterer, Steven, and Galen Cranz. "The Picture Postcard: Its Development and Role in American Urbanization." *Journal of American Culture* 5, no. 1 (1982): 44–50. http://dx.doi.org/10.1111/j.1542-734X.1982.0501_44.x.

Durland, Kellogg. *The Red Reign: The True Story of an Adventurous Year in Russia*. New York: Century Co., 1907.

Eager, M. *Six Years at the Russian Court*. London: Hurst and Blackett, 1906.

Edmondson, Linda. *Feminism in Russia, 1900–1917*. Stanford: Stanford University Press, 1984.

– "Women's Rights, Civil Rights and the Debate over Citizenship in the 1905 Revolution." In *Women and Society in Russia and the Soviet Union*, ed. L. Edmondson, 77–100. Cambridge: Cambridge University Press, 1992. http://dx.doi.org/10.1017/CBO9780511520877.006

Ehrenburg, Ilya. *People and Life, 1891–1921*. New York: Alfred A. Knopf, 1962.

Elwood, R.C. *Roman Malinovsky: A Life without a Cause*. Newtonville, MA: Oriental Research Partners, 1977.

Ely, Christopher. *This Meager Nature: Landscape and National Identity in Imperial Russia*. DeKalb: Northern Illinois University Press, 2002.

– "The Origins of Russian Scenery: Volga River Tourism and Russian Landscape Aesthetics." *Slavic Review* 62, no. 4 (2003): 666–82. http://dx.doi.org /10.2307/3185650.

Engel, Barbara A. *Between the Fields and the City: Women, Work, and Family in Russia, 1861–1914*. Cambridge: Cambridge University Press, 1996.

Engelstein, Laura. *The Keys to Happiness: Sex and the Search for Modernity in Fin-de-Siècle Russia*. Ithaca: Cornell University Press, 1992.

Erickson, Carolly. *Alexandra: The Last Tsarina.* New York: St. Martin's Griffin, 2001.

Evans, Eric J., and Jeffrey Richards. *A Social History of Britain in Postcards 1870–1930.* London: Longman, 1980.

Fainshtein, E.B. "Russkie revoliutsionnye otkrytki (1905–1907)." *Sovetskii kollekstioner* (1967): 86–90.

Farrell, Dianne Ecklund. "The Bawdy Lubok: Sexual and Scatalogical Content in Eighteenth-Century Russian Popular Prints." In *Eros i pornografiia v russkoi kul'ture*, eds. M. Levitt and A. Toporkov, 16–41. Moscow: Ladomir, 1999.

Ferenczi, Caspar. "Freedom of the Press under the Old Regime, 1905–1914." In *Civil Rights in Imperial Russia*, eds. O. Crisp and L. Edmondson, 191–214. Oxford: Clarendon Press, 1989.

Field, Daniel. *Rebels in the Name of the Tsar.* Boston: Unwin Hyman, 1989.

Figes, Orlando. *The Whisperers: Private Life in Stalin's Russia.* New York: Metropolitan Books, 2007.

Figes, Orlando, and Boris Kolonitskii. *Interpreting the Russian Revolution: The Language and Symbols of 1917.* New Haven: Yale University Press, 1999.

Findlen, Paula. "Humanism, Politics and Pornography in Renaissance Italy." In *The Invention of Pornography: Obscenity and the Origins of Modernity, 1500–1800*, ed. L. Hunt, 49–108. New York: Zone Books, 1993.

Fraser, John Foster. *Red Russia.* London: Cassell, 1907.

Fürst, Julianne. *Stalin's Last Generation.* Oxford: Oxford University Press, 2010. http://dx.doi.org/10.1093/acprof:oso/9780199575060.001.0001

Fussell, Paul. *The Great War and Modern Memory.* New York: Oxford University Press, 1975.

G. B-n, "Bor'ba s pornografiei." *Peterburgsksia gazeta* (6 Aug. 1906).

Gaines, Jane. "Costume and Narrative: How Dress Tells the Woman's Story." In *Fabrications: Costume and the Female Body*, eds. J. Gaines and C. Herzog, 180–211. New York: Routledge, 1990.

Gatrell, Peter. *A Whole Empire Walking: Refugees in Russia during World War I.* Bloomington: Indiana University Press, 1999.

– *Russia's First World War.* Harlow: Pearson, 2005.

Geary, C.M., and V.-L. Webb, eds. *Delivering Views: Distant Cultures in Early Postcards.* Washington, DC: Smithsonian Institution Press, 1998.

Ginzburg, S. *Kinematografiia dorevoliutsionnoi Rossii.* Moscow: Izdatel'stvo iskusstvo, 1963.

Goldschmidt, Paul. "Pornography in Russia." In *Consuming Russia*, ed. Adele Barker, 318–39. Durham: Duke University Press, 1999.

Good, Jane E. "America and the Russian Revolutionary Movement, 1888–1905." *Russian Review* 41, no. 3 (1982): 273–87. http://dx.doi.org/10.2307/129602.

Good, Jane E., and David R. Jones. *Babushka: The Life of Russian Revolutionary Ekaterina K. Breshko-Breshkovskaia (1844–1934)*. Newtonville, MA: Oriental Research Partners, 1991.

Gorsuch, Anne, and Diane Koenker, eds. *Turizm: The Russian and East European Tourist under Capitalism and Socialism*. Ithaca: Cornell University Press, 2006.

Got'e, Iurii. *Time of Troubles: The Diary of Iurii Vladimirovich Got'e*. Trans. and ed. T. Emmons. Princeton: Princeton University Press, 1988.

Goulzadian, Anne. *L'empire du dernier Tsar*. Paris: Editions Astrid, 1982.

Grabbe, Paul. *Windows on the River Neva*. New York: Pomerica Press, 1977.

Graham, Stephen. *A Vagabond in the Caucasus*. London: John Lane, 1911.

Grand-Carteret, John. *Le musée pittoresque du voyage du Tsar*. Paris: Librairie Charpentier et Fasquelle, 1896.

Grant, Jonathan. "The Socialist Construction of Philately in the Early Soviet Era." *Comparative Studies in Society and History* 37, no. 3 (1995): 476–93. http://dx.doi.org/10.1017/S0010417500019770.

Greenfield, Douglas. "From the Hothouse to the Harem: Rozanov and Decadence." *Ulbandus* 8 (2004): 67–86.

Groberg, Kristi. "Crucified Women in Russian Fin-de-Siècle Art: Why Demons Cling to the Cross." Paper presented at the annual conference of the Canadian Association of Slavists, Concordia University, Montreal, 30 May 2010.

Grow, Malcolm. *Surgeon Grow: An American in the Russian Fighting*. New York: Frederick A. Stokes, 1918.

Hamilton, Peter, and Roger Hargreaves. *The Beautiful and the Damned: The Creation of Identity in Nineteenth-Century Photography*. London: National Portrait Gallery, 2001.

Hamm, Michael. "Introduction." In *The City in Late Imperial Russia*, ed. M. Hamm, 1–8. Bloomington: Indiana University Press, 1986.

Hammon, Paul. *French Undressing: Naughty Postcards from 1900 to 1920*. London: Jupiter Books, 1976.

Hargrove, June. "Shaping the National Image: The Cult of Statues to Great Men in the Third Republic." In *Nationalism in the Visual Arts*, ed. R. Etlin, 49–63. Washington: National Gallery of Art, 1991.

Harley, J.B. "Maps, Knowledge, and Power." In *The Iconography of Landscape*, eds. D. Cosgrove and S. Daniels, 277–312. Cambridge: Cambridge University Press, 1988.

Harris, Carolyn. "The Succession Prospects of Grand Duchess Olga Nikolaevna (1895–1918)." *Canadian Slavonic Papers* 54, no. 1–2 (2012): 61–85.

Hatch, Alden. *American Express: A Century of Service*. Garden City, NY: Doubleday, 1950.

Healey, Dan. *Homosexual Desire in Revolutionary Russia*. Chicago: University of Chicago Press, 2001.

Heffer, Simon. *Power and Place: The Political Consequences of King Edward VII.*
London: Phoenix, 1998.

Heldt, Barbara. *Terrible Perfection: Women and Russian Literature.* Bloomington:
Indiana University Press, 1987.

Hellberg-Hirn, Elena. "Imperial Places and Stories." In *Imperial and National
Identities in Pre-Revolutionary, Soviet, and Post-Soviet Russia,* eds. C.J. Chulos and
J. Remy, 19–44. Helsinki: SKS, 2002.

Hobsbawm, Eric. "Mass-Producing Traditions: Europe, 1870–1914." In *The
Invention of Tradition,* eds. E. Hobsbawm and T. Ranger, 263–307. Cambridge:
Cambridge University Press, 1983.

Holmgren, Beth. *Rewriting Capitalism: Literature and the Market in Late Tsarist
Russia and the Kingdom of Poland.* Pittsburgh: University of Pittsburgh Press,
1998.

Holquist, Peter. "What's so Revolutionary about the Russian Revolution? State
Practices and the New-Style Politics, 1914–21." In *Russian Modernity,* eds.
D. Hoffmann and Y. Kotsonis, 87–114. New York: St. Martin's Press, 2000.

Holt, Tonie, and Valmai Holt. *Till the Boys Come Home: The Picture Postcards of the
First World War.* London: Macdonald and Jane's, 1977.

Hopkins, William. "The Development of 'Pornographic' Literature in
Eighteenth- and Early Nineteenth-Century Russia." PhD dissertation, Indiana
University, 1977.

Houston, Gail Turley. *Royalties: The Queen and Victorian Writers.* Charlottesville:
University Press of Virginia, 1999.

Hughes, Lindsey. "Monuments and Identity." In *National Identity in Russian
Culture,* eds. S. Franklin and E. Widdis, 171–96. Cambridge: Cambridge
University Press, 2004. http://dx.doi.org/10.1017/CBO9780511720116.017

Hunt, Lynn. "Introduction." In *The Invention of Pornography: Obscenity and the Origins
of Modernity, 1500–1800,* ed. L. Hunt, 9–45. New York: Zone Books, 1993.

– "Pornography and the French Revolution." In *The Invention of Pornography:
Obscenity and the Origins of Modernity, 1500–1800,* ed. L. Hunt, 301–39. New
York: Zone Books, 1993.

Huss, Marie-Monique. "Pronatalism and the Popular Ideology of the Child in
Wartime France: The Evidence of the Picture Postcard." In *The Upheaval of
War,* eds. R. Wall and J. Winter, 329–67. Cambridge: Cambridge University
Press, 1988.

International Sleeping Car and European Express Trains Ry. *Guide for the Use of
Travellers to the Far-East by the Trans-Siberian Ry.* London: privately published,
1910.

Iogolevitch, Paul. *The Youngest Russian Corporal.* New York: Harper and Brothers,
1919.

Isitt, Benjamin. *From Victoria to Vladivostok: Canada's Siberian Expedition, 1917–19.* Vancouver: UBC Press, 2010.

Jahn, Hubertus F. "For Tsar and Fatherland: Russian Popular Culture and the First World War." In *Cultures in Flux*, eds. S.P. Frank and M.D. Steinberg. 131–46. Princeton: Princeton University Press, 1994.

– *Patriotic Culture in Russia during World War I.* Ithaca: Cornell University Press, 1995.

Jakle, John A. *City Lights: Illuminating the American Night.* Baltimore: Johns Hopkins University Press, 2001.

– *Postcards of the Night: Views of American Cities.* Santa Fe: Museum of New Mexico Press, 2003.

Jakle, John A., and Keith Sculle. "The American Hotel in Postcard Advertising: An Image Gallery." *Material Culture* 37, no. 2 (2005): 1–25.

Jansen, Marc. *A Show Trial under Lenin: The Trial of the Socialist Revolutionaries, Moscow 1922.* Trans. J. Sanders. The Hague: Martinus Nijhoff, 1982.

Johanson, Christine. *Women's Struggle for Higher Education in Russia.* Montreal: McGill-Queen's University Press, 1987.

Jordanova, Ludmilla. *Sexual Visions: Images of Gender in Science and Medicine between the Eighteenth and Twentieth Centuries.* Madison: University of Wisconsin Press, 1989.

Kanatchikov, Semen. *A Radical Worker in Tsarist Russia.* Trans. R. Zelnik. Stanford: Stanford Stanford University Press, 1986.

Kandaouroff, Prince Dimitry. *Collecting Postal History.* New York: Larousse, 1974.

Keeling, H.V. *Bolshevism: Mr. Keeling's Five Years in Russia.* London: Hodder and Stoughton, 1919.

Keller, Shoshana. *To Moscow, Not Mecca: The Soviet Campaign against Islam in Central Asia, 1917–1941.* Westport: Praeger, 2001.

Kelly, Veronica. "Beauty and the Market: Actress Postcards and Their Senders in Early Twentieth-Century Australia." *New Theater Quarterly* 20, no. 2 (2004): 99–116. http://dx.doi.org/10.1017/S0266464X04000016.

Kenez, Peter. *Cinema and Soviet Society, 1917–1953.* Cambridge: Cambridge University Press, 1992.

Kent, Christopher. "Image and Reality: The Actress and Society." In *A Widening Sphere: Changing Roles of Victorian Women*, ed. M. Vicinus, 94–116. Bloomington: Indiana University Press, 1977.

Kernan, Michael. "Pushing the Envelope." *Smithsonian Magazine* (Oct. 1997). http://www.smithsonianmag.si.edu/smithsonian/issues97/oct97/mall_oct97.html. Accessed 18 June 2002.

Kivelson, Valerie. *Cartographies of Tsardom: The Land and Its Meanings in Seventeenth-Century Russia.* Ithaca: Cornell University Press, 2006.

Kivelson, Valerie, and Joan Neuberger, eds. *Picturing Russia: Explorations in Visual Culture*. New Haven: Yale University Press, 2008.

Kleinmichel, Countess. *Memories of a Shipwrecked World*. New York: Brentano's, 1923.

Kokorina, Z. *Rabotnitsa izuchai voennoe delo*. Moscow: Gosudarstvennoe izdatel'stvo otdel voennoi literatury, 1930.

Kolonitskii, Boris. *"Tragicheskaia erotica": Obrazy imperatorskoi sem'i v gody pervoi mirovoi voiny*. Moscow: Novoe Literaturnoe Obozrenie, 2010.

Komitet populiarizatsii khudozhestvennykh izdaniii. *Za tridtsat' let, 1896–1926*. Leningrad: published by the author, 1928.

Konovich, A.A. *Teatralizovannye prazdniki i obriady v SSSR*. Moscow: Vyshaia shkola, 1990.

Kotkin, Stephen. *Magnetic Mountain: Stalinism as a Civilization*. Berkeley: University of California Press, 1995.

Kravitz, Samantha. "The Business of Selling the Soviet Union: Intourist and the Wooing of American Travelers, 1929–1939." MA thesis, Concordia University, 2006.

Krichevskii, M., ed. *Dnevnik A.S. Suvorina*. Moscow: Izdatel'stvo L.D. Freikel, 1923.

Kudrina, Iuliia. *Imperatritsa Mariia Fedorovna (1847–1928 gg)*. Moscow: Olma-Press, 2001.

Kulagina, A.V. ""Russkaia eroticheskaia chastushki." In *Eros i pornografiia v russkoi kul'ture*, eds. M. Levitt and A. Toporkov, 94–120. Moscow: Ladomir, 1999.

Kyrou, Ado. *L'âge d'or de la carte postale*. Paris: André Balland, 1966.

Lahti, Katherine. "On Living Statues and Pandora, *Kamennye baby* and Futurist Aesthetics – The Female Body in *Vladimir Mayakovsky: A Tragedy*." *Russian Review* 58, no. 3 (1999): 432–55. http://dx.doi.org/10.1111/0036-0341.00083.

Lavrov, V.M. *Mariia Spiridonova: Terroristka i zhertva terrora*. Moscow: Arkheograficheskii tsentr, 1996.

Layton, Susan. "The Creation of an Imaginative Caucasian Geography." *Slavic Review* 45, no. 3 (1986): 470–88. http://dx.doi.org/10.2307/2499052.

Leikina-Svirskaia, V.R. *Russkaia intelligentsiia v 1900–1917 godakh*. Moscow: Mysl', 1981.

Lengyel, Emil. *Siberia*. New York: Random House, 1943.

Lensen, George A. "The Attempt on the Life of Nicholas II in Japan." *Russian Review* 20, no. 3 (1961): 232–53. http://dx.doi.org/10.2307/126401.

Levitt, M., and A. Toporkov, eds. *Eros i pornografiia v russkoi kul'ture*. Moscow: Ladomir, 1999.

Lewinski, Jorge. *The Camera at War*. London: W.H. Allen, 1978.

Leyda, Jay. *Kino: A History of the Russian and Soviet Film.* Princeton: Princeton University Press, 1973.

Liddell, R. Scotland. *On the Russian Front.* London: Simpkin, Marshall, Hamilton, Kent, 1916.

Lindenmeyr, Adele. *Poverty Is Not a Vice: Charity, Society, and the State in Imperial Russia.* Princeton: Princeton University Press, 1996.

Liubov' Orlova. Mosfilm, 1983.

Livers, Keith A. *Constructing the Stalinist Body: Fictional Representations of Corporeality in the Stalinist 1930s.* Lanham: Lexington Books, 2004.

Lobanov-Rostovsky, Prince A. *The Grinding Mill: Reminiscences of War and Revolution in Russia, 1913–1920.* New York: Macmillan, 1935.

Lukomskii, Aleksandr Sergeevich. *Memoirs of the Russian Revolution.* Westport: Hyperion Press, 1975.

Marcus, Steven. *The Other Victorians: A Study of Sexuality and Pornography in Mid-Nineteenth-Century England.* New Brunswick, NJ: Transaction Publishers, 2009.

Marks, Steven. *Road to Power: The Trans-Siberian Railroad and the Colonization of Asian Russia, 1850–1917.* Ithaca: Cornell University Press, 1991.

Marshak, Samuel. *At Life's Beginning: Some Pages of Reminiscence.* New York: E.P. Dutton, 1964.

Martin, A.G. *Mother Country Fatherland: The Story of a British-Born German Soldier.* London: Macmillan, 1936.

Marullo, Thomas Gaiton. *Ivan Bunin: The Twilight of Émigré Russia, 1934–1953.* Chicago: Ivan R. Dee, 2002.

Marye, George Thomas. *Nearing the End in Imperial Russia.* London: Selwyn and Blount, 1929.

Masing-Delic, Irene. "Creating the Living Work of Art: The Symbolist Pygmalion and His Antecedents." In *Creating Life: The Aesthetic Utopia of Russian Modernism,* eds. I. Paperno and D.D. Grossman, 51–82. Stanford: Stanford University Press, 1994.

Mathew, Tobie. "'Wish You Were (Not) Here': Anti-Bolshevik Postcards of the Russian Civil War, 1918–21." *Revolutionary Russia* 23, no. 2 (2010): 183–216. http://dx.doi.org/10.1080/09546545.2010.523070.

– "The Hundred Year War: Russian Political Postcards 1905–2005." www.passportmagazine.ru/article/367.

Matich, Olga. *Erotic Utopia: The Decadent Imagination in Russia's Fin-de-Siècle.* Madison: University of Wisconsin Press, 2005.

Mazur, P. "O pochtovom obrashchenii revoliutsionnykh marok vypuska 1918 goda." *Filateliia SSSR,* no. 12 (1972): 34–6.

McCannon, John. *Red Arctic: Polar Exploration and the Myth of the North in the Soviet Union, 1932–1939*. New York: Oxford University Press, 1998.

McCauley, Elizabeth Anne. *A.A.E. Disdéri and the Carte de Visite Portrait Photograph*. New Haven: Yale University Press, 1985.

McCormick, Robert. *With the Russian Army*. New York: Macmillan, 1915.

McDonald, Ian. *The Boer War in Postcards*. London: Wren's Park Publishing, 2000.

McDonald, Paul. *The Star System: Hollywood's Production of Popular Identities*. London: Wallflower, 2000.

McLean, Roderick. *Royalty and Diplomacy in Europe, 1890–1914*. Cambridge: Cambridge University Press, 2001.

McReynolds, Louise. *The News under Russia's Old Regime*. Princeton: Princeton University Press, 1991.

– *Russia at Play*. Ithaca: Cornell University Press, 2003.

Melancon, Michael. "The Ninth Circle: The Lena Goldfields Workers and the Massacre of 4 April 1912." *Slavic Review* 53, no. 3 (1994): 766–95. http://dx.doi.org/10.2307/2501519.

– *The Lena Goldfields Massacre and the Crisis of the Late Tsarist State*. College Station: Texas A & M University Press, 2006.

Melitonian, A., P. Sukanov, S. Velichko, and A. Larina. *Privet iz Moskvy*. Moscow: Magma, 2004.

Merridale, Catherine. *Night of Stone: Death and Memory in Twentieth-Century Russia*. New York: Viking, 2000.

Mikhailova, Yulia. "Images of Enemy and Self: 'Popular Prints' of the Russo-Japanese War." *Acta Slavic Iaponica* 16 (1998): 30–53.

Miliukov, Paul. *Political Memoirs, 1905–1917*. Ann Arbor: University of Michigan Press, 1967.

Milne, Esther. *Letters, Postcards, Email: Technologies of Presence*. New York: Routledge, 2010.

Milter, Katalin Szoverfy, and Joseph W. Slade. "Global Traffic in Pornography: The Hungarian Example." In *International Exposures: Perspectives on Modern European Pornography, 1800–2000*, ed. Lisa Z. Sigel, 173–204. New Brunswick, NJ: Rutgers University Press, 2005.

Moriarty, Catherine. "Private Grief and Public Remembrance: British First World War Memorials." In *War and Memory in the Twentieth Century*, eds. M. Evans and K. Lunn, 125–42. Oxford: Berg, 1997.

– "'Though in a Picture Only': Portrait Photography and the Commemoration of the First World War." In *Evidence, History and the Great War*, ed. G. Braybon, 30–42. New York: Berghahn, 2003.

Morozov, S. "Early Photography in Eastern Europe: Russia." *History of Photography* 1, no. 4 (1977): 327–47.

Morris, Marcia. *Saints and Revolutionaries: The Ascetic Hero in Russian Literature.* Albany: State University of New York Press, 1993.

Nabokov, Nicholas. *Bagazh: Memoirs of a Russian Cosmopolitan.* New York: Atheneum, 1975.

Nagornaja, Oxana. "United by Barbed Wire: Russian POWs in Germany, National Stereotypes, and International Relations, 1914–22." *Kritika* 10, no. 3 (2009): 475–98. http://dx.doi.org/10.1353/kri.0.0111.

Nevinson, Henry W. *The Dawn in Russia.* Reprint ed. New York: Arno Press and New York Times, 1971.

Nikon, Bishop. "Vera Khristova ne terpit dvoedushiia." *Tserkovnym vedomostiam* 9 (Feb. 1913): 282–91.

Norberg, Kathryn. "The Libertine Whore: Prostitution in French Pornography from Margot to Juliette." In *The Invention of Pornography: Obscenity and the Origins of Modernity, 1500–1800,* ed. L. Hunt, 225–52. New York: Zone Books, 1993.

Nørgaard, Erik. *With Love to You: A History of the Erotic Postcard.* New York: Clarkson N. Potter, 1969.

Norris, Stephen. *A War of Images: Russian Popular Prints, Wartime Culture, and National Identity, 1812–1945.* DeKalb: Northern Illinois University Press, 2006.

Orlovsky, Daniel T. "The Provisional Government and Its Cultural Work." In *Bolshevik Culture,* eds. A. Gleason, P. Kenez, and R. Stites, 39–56. Bloomington: Indiana University Press, 1985.

Osborne, Peter. *Traveling Life: Photography, Travel and Visual Culture.* Manchester: Manchester University Press, 2000.

Oskine, J. *Le carnet d'un soldat russe.* Paris: Albin Michel, 1931.

Ouellette, William, and Barbara Jones. *Erotic Postcards.* New York: Excalibur Books, 1977.

Parr, Martin. *Boring Postcards.* London: Phaidon, 1999.

Paustovsky, Konstantin. *Slow Approach of Thunder.* Trans. M. Harari and M. Duncan. London: Harvill, 1965.

– *In That Dawn.* Trans. M. Harari and M. Duncan. London: Harvill, 1967.

Pease, Allison. *Modernism, Mass Culture, and the Aesthetics of Obscenity.* Cambridge: Cambridge University Press, 2000.

Pennington, Reina. *Wings, Women, and War: Soviet Airwomen in World War II.* Lawrence: University of Kansas Press, 2001.

Percival, Nora Lourie. *Weather of the Heart: A Child's Journey Out of Revolutionary Russia.* Boone, NC: High Country Publishers, 2001.

Petrone, Karen. *The Great War in Russian Memory.* Bloomington: Indiana University Press, 2011.

Petrov, B.N. *Rezhissura massovogo sportivno-khudozhestvennogo teatra.* Leningrad: Leningradskii Gosudarstvennyi institut N.K. Krupskoi, 1986.

Pil'niak, Boris. *The Naked Year.* Trans. A.R. Tulloch. Ann Arbor: Ardis, 1975.

Plokhy, Serhii. "The City of Glory: Sevastopol in Russian Historical Mythology." *Journal of Contemporary History* 35, no. 3 (2000): 369–83. http://dx.doi.org/10.1177/002200940003500303.

Pogorelskin, Alexis. "Kamenev in Early NEP: The Twelfth Party Congress." In *Rude and Barbarous Kingdom Revisited: Essays in Russian History and Culture in Honor of Robert O. Crummey,* eds. C. Dunning, R. Martin, and D. Rowland, 173–87. Bloomington: Slavica, 2008.

Polikarpova, G.A., and L.A. Protsai. "Iz istorii izdatel'stva Obshchiny sviatoi Evgenii." In *Izdaniia Obshchiny sviatoi Evgenii,* ed. Irina Zolotinkina, 7–12. St. Petersburg: Palace Editions and Graficart, 2008.

Pratt, Mary Louise. *Imperial Eyes: Travel Writing and Transculturation.* London: Routledge, 1992.

Prochaska, Frank. *Royal Bounty: The Making of a Welfare Monarchy.* New Haven: Yale University Press, 1995.

Prochno, Renate. "Nationalism in British Eighteenth-Century Painting: Sir Joshua Reynolds and Benjamin West." In *Nationalism in the Visual Arts,* ed. R. Etlin, 27–47. Washington, DC: National Gallery of Art, 1991.

Prokof'eva, Elena. *Koroleva ekrana.* Moscow: Izdatel'skii dom "I.G.S.," 2001.

Prokofiev, Sergei. *Sergei Prokofiev Diaries 1907–1914: Prodigious Youth.* Trans. and ed. A. Phillips. Ithaca: Cornell University Press, 2006.

– *Sergey Prokofiev Diaries, 1915–1923: Behind the Mask.* Trans. and ed. A. Phillips. Ithaca: Cornell University Press, 2008.

Punin, Nikolai. *The Diaries of Nikolai Punin, 1904–1953.* Eds. S. Monas and J.G. Krupala. Austin: University of Texas Press, 1999.

Rabinowitch, Alexander. "Maria Spiridonova's 'Last Testament.'" *Russian Review* 54, no. 3 (1995): 424–46. http://dx.doi.org/10.2307/131440.

Radzinsky, Edvard. *Alexander II.* New York: Free Press, 2005.

Raeff, Marc. *Russia Abroad: A Cultural History of the Russian Emigration, 1919–1939.* Oxford: Oxford University Press, 1990.

Richards, Sandra. *The Rise of the English Actress.* New York: St. Martin's Press, 1993.

Robins, Jane. *The Trial of Queen Caroline.* New York: Free Press, 2006.

Robinson, Paul. *The White Russian Army in Exile, 1920–1941.* Oxford: Oxford University Press, 2002. http://dx.doi.org/10.1093/acprof:oso/9780199250219.001.0001

Roosevelt, Priscilla. *Life on the Russian Country Estate.* New Haven: Yale University Press, 1995.

Rosenman, Ellen Bayuk. *Unauthorized Pleasures: Accounts of Victorian Erotic Experiences.* Ithaca: Cornell University Press, 2003.

Rowley, Alison. "Miniature Propaganda: Self-Definition and Soviet Postage Stamps, 1917–41." *Slavonica* 8, no. 2 (2002): 135–57. http://dx.doi.org/10.1179/136174202790108162.

– "Popular Culture and Visual Narratives of Revolution: Russian Postcards, 1905–1922." *Revolutionary Russia* 21, no. 1 (2008): 1–31. http://dx.doi.org/10.1080/09546540802085495.

– "Masha Grab Your Gun: 1930s Images of Soviet Women and the Defense of Their Country." *Minerva: Journal of Women and War* 2, no. 1 (2008): 54–69. http://dx.doi.org/10.3172/MIN.2.1.54.

– "Monarchy and the Mundane: Picture Postcards and Images of the Romanovs, 1890–1970." *Revolutionary Russia* 22, no. 2 (2009): 125–52.

– "Picture Postcards as Recorders of the Changing Cult of Lenin, 1918–1930." *NEP Era: Soviet Russia, 1921–1928*, 4 (2010): 11–29.

Ruane, Christine. "Clothes Shopping in Imperial Russia: The Development of a Consumer Culture." *Journal of Social History* 28, no. 4 (1995): 765–82. http://dx.doi.org/10.1353/jsh/28.4.765.

– "The Development of a Fashion Press in Late Imperial Russia: *Moda – Zhurnal dlia svetskikh liudei.*" In *An Improper Profession: Women, Gender, and Journalism in Late Imperial Russia*, eds. B. Norton and J. Gheith, 74–92. Durham: Duke University Press, 2001.

Ruane, Christine. *The Empire's New Clothes: A History of the Russian Fashion Industry, 1700–1917*. New Haven: Yale University Press, 2009.

Ruder, Cynthia A. *Making History for Stalin: The Story of the Belomor Canal.* Gainesville: University Press of Florida, 1998.

"Russkii amerikanets." *Teatr i kino* 8 (Oct. 1916): 14.

Ruud, Charles. *Fighting Words: Imperial Censorship and the Russian Press, 1804–1906.* Toronto: University of Toronto Press, 1982.

Sablinsky, Walter. *The Road to Bloody Sunday.* Princeton: Princeton University Press, 1976.

Safonov, N., and V. Karlinskii. *Pis'mo otpravliaetsia v put': Rasskazy o zarozhdenii i razvitii otechestvennoi pochty.* Moscow: Izdatel'stvo sviaz', 1965.

Sampson, Gary D. "Unmasking the Colonial Picturesque: Samuel Bourne's Photographs of Barrackpore Park." In *Colonial Photography: Imag(in)ing Race and Place*, eds. E.M. Hight and G.D. Sampson, 84–106. London: Routledge, 2002.

Sayn-Wittgenstein, Princess Catherine. *La fin de ma Russie: Journal, 1914–1919.* Montricher, Switzerland: Les éditions noir sur blanc, 1990.

Schama, Simon. "The Domestication of Majesty: Royal Family Portraiture, 1500–1850." In *Art and History: Images and Their Meaning*, eds. R. Rotberg and T. Rabb, 155–83. Cambridge: Cambridge University Press, 1988.

Schönle, Andrea. *The Ruler in the Garden: Politics and Landscape Design in Imperial Russia.* Bern: Peter Lang, 2007.

Schor, Naomi. "Collecting Paris." In *The Cultures of Collecting,* eds. J. Elsner and R. Cardinal, 151–74. London: Reaktion Books, 1994.

Schuler, Catherine. *Women in Russian Theatre: The Actress in the Silver Age.* London: Routledge, 1996.

– "Actresses, Audience and Fashion in the Silver Age: A Crisis of Costume." In *Women and Russian Culture,* ed. R. Marsh, 107–21. New York: Berghahn, 1998.

Schwartz, Joan M. "*The Geography Lesson*: Photographs and the Construction of Imaginative Geographies." *Journal of Historical Geography* 22, no. 1 (1996): 16–45. http://dx.doi.org/10.1006/jhge.1996.0003.

Schwarzenbach, Alexis. "Royal Photographs: Emotions for the People." *Contemporary European History* 13, no. 3 (2004): 255–80. http://dx.doi.org/10.1017/S0960777304001729.

Seaton, Beverly. *The Language of Flowers: A History.* Charlottesville: University Press of Virginia, 1995.

Semmerling, Tim Jon. *Israeli and Palestinian Postcards: Presentations of National Self.* Austin: University of Texas Press, 2004.

Senelick, Laurence. "The Erotic Bondage of Serf Theatre." *Russian Review* 50, no. 1 (1991): 24–34. http://dx.doi.org/10.2307/130208.

– "Eroticism in Early Theatrical Photography." *Theatre History Studies* 11 (1991): 1–49.

Sergeev, Evgenii. "Russkie voennoplennye v Germanii i Avstro-Vengrii v gody pervoi mirovoi voiny." *Novaia i Noveishaia Istoriia,* no. 4 (1996): 65–78.

Shalimoff, G.V., and G.B. Shaw, eds. *Catalogue of Propaganda-Advertising Postal Cards of the USSR, 1927–1934.* Norfolk, VA: United Postal Stationery Society, 2002.

Shleev, V.V., and E.B. Fainshtein. *Khudozhestvennye otkrytki i ikh sobiranie.* Moscow: Gosudarstvennoe izdatel'stvo izobrazitel'nogo iskusstva, 1960.

Showalter, Elaine. *Sexual Anarchy: Gender and Culture at the Fin de Siècle.* Harmondsworth: Penguin, 1990.

Shulman, Elena. *Stalinism on the Frontier of Empire: Women and State Formation in the Soviet Far East.* Cambridge: Cambridge University Press, 2008. http://dx.doi.org/10.1017/CBO9780511497131

Sigel, Lisa Z. "Filth in the Wrong People's Hands: Postcards and the Expansion of Pornography in Britain and the Atlantic World, 1880–1914." *Journal of Social History* 33, no. 4 (2000): 859–85. http://dx.doi.org/10.1353/jsh.2000.0084.

Skipton, David, and Peter Michalove. *Postal Censorship in Imperial Russia,* vol. I. Urbana: John H. Otten, 1989.

Smith, John T. "Russian Military Censorship during the First World War." *Revolutionary Russia* 14, no. 1 (2001): 71–95. http://dx.doi.org/10.1080/09546540108575734.

Smith, Steve, and Catriona Kelly. "Commercial Culture and Consumerism." In *Constructing Russian Culture in the Age of Revolution, 1881–1940*, eds. C. Kelly and D. Shepherd, 106–55. Oxford: Oxford University Press, 1998.

Snopkov, A.E., P.A. Snopkov, A.F. Shkliaruk, N.I. Baburina, S.N. Artamonova, Rossiiskaia gosudarstvennaia biblioteka. *Zhenshchiny v russkom plakate.* Moscow: Kontakt-kul'tura, 2001.

Snopkov, A.E., P.A. Snopkov, and A.F. Shkliaruk. *Russkii kinoplakat.* Moscow: Kontakt-kul'tura, 2002.

Sorokin, Pitrim A. *Leaves from a Russian Diary – and Thirty Years After.* Boston: Beacon Press, 1950.

Staff, Frank. *The Picture Postcard and Its Origins.* New York: Praeger, 1966.

Stark, Gary D. "Pornography, Society, and the Law in Imperial Germany." *Central European History* 14, no. 3 (1981): 200–29. http://dx.doi.org/10.1017/S000893890000131X.

Stasova, Elena. *Vospominaniia.* Moscow: Mysl', 1969.

Steinberg, Mark, and Vladimir Khrustalev. *The Fall of the Romanovs.* New Haven: Yale University Press, 1995.

Sternin, G.Iu. *Khudozhestvennaia zhizn' Rossii: Na rubezhe XIX–XX vekov.* Moscow: Izdatel'stvo "Iskusstvo," 1970.

Stibbe, Matthew. "The Internment of Civilians by Belligerent States during the First World War and the Response of the International Committee of the Red Cross." *Journal of Contemporary History* 41, no. 1 (2006): 5–19. http://dx.doi.org/10.1177/0022009406058669.

Stigneev, Valerii. *Vek fotografii, 1894–1994: Ocherki istorii otechestvennoi fotografii.* Moscow: URSS, 2005.

Stites, Richard. "Days and Nights in Wartime Russia: Cultural Life, 1914–1917." In *European Culture in the Great War: The Arts, Entertainment, and Propaganda, 1914–1918*, eds. A. Roshwald and R. Stites, 8–31. Cambridge: Cambridge University Press, 1999.

Stoff, Laurie. *They Fought for the Motherland.* Lawrence: University Press of Kansas, 2006.

Stolarski, Christopher. "Picturing War, Representing Empire: Russian Photojournalism during the First World War." Paper presented at the Canadian Association of Slavists Annual Conference, Carleton University, Ottawa, May 2009.

– "Another Way of Telling the News: The Rise of Photojournalism in Russia, 1900–1914." *Kritika: Explorations in Russian and Eurasian History* 12, no. 3 (2011): 561–90. http://dx.doi.org/10.1353/kri.2011.0038.

Strasser, Susan. *Satisfaction Guaranteed: The Making of the American Mass Market.* New York: Pantheon Books, 1989.

– *Waste and Want: A Social History of Trash.* New York: Owl Books, 1999.

Sudakov, A.N. "Sovetskaia filateliia." In *Sto let russkoi pochtovoi marki, 1858–1958*, ed. I.G. Papinako. Moscow: Sviaz'izdat, 1958: 87–99.

Swift, E. Anthony. *Popular Theater and Society in Tsarist Russia.* Berkeley: University of California Press, 2002.

Swinglehurst, Edmund. *Cook's Tours: The Story of Popular Travel.* Poole: Blandford Press, 1982.

Tagrin, N. "Obraz Lenina v illiustrirovannoi otkrytke." *Sovetskaia knizhnaia torgovlia*, no. 4 (1960): 8–10.

Tagrin, N. *Mir v otkrytke.* Moscow: Izobrazitel'noe iskusstvo, 1978.

Teleshov, N. *A Writer Remembers.* London: Hutchinson, 1946.

Terret, T., and C. Nafziger. "Sports and Erotica: Erotic Postcards of Sportswomen during France's *années folles.*" *Journal of Sport History* 29, no. 2 (2002): 271–87. Medline:17265584

Thyrêt, Isolde. *Between God and Tsar: Religious Symbolism and the Royal Women of Muscovite Russia.* DeKalb: Northern Illinois University Press, 2001.

Tiersten, Lisa. *Marianne and the Market: Envisioning Consumer Society in Fin-de-Siècle France.* Berkeley: University of California Press, 2001.

Toepfer, Karl. "Nudity and Modernity in German Dance, 1910–1930." *Journal of the History of Sexuality* 3, no. 1 (1992): 58–108.

– *Empire of Ecstasy: Nudity and Movement in German Body Culture, 1910–1935.* Berkeley: University of California Press, 1997.

Tsivian, Yuri. *Early Cinema in Russia and Its Cultural Reception.* London: Routledge, 1994.

Tumarkin, Nina. *Lenin Lives!: The Lenin Cult in Soviet Russia,* enlarged ed. Cambridge, MA: Harvard University Press, 1997.

Tweedy, Owen. *Russia at Random.* London: Jarrolds, 1931.

Vaha, Eliisa. "Out of Oppression into Brotherhood: The Meaning of the October Revolution as Part of National Identity in Soviet History Textbooks." In *Imperial and National Identities in Pre-Revolutionary, Soviet, and Post-Soviet Russia,* eds. C.J. Chulos and J. Remy, 100–11. Helsinki: SKS, 2002.

Vanderwood, Paul. "The Picture Postcard as Historical Evidence: Veracruz, 1914." *Americas* [Academy of American Franciscan History] 45, no. 2 (1988): 201–25. http://dx.doi.org/10.2307/1006785.

Varakin, Aleksandr. *V luchakh slavy: zvezdy russkogo kino.* Moscow: Veche, 2006.

Vaule, Rosamund B. *As We Were: American Photographic Postcards, 1905–1930.* Boston: David R. Godine, 2004.

Vera Kholodnaia: K 100-letiiu so dnia rozhdeniia. Ed. B.B. Ziukov. Moscow: Iskusstvo, 1995.

Viroubova, Anna. *Memories of the Russian Court.* New York: Macmillan, 1923.

Vitashevskaia, M.N. *Starinnaia russkaia pochta.* Moscow: Sviaz' izdat', 1969.

Vittenberg, E. "Lenin protiv kulta Lenina." *Nauka i zhizn'* 4 (1989): 12–14.

Vladimirov, V.N. *Mariia Spiridonova s portretem i risunkami*. Moscow: Vserossiiskago Soiuz ravnopraviia zhenshchin, 1906.

Vladinets, N.I. *Filatelisticheskaia geografiia*. Moscow: Radio i sviaz', 1982.

Vodopyanov, M. *Outstanding Flights by Soviet Airmen*. Moscow: Foreign Languages Publishing House, 1939.

Volkogonov, Dmitri. *Lenin*. New York: Free Press, 1994.

von Geldern, James. *Bolshevik Festivals, 1917–1920*. Berkeley: University of California Press, 1993.

Vygodskaia, Anna Pavlovna. *The Story of a Life: Memoirs of a Young Jewish Woman in the Russian Empire*. Trans. and ed. E.M. Avrutin and R.H. Greene. DeKalb: Northern Illinois University Press, 2012.

Warwick, Christopher. *Ella: Princess, Saint and Martyr*. Chichester: Wiley, 2006.

Watson, Janet. *Fighting Different Wars: Experience, Memory, and the First World War in Britain*. Cambridge: Cambridge University Press, 2004.

West, Sally. *I Shop in Moscow: Advertising and the Creation of Consumer Culture in Late Tsarist Russia*. DeKalb: Northern Illinois University Press, 2011.

White, Elizabeth. *The Socialist Alternative to Bolshevik Russia: The Socialist Revolutionary Party, 1921–1939*. London: Routledge, 2011.

Wichard, Robin, and Carol Wichard. *Victorian Cartes-de-Visite*. Risborough: Shire Publications, 1999.

Widdis, Emma. "To Explore or Conquer?" In *The Landscape of Stalinism: The Art and Ideology of Soviet Space*, eds. E. Dobrenko and E. Naiman, 219–40. Seattle: University of Washington Press, 2003.

Williams, Albert Rhys. *Journey into Revolution: Petrograd, 1917–1918*. Chicago: Quadrangle Books, 1969.

Williams, Richard. *The Contentious Crown: Public Discussion of the British Monarchy in the Reign of Queen Victoria*. Aldershot: Ashgate, 1997.

Williams, Robert C. *Culture in Exile: Russian Émigrés in Germany, 1881–1941*. Ithaca: Cornell University Press, 1972.

Wisdom, J.H. *The Briton in Russia*. London: Leopold B. Hill, 1915.

Wood, Ruth Kedzie. *Honeymooning in Russia*. New York: Dodd, Mead, 1911.

– *The Tourist's Russia*. New York: Dodd, Mead, 1912.

Woody, Howard. "International Postcards: Their History, Production, and Distribution (Circa 1895 to 1915)." In *Delivering Views: Distant Cultures in Early Postcards*, eds. C.M. Geary and V.L. Webb, 13–45. Washington, DC: Smithsonian Institution Press, 1998.

Wortman, Richard. "Publicizing the Imperial Image in 1913." In *Self and Story in Russian History*, eds. L. Engelstein and S. Sandler, 94–119. Ithaca: Cornell University Press, 2000.

– *Scenarios of Power: Myth and Ceremony in Russian Monarchy*, vol. II. Princeton: Princeton University Press, 2000.

Youngblood, Denise. *The Magic Mirror: Moviemaking in Russia, 1908–1918*. Madison: University of Wisconsin Press, 1999.

Youssoupoff, Felix. *Lost Splendor*. New York: Helen Marx, 2003.

Zabochen', M. "Otkrytki – propagandisty." *Tvochestvo* 10 (1965): 24.

Zasosov, D.A., and V.I. Pyzin. *Iz zhizni Peterburga 1890–1910x godov*. Leningrad: Lenizdat, 1991.

Zhurnal "Sredi kollektsionerov" (1921–1924) ukazatel' soderzhaniia. Leningrad: DOK RSFSR, 1986.

Zichy, Mihaly. *The Erotic Drawings of Mihaly Zichy*. New York: Grove Press, 1969.

Zolotinkina, I.A. "Otkrytye pis'ma Obshchiny sviatoi Evgenii i russkaia grafika nachala XX veka." In *Izdaniia Obshchiny sviatoi Evgenii*, 23–33. St. Petersburg: Palace Editions and Graficart, 2008.

Zolotonosov, Mikhail. *Gliptokpratos: Issledovanie nemnogo diskursa*. St. Petersburg: Inapress, 1999.

Zorkaia, N.M. *Na rubezhe stoletii: U istokov massovogo iskusstva v Rossii 1900–1910 godov*. Moscow: Izdatel'stvo Nauka, 1976.

Index

www.ingramcontent.com/pod-product-compliance
Ingram Content Group UK Ltd.
Pitfield, Milton Keynes, MK11 3LW, UK
UKHW032117310125
454513UK00001B/89